EQ6 SIMPLIFIED

An Easy Learning Guide by Fran Iverson Gonzalez

COMPANION BOOK 2

The Electric Quilt Company

419 Gould Street, Suite 2

Bowling Green, Ohio 43402

EQ6 Simplified

The Electric Quilt Company
419 Gould Street, Suite 2
Bowling Green, OH 43402 USA

419/352-1134 (general)
800/356-4219 (sales only)
419/352-4332 (fax)
Find us online at: www.electricquilt.com

Any corrections and/or clarifications to sections of this book after it has been printed can be found online at: www.electricquilt.com > Support > Frequently Asked Questions > EQ6

CREDITS:

Book Editor:	Sara Seuberling
Book and Cover Design:	Sara Seuberling
Book Layout:	Whitney Taylor
Technical Reviewers:	Jenny Novinsky, Heidi Kory

Quilt design shown on the front cover designed by Fran Iverson Gonzalez.

Acknowledgments

My special thanks to:

Larry Gonzalez, as always, for his flawless logic and exceptional tech support, for his willingness to learn all about fabric and design over the years, for doing all the cooking when I was busy writing, and for always suggesting a slow dance when the time was right.

Karen and **David**, our daughter and son-in-law, for giving us something so right and so beautiful to celebrate during the writing of this book...their marriage.

Betsy Meyer, for being a one-woman cheering section and complete fan club and especially for being a world-class sister and friend.

Carol and **Roger Miller** at Quilt University, for making it so easy for me to teach EQ worldwide.

The community of **Quilt University students** for their boundless enthusiasm and passion for EQ.

My fabulous testers: **Gordon Cooper**, **Jean Folkes**, **Ethel Mecklem**, and **Libby Swoope** for happily investing so much time and energy to thoroughly test each lesson of this book, often on short notice and always with looming deadlines. Any mistakes that remain are mine alone.

Sara Seuberling, my wonderful editor at EQ, for being so skilled, so efficient, and so nice that she made this publishing experience a pleasure.

Whitney Taylor for her excellent typesetting, and **Jenny Novinsky** and **Heidi Kory** for their exceptional skills as technical reviewers.

Penny McMorris and **Ann Rutter** at The Electric Quilt Company for keeping me on track...sweetly, firmly, and with gentle humor...when I got carried away with all that EQ6 can do.

Dean Neumann for continually raising the creative bar with each new version of EQ.

About the Author

Fran Iverson Gonzalez has been writing the popular EQ Simplified series since her first tutorial, *EQ2 Simplified*. She is a professional quilt designer and teacher with over 30 years of quilting experience. Fran teaches a series of dynamic Electric Quilt classes online at Quilt University (www.quiltuniversity.com) and has taught EQ lab classes at the International Quilt Festival in Houston, Texas for years.

Fran lives in Edmond, Oklahoma with her husband Larry, a neuroscientist and university professor. They have a brilliant and beautiful daughter, Karen, and an exceptionally talented and versatile son-in-law, David, who are both working toward their doctoral degrees.

Introduction

Electric Quilt 6 (EQ6) is the latest version of a very powerful and versatile quilt design program that has achieved artistic acceptance throughout the quilting world while also earning an excellent reputation for quality and support. This is the perfect design software package for creating, editing, coloring, saving, and printing original and traditional quilt patterns. With EQ6's wide range of features and tools, the design possibilities are unlimited. Whether you are a beginner or a professional, the program makes it easy for you to experiment with various design factors at the same time that you are considering practical matters such as construction techniques and fabric yardage.

In writing this tutorial, I have relied upon my extensive experience as a quilter, designer, teacher, and long-time EQ user to create a series of instructive quilts in EQ6. I have broken down the design process into simple steps, while applying EQ6's tools in many different ways. I hope that this will make the learning experience fun and exciting and inspire creativity and confidence in my readers.

This is a progressive, project-oriented tutorial so you should work through these lessons in sequence. The quilts in this book are designed to expand and strengthen your EQ skills gradually, as you learn how to use the program. In Lessons 1 through 4, you will use EQ6's basic tools to develop a series of quilts that range from beginner to intermediate skill level. In Lessons 5 through 8, you will develop advanced skills as you create more complex designs.

My strategy for building the quilts in this tutorial is to collect the blocks, appliqué, fabrics and layouts, and then to add borders and designs on layers. In teaching you how to use EQ6, I assume that you already have elementary computer skills and a basic understanding of computer operation. I also assume that you are familiar with basic quilting terminology and have some experience with block or quilt construction.

To optimize your learning experience, please take your time and read these lessons very carefully. Follow the directions exactly. Every step is important! Stop when you are tired.

When you need information or help, check the EQ6 Help file, the *EQ6 User Manual*, or contact EQ's online Tech Support at techsupport@electricquilt.com

If you are using a touchpad instead of a mouse, read the section entitled "Notes for Laptop/Touchpad Users" on page 9 of the *EQ6 User Manual*.

There are many ways to accomplish specific tasks in EQ6, so feel free to venture beyond the methods and techniques described here. Commit to learning EQ6 and, with just a little practice, you will develop more artistic confidence, strengthen your design skills, and boost your creativity and productivity to amazing new levels!

Table of Contents

EQ6 Simplified

EQ6 SIMPLIFIED

An Easy Learning Guide by Fran Iverson Gonzalez

Color Quilts

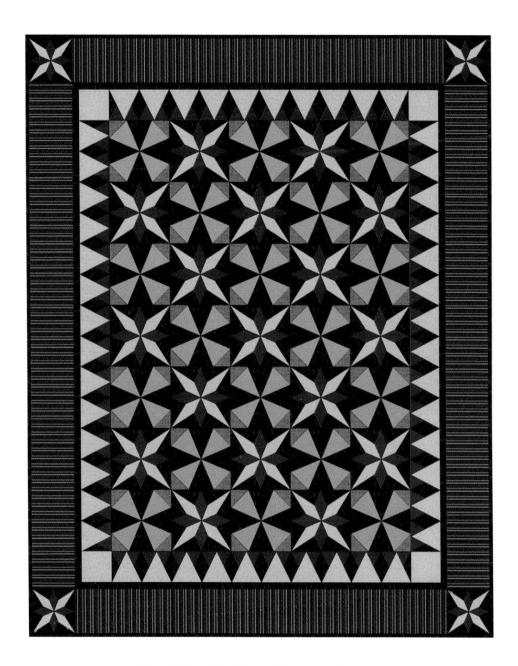

LESSON 1
Colliding Stars

LESSON 2
Celtic Crossroads

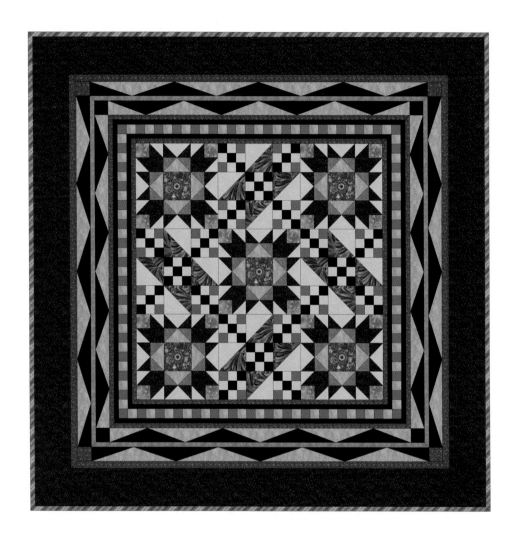

LESSON 3
Voodoo Queen

LESSON 4
Wildflower Wheelies

LESSON 5
Beaucoup Begonias

LESSON 6
Nebraska Sunrise

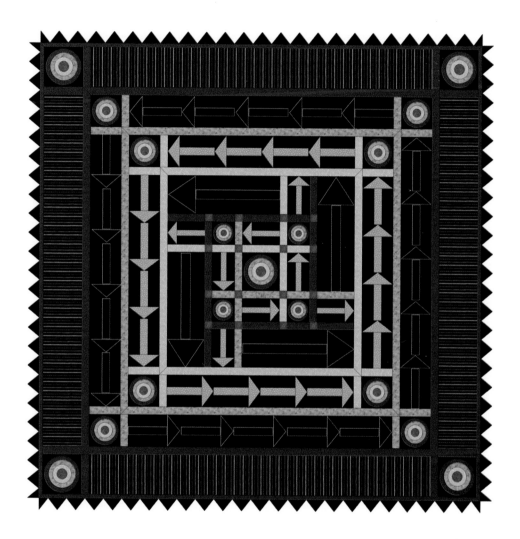

LESSON 7
Gearing Up

LESSON 8
Shady Apple Farm

EQ6 SIMPLIFIED

An Easy Learning Guide by Fran Iverson Gonzalez

Lessons

Starting with the Libraries

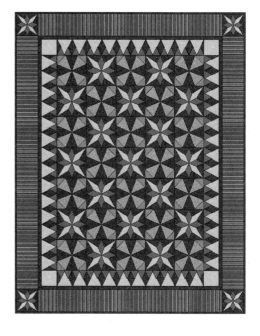

In this lesson, you will create three quilts based on designs that you will add from the EQ6 Block and Layout Libraries. The first quilt is *Kaleidoscope*, a simple design that will introduce you to EQ6's basic features. The second quilt is *Kaleidoscope Cartwheels*, which will give you more practice using the main color tools. The third quilt is *Colliding Stars*, a modified version of the first design, and it will help you to explore the program even further. You will learn to:

- Start a new project

- Find help and other resources

- Restore the default settings

- Add designs from the EQ6 Libraries

- View the Project Sketchbook

- Set blocks into a horizontal layout

- Undo an action

- Save your designs

- Color on the Quilt worktable

- Modify a quilt

    - Change the layout and borders

    - Change a block in the layout

- Customize the Quilt toolbar

- Rotate directional fabrics

- Complete quilt notecards

- Delete and sort layouts

- Print a quilt

- Calculate fabric yardage

- Exit EQ6

Lesson 1

Starting a New Project

1   Run Electric Quilt 6. The Tip of the Day box will open, giving you useful information about EQ6. Click **Close**.

After you close the Tip of the Day box, the EQ6 Project Helper will open with three tabs: Create a new project, Open an existing project, and Start with a quick-quilt project.

2   Click the **Create a new project** tab and then type *Colliding Stars* in the project name box. Click **OK**.

Your project is now stored on your hard drive and is identified by the name *Colliding Stars.PJ6*. The .PJ6 extension is added automatically to all of your project files.

> **Notes**
> EQ6, like any Windows® program, allows long file names that can include spaces. There are nine symbols that are invalid, however, and should never be used: / \ : * ? " < > |

After the Project Helper closes, the program will open to either the **Quilt worktable** or one of the **Block worktables**. If EQ6 opens to the Quilt worktable, you will see the Quilt toolbar displayed vertically on the right side of the screen. If EQ6 opens to one of the Block worktables, you will see one of the drawing toolbars displayed vertically on the left side of the screen.

Notice that the *Colliding Stars.PJ6* project file name is displayed in the upper-left corner of the screen.

The main menu is displayed horizontally, across the upper-left of the screen, just below the EQ6 logo and the project file name. The main menu items are: FILE, EDIT, VIEW, WORKTABLE, LIBRARIES, QUILT or BLOCK, VIDEOS, and HELP.

This main menu is organized in a tree-like structure in which each item branches to more options when it is selected.

Step 1

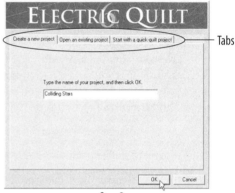

Tabs

Step 2

Project Tools

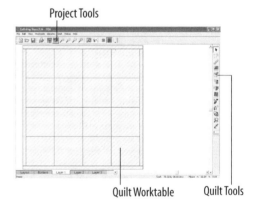

Quilt Worktable   Quilt Tools

Project File Name

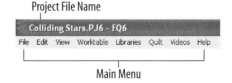

Main Menu

FILE > Print > Quilt

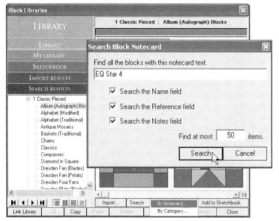

LIBRARIES > Block Library > Search > By Notecard >
type *EQ Star 4* > Search > OK

Project Toolbar

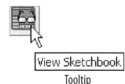

View Sketchbook

Tooltip

Status Bar

All of the main menu items are capitalized in this tutorial. **Carets (>)** are used to shorten the text in a series of sequential main menu instructions.

Here is an example of a menu instruction:

- Click **FILE** in the main menu, click **Print** in the drop-down menu, and then click **Quilt**.

Here is the shortened version of this instruction:

- Click **FILE > Print > Quilt**.

Here is a longer example of a main menu instruction:

- Click **LIBRARIES** in the main menu, click **Block Library** in the drop-down menu, click the **Search** button and then click **By Notecard** in the extended menu.

- Type *EQ Star 4* in the Search Block Notecard box and then click the **Search** button at the bottom of the Search Block Notecard box. Click **OK** when EQ6 tells you how many block notecards contain these words.

Here is the shortened version of this instruction:

- Click **LIBRARIES > Block Library > Search > By Notecard > type *EQ Star 4* > Search > OK**.

In the beginning of this first lesson, both the long and short versions of menu instructions are given. By the end of this lesson, only the shortened versions are given.

The **Project** toolbar is displayed horizontally at the top of the screen, under the main menu. You will find a quick, illustrated reference guide for all of the EQ6 toolbars at the back of this book and at the back of the *EQ6 User Manual*.

To identify a tool on the Project toolbar, place the cursor over that button *without clicking*. EQ6 will display the tool name in a tooltip and describe its function on the status bar on the lower-left of the screen.

Finding Help and Other Resources

HELP is the last item in the main menu and is one of the most valuable resources for EQ6 users. Click **HELP** to open the drop-down menu. This extended menu offers you three methods for searching the HELP file and gives you access to the built-in instructional features *Dynamic Tool Help* and *Tip of the Day*. There is a wonderful overview of EQ6 under *What's New?* and you will also find contact information for The Electric Quilt Company under *Tech Support*.

Help Menu

Be sure to explore the HELP file thoroughly since it is a complete and convenient resource that contains extensive, well-illustrated information about EQ6. If you opened the HELP file, you can close it now by clicking the **X** in the upper-right corner of the screen.

Close Help File

HELP File

There are many excellent resources for EQ6 users in addition to the HELP file and the *EQ6 User Manual*.

There is an extensive collection of instructional videos within the program that illustrates many of EQ6's design features. Click **VIDEOS** on the main menu or click the **Watch a Video** button on the Project toolbar to access these files.

The Electric Quilt Company (**www.electricquilt.com**) maintains an exciting, dynamic website that offers valuable information, instructive projects, free downloads, excellent products, and continuous, interactive technical support. Be sure to explore this site completely and return to it often!

Planet Patchwork (**www.planetpatchwork.com**) sponsors Info-EQ, a very active and informative free mailing list for EQ users. You can subscribe to Info-EQ here: http://www.electricquilt.com/Users/ InfoEQ/InfoEQ.asp

Videos Menu

Watch a Video Button

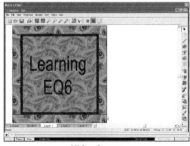

Video Screen

Quilt University (www.quiltuniversity.com) is a unique online resource that offers a wide variety of quilt-related classes, including a full range of EQ classes. I teach a series of in-depth EQ classes at QU starting with the basic skills, progressing through beginning/intermediate drawing and block analysis, and then advancing to complex layout design. This online learning experience differs from other instructional material because it is taught in a highly interactive classroom setting that is geared to give students personalized attention at their own convenience. I have taught at QU for years and have found it to be a very effective venue for helping thousands of students to master EQ.

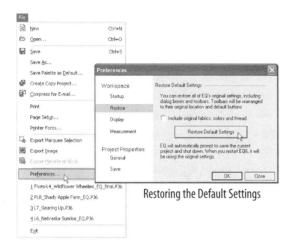

Restoring the Default Settings

Restoring the Default Settings

This tutorial was written with the default or factory settings in place, so you should restore these settings now if you have changed any of them in the past. To restore the default settings: Click **FILE**, then click on **Preferences** in the drop-down menu. Click **Restore** and then click **Restore Default Settings**. Click **OK**. The program will close.

Run EQ6 and click the **Open an existing project** tab. Click the *Colliding Stars.PJ6* file in the *Most recently used projects* list or in the *Existing projects* list. The default settings will be in place.

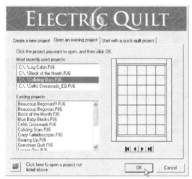

Open the *Colliding Stars* File

Adding Designs from the EQ6 Libraries

Now you will begin designing quilts in EQ6! Your first task in creating the *Kaleidoscope* quilt is to add the designs from the EQ6 Libraries that you will need to the current Sketchbook. You must save a design in the Sketchbook before you can use it to create a quilt.

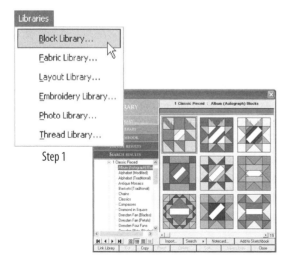

Step 1

1   Click **LIBRARIES** in the main menu and then click **Block Library** in the drop-down menu to open the **Block Library**. (**LIBRARIES > Block Library**)

There are *six libraries* in EQ6 and they contain thousands of designs. These libraries are: Block, Fabric, Layout, Embroidery, Photo, and Thread.

There are *five sections* within each of the EQ6 Libraries. The sections are the same in all of the libraries except the Thread Library, which does not have an Import Results section. You must open each library separately in order to view the sections within it. These sections are:

- **Library**, which contains the designs included with the program.

- **My Library**, which is your personal space for storing designs.

- **Sketchbook**, which contains the designs that are in the current project file.

- **Import Results**, which contains designs that you add to the library from other project files. You can also import image files into the Fabric, Photo, and Embroidery Libraries through this section.

- **Search Results**, which contains the designs that are found when you search the libraries. The number of designs that EQ6 will find in a search is dependent upon the libraries that you have linked to EQ6. Add-on collections, such as BlockBase and the Classic Appliqué Block series, will be included in the search if you have these libraries linked to EQ6. Designs in My Library will also be included.

There are five different Library Sections

Notes
- In the Block Library, the selected library style (e.g., Album (Autograph) Blocks under 1 Classic Pieced) is highlighted. The designs in this selected library style are displayed in the viewing area of the Block Library. The name of the selected style is displayed above the designs.

- There are four viewing options under the library list on the left side of the Block Library. They allow you to view four, nine, sixteen, or twenty-five designs simultaneously.

2   Click the **Search** button at the bottom of the Block Library and then click **By Notecard** in the extended menu (**Search > By Notecard**). The Search Block Notecard box will open.

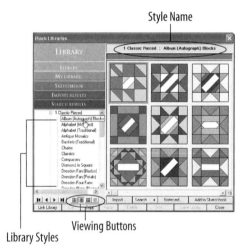

Style Name

Library Styles   Viewing Buttons

Step 2

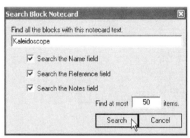

Steps 3 and 4

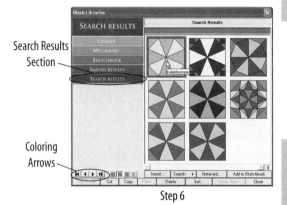

Search Results Section

Coloring Arrows

Step 6

Notecard... | Add to Sketchbook
Sort... | Save Library | Close

Step 7   Step 8

Libraries
Block Library...
Fabric Library...
Layout Library...
Embroidery Library...
Photo Library
Thread Library

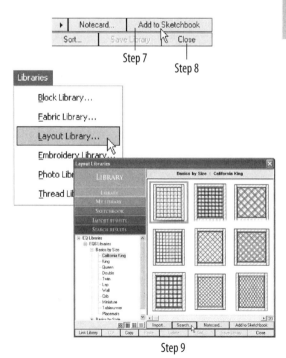

Step 9

3   Type ***Kaleidoscope*** in the Search Block Notecard box.

4   Click the **Search** button at the bottom of the Search Block Notecard box. EQ6 will perform the search and then tell you how many block notecards contain this word.

Notes
Each design in the EQ6 Libraries has a notecard that contains information about that specific design. You will learn more about notecards as you work through this tutorial.

5   Click **OK** and the Search Results section will open with these designs displayed.

6   Click the ***Kaleidoscope*** block at the top of the first column on the Search Results section. It is the green and purple block in the upper-left corner.

Notes
The four Coloring Arrows ◄◄ ◄ ► ►► below the library style list allow you to navigate through the first, previous, next, and last colorings saved under a selected design. In the Library, this includes the line drawing, the grayscale coloring, and the default coloring of the designs in the selected library style.

7   Click the **Add to Sketchbook** button at the bottom of the Block Library. The selected design will disappear from the Search Results section when it is added to the Blocks section of the current Sketchbook. The block is still in the library and you will see it the next time that you open that library.

8   Click **Close** to close the Block Library.

Now you will search the **Layout Library** for the layout that you will use for your *Kaleidoscope* quilt.

9   Click **LIBRARIES** in the main menu and then click **Layout Library**. Click the **Search** button at the bottom of the Layout Library. (**LIBRARIES > Layout Library > Search**)

Lesson 1

10 Type **35 total** in the Search Layout Notecard box.

11 Click the **Search** button at the bottom of the Search Layout Notecard box. EQ6 will tell you how many layout notecards contain these words.

12 Click **OK** and the Search Results section will open with these layouts displayed.

13 Use the **tooltip** feature to identify the layout that is labeled *11.5" Blocks – 35 Total*. Click this layout to select it.

Notes
Place the cursor over a library design without clicking to display the name.

14 Click the **Add to Sketchbook** button at the bottom of the Layout Library. The selected layout will disappear from the Search Results section when it is added to the Quilts section of the current Sketchbook. The layout is still in the Layout Library and you will see it the next time that you open that library.

15 Click **Close** to close the Layout Library.

Viewing the Project Sketchbook

You now have the block and layout designs that you need to create your *Kaleidoscope* quilt. You will open the **Project Sketchbook** to view the block and the layout that you added to this file.

In each EQ6 project file (PJ6) is a Project Sketchbook that contains all of the design elements that you save in that particular file: quilts, blocks, motifs, stencils, fabrics, embroidery, photos, and thread. The Project Sketchbook is stored as a project file on your hard drive. You can easily view, sort, document, retrieve, edit, and delete the designs that you save there.

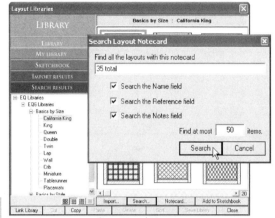

Steps 10 and 11

Step 12

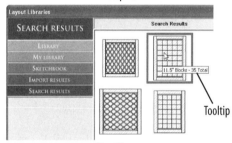

Tooltip

Step 13

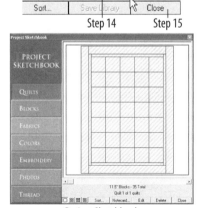

Step 14 Step 15

Project Sketchbook

VIEW > Sketchbook

Step 1
View Sketchbook

Project Sketchbook

PROJECT
SKETCHBOOK

QUILTS

BLOCKS

FABRICS

COLORS

EMBROIDERY

PHOTOS

THREAD

Project Sketchbook Sections

1 Open the Project Sketchbook using one of the following methods:

- Click the **View Sketchbook** button, the sixth button from the left on the Project toolbar. The icon is a pair of eyeglasses superimposed over an image of the Project Sketchbook.

- Click **VIEW** in the main menu and then click **Sketchbook** in the drop-down menu. (**VIEW > Sketchbook**)

- Press the **F8** function key on the top row of your keyboard.

The **Project Sketchbook** is divided into seven sections: Quilts, Blocks, Fabrics, Colors, Embroidery, Photos, and Thread. These sections contain all of the designs that you add to this project file.

- The **Quilts** section contains quilt layouts.

- The **Blocks** section contains blocks, motifs, and stencils.

- The **Fabrics** section contains a default palette that is included in every new project file, as well as any additional fabrics that you add to the Sketchbook.

- The **Colors** section contains the individual solid colors that comprise the multicolored fabrics in the Fabrics section. It also contains any solid colors that you create within EQ6 and add to the Sketchbook.

- The **Embroidery** section contains embroidery designs.

- The **Photos** section contains photographs.

- The **Thread** section contains a default palette that is included in every new project file, as well as any other quilting and embroidery threads that you add from the EQ6 Libraries.

Lesson 1

Notes
To move the Project Sketchbook, click the blue bar at the top and, holding down the mouse button, drag the box to the desired location on the worktable.

2 Click the **Quilts** button to open the Quilts section of the Sketchbook. You will see the layout that you added from the Layout Library. You will also see buttons in the Quilts section that give you a variety of options:

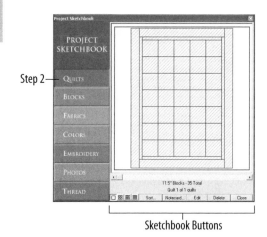

Step 2

Sketchbook Buttons

- The **viewing buttons** 🔲 🟦 ⊞ ⊞ allow you to view one, four, nine, or sixteen layouts simultaneously.

- The **Sort** button is available in all of the Sketchbook sections and it allows you to organize the contents of a section in any order that you desire.

- The **Notecard** feature is available in these Sketchbook sections: Quilts, Blocks, Fabrics, Embroidery, and Photos. Library designs contain notecard information that is transferred automatically when they are added to the Project Sketchbook. You can add text to notecards for any design in the Sketchbook.

- The **Edit** button places the selected design on the appropriate worktable.

- The **Delete** button removes a design from the section.

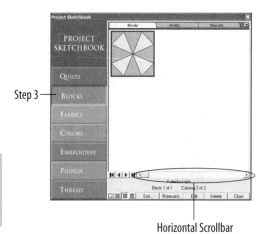

Step 3

Horizontal Scrollbar

- The **Close** button closes the Sketchbook.

Notes
Click and drag the horizontal scrollbar at the bottom of the Sketchbook to view saved quilts that are outside of the display area of the Sketchbook.

3 Click the **Blocks** button to open the Blocks section of the Sketchbook. You will see the *Kaleidoscope* block that you added from the Block Library. It is selected automatically because it is the only design in this section.

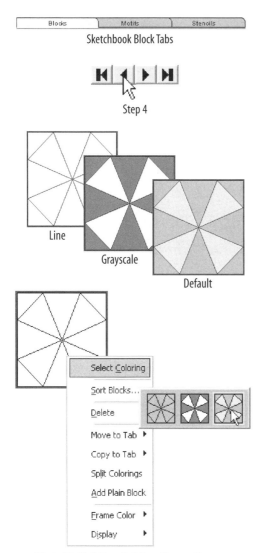

Sketchbook Block Tabs

Step 4

Line

Grayscale

Default

Blocks, Motifs, & Stencils Palette Context Menu

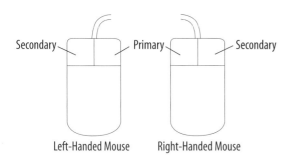

Secondary   Primary   Secondary

Left-Handed Mouse   Right-Handed Mouse

Notes

- There are three tabs at the top of the Blocks section of the Sketchbook: Blocks, Motifs, and Stencils. Click a tab to open a section. The Motifs and Stencils tabs are empty because you have not saved any designs of these types in this file.

- The viewing buttons □ ▦ ▦ ▦ at the bottom of the Blocks section of the Sketchbook allow you to view one, four, nine, or sixteen designs simultaneously.

4   Use the set of four **Coloring Arrows** next to the horizontal scrollbar to view the **line drawing**, the **grayscale coloring**, and the **default coloring** of the *Kaleidoscope* block.

Notes

- New colorings in the Blocks section of the Sketchbook are saved in sequence after the line drawing, the grayscale coloring, and the default coloring.

- To view the line drawing and all colorings of a design simultaneously, click the design in the Blocks section of the Sketchbook, then right-click on the mouse. The Blocks, Motifs, & Stencils Palette Context Menu will open. Click Select Coloring. A box that contains the line drawing and all of the saved colorings of the selected block will appear. Click the coloring that you want to display in the Blocks section of the Sketchbook.

Throughout this tutorial you will be instructed to click on various items with your mouse. Except where specified otherwise, you will always click your *primary mouse button*.

- The **primary button** on a *right-handed mouse* is the **left** button on the left side.

- The **primary button** on a *left-handed mouse* is the **right** button on the right side. A left-handed mouse must be selected in the Windows® Control Panel.

- The remaining button on either type mouse is the **secondary button**.

- When you are instructed to **right-click**, you should use your **secondary mouse button**.

Setting Blocks in a Horizontal Layout

It is time to retrieve the layout that you added from the Layout Library and set your *Kaleidoscope* block in it!

1   With the Project Sketchbook still open, click the **Quilts** button. The *11.5" Blocks – 35 Total* layout that you added to the Layout Library is displayed in the Quilts section of the Sketchbook. Click the **Edit** button at the bottom of the Sketchbook to place this layout on the Quilt worktable.

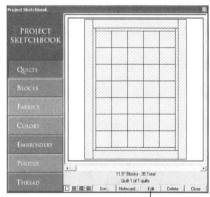
Step 1

Notes
You can also double-click the quilt to place it on the worktable.

On the Quilt worktable, the *Project toolbar* is displayed horizontally at the top of the screen and the *Quilt toolbar* is displayed vertically, at the right side of the screen.

There are five tabs at the bottom of the worktable that you will explore as you work through this tutorial: Layout, Borders, Layer 1, Layer 2 and Layer 3.

- The **Layout** tab contains options that are specific to the selected quilt layout style, including basic settings such as the *number of horizontal and vertical blocks in the layout*, the *finished size of the blocks*, and the *finished width of sashing*.

- The **Borders** tab contains *border style* and *border size* options.

- The **Layer 1** tab is the basic design layer and it contains the *pieced and/or appliqué blocks and the borders* that comprise the base layer of the quilt. The Layer 1 tab is also the basic layer for the advanced *Custom Set layout* which you will explore later in this tutorial.

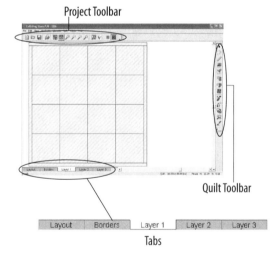
Tabs

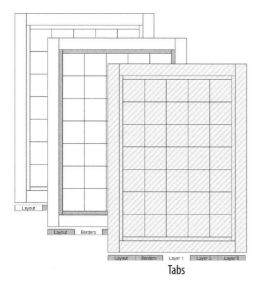

Tabs

Quilt: 73.50 by 96.50 (ins)	Mouse H: 26.12 V: 49.30
Size of the Quilt	Mouse Coordinates

Layout   Borders   Layer 1   Layer 2   Layer 3

Step 2

Step 3
Set Block

Blocks Palette

- The **Layer 2** tab is the second layer of the quilt and it consists of *designs that "float" over Layer 1*, such as appliqué motifs. An appliqué motif is an appliqué design that has no background square.

- The **Layer 3** tab is the third layer of the quilt and it contains *quilting stencils* and *embroidery designs* that are superimposed over Layers 1 and 2.

Notes

- Notice that the *size of the quilt* is displayed in the Status bar on the lower-right side of the screen, next to the *mouse coordinates*. (e.g. Quilt: 70.00 by 88.00 (ins))

- If you want to convert the quilt size to centimeters, click FILE > Preferences > Measurement > Centimeters > OK.

2   Click the **Layer 1** tab.

3   Click the **Set Block** tool, the fourth tool from the top on the Quilt toolbar. The icon is a colored block and a curved arrow superimposed over a layout grid. The Blocks palette will open with the *Kaleidoscope* block displayed. The Blocks palette contains all of the designs and colorings that you add to your Blocks section of the Sketchbook. The *Kaleidoscope* is selected automatically because it is the only design in the Blocks palette.

Notes

- There are three tabs on the Blocks palette that correspond to the same tabs in the Blocks section of the Sketchbook: Blocks, Motifs, and Stencils.

- To change the number of designs displayed simultaneously, click the viewing buttons at the bottom of the Blocks palette. The viewing buttons work the same way as the viewing buttons in the EQ6 Libraries and the Quilts section of the Sketchbook.

- To view the saved colorings of the selected design, use the Coloring Arrows in the Blocks palette. These Coloring Arrows function the same way as those in the Blocks section of the Sketchbook: first, previous, next, and last.

- To view designs in the Blocks palette that are outside of the display area, click and drag the horizontal scrollbar button at the bottom of the palette.

- To move the Blocks palette, click on the blue bar at the top and, holding down the mouse button, drag the palette to a new location.

- To resize the Blocks palette, move the cursor to any edge of the palette until the cursor changes to a two-headed arrow. Click and drag this arrow to stretch or shrink the palette.

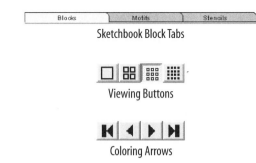

Sketchbook Block Tabs

Viewing Buttons

Coloring Arrows

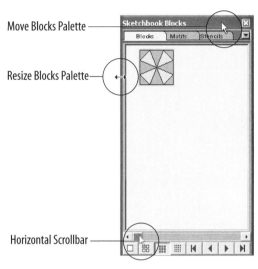

Move Blocks Palette

Resize Blocks Palette

Horizontal Scrollbar

4   Be sure that the **default coloring** (green and purple) of the *Kaleidoscope* block is displayed in the Blocks palette. You will use the default coloring of this block in your quilt because this will make it easier for you to follow my instructions as you experiment with the EQ6 color tools.

With the **Set Block** tool still engaged, **click any space in the quilt's center layout area** to set the default coloring of the *Kaleidoscope* block. You have just set one block in the layout.

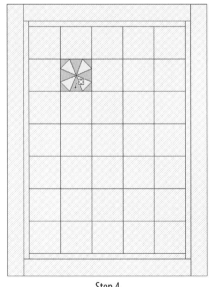

Step 4

EDIT > Undo

Erase Block Tool

Step 5
Set Block

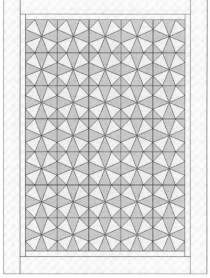

Step 5
CTRL+click

Add to Sketchbook Button

Notes

- To undo a single action in EQ6, click EDIT in the main menu and then click Undo in the drop-down menu (EDIT > Undo). You can also use the keyboard shortcut CTRL+Z to undo an action. You can undo ten actions in reverse sequence by repeating using EDIT > Undo or CTRL+Z. There are certain actions that cannot be undone. For example, you cannot undo Add to Sketchbook and you cannot undo an action after you have changed worktables.

- To erase a block in the layout, click the Erase Block tool, the fifth tool on the Quilt toolbar. It is directly under the Set Block tool and the icon is a pencil eraser superimposed on a blank block. Click the design in the layout that you want to erase.

5   Click the **Set Block** tool and then hold down the **CTRL key and click any space in the layout**. All of the block spaces in the center design area will fill with the *Kaleidoscope* block.

Notes

To erase all blocks in the layout, click the Erase Block tool and CTRL+click any block in the layout.

Saving Your Designs

As you can see, your design is unfinished. Your blocks are set in the layout, but your borders are still uncolored. Even though this design is unfinished, it is very important to save it now and often during the design process.

The **Add to Sketchbook** button allows you to add a copy of your design to the Project Sketchbook, the permanent file on your hard drive. When you change the Project Sketchbook, by adding or deleting designs for example, you change the permanent project file on your hard drive.

Each time that you add an unfinished design to the Sketchbook, this action adds a copy of the design, at that stage of its development, to the project file on your hard drive. Your project file contains all of the copies that you add to the Sketchbook while you are working.

If you make a mistake that isn't easy to correct or want to develop a design differently, you can retrieve an earlier version of your design from the Sketchbook. When your design is finished to your satisfaction, you can delete the unwanted versions from the Project Sketchbook easily. You will learn how to do this at the end of this lesson.

If you've named your project, by default, EQ6 will **save the project file automatically any time the Project Sketchbook is changed**. Also, EQ6 backs up your project file automatically every three minutes. These settings can be changed in **FILE > Preferences > Save**. See the *EQ6 User Manual* or the HELP file for more information.

You will now add the changes that you have made in your layout to your Project Sketchbook.

Notes

Once you have clicked Add to Sketchbook, no previous actions can be reversed with the Undo feature.

1   Click **Add to Sketchbook**, the fifth button on the Project toolbar, to save this design in the Quilts section of the Sketchbook. The Add to Sketchbook icon is a large red arrow superimposed over the image of the Project Sketchbook.

Notes

• You can also save a quilt by clicking QUILT > Add Quilt to Sketchbook.

• You cannot save when the Project Sketchbook is open.

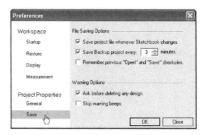

FILE > Preferences > Save

Step 1
Add to Sketchbook

QUILT > Add Quilt to Sketchbook

Double Nine Patch Block

Paintbrush Tool
(One Dot Brush)

2 x 2 Double Nine Patch Block Layout

Spraycan Tool

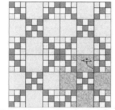

2 x 2 Double Nine Patch Block Layout

Swap All Colors Tool

2 x 2 Double Nine Patch Block Layout

Eyedropper Tool

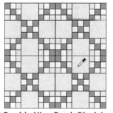

2 x 2 Double Nine Patch Block Layout

Coloring on the Quilt Worktable

Your unfinished quilt is now saved in the Quilts section of the Sketchbook and in your project file. You are ready to experiment with EQ6's powerful color tools! The four basic color tools on the Quilt toolbar function like this:

- The **Paintbrush** tool recolors *individual patches within a single design*. It is the ninth tool on the Quilt toolbar and the icon is a paintbrush. There are several tools available on the Paintbrush flyout bar on the Quilt worktable. Whenever you are instructed to use the Paintbrush tool in this tutorial, you should select the **One Dot Brush** tool on this flyout bar. To access the flyout bar, click and hold on the Paintbrush tool on the Quilt toolbar. The Paintbrush tool is available on the Block and Quilt worktables.

- The **Spraycan** tool recolors all *identically colored patches within a single design*. It is located just below the Paintbrush on the Quilt toolbar and the icon is a spraycan. The Spraycan tool is available on the Block and Quilt worktables.

- The **Swap All Colors** tool recolors all *identically colored patches in the entire layout, including borders and designs on Layers 1, 2, and 3*. It is located just below the Spraycan tool and the icon is two colored squares with two curved arrows. The Swap All Colors tool is available only on the Quilt worktable.

- The **Eyedropper** tool finds *previously used samples in the Fabrics and Colors palette*. It is located just below the Swap All Colors tool and the icon is an eyedropper. The Eyedropper tool is available on the Block and Quilt worktables.

Lesson 1

1   With your *Kaleidoscope* quilt still on the
worktable, click the **Paintbrush** tool. The
Fabrics and Colors palette will open with the
default palette.

Step 1
Paintbrush

There is a small black triangle on the Paintbrush
tool button. This arrow indicates that there are more
tools available under this button. **Click and hold
down the Paintbrush** tool and a flyout toolbar
will open, giving you access to these additional
Paintbrush tools. Click the **One Dot Brush** tool
button to close the flyout toolbar. The One Dot
Brush tool has no red markings on the button. See
Paintbrush Flyout tools in the HELP file or the *EQ6
User Manual* for more information.

One Dot Brush

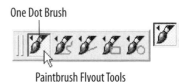

Paintbrush Flyout Tools

Notes

- The Fabrics and Colors Palette contains a large sample
  window that displays the selected fabric, an area where
  the most recently used fabric and color samples are
  displayed, a Fabrics tab, a Colors tab, and the area where the
  complete palette is displayed. There are viewing buttons
  at the bottom of the Fabrics and Colors palette that allow
  you to change the number of samples that you can view
  simultaneously.

- To view fabrics that are not visible in the display area, click
  and drag the horizontal scrollbar at the bottom of the
  Fabrics and Colors Palette.

- To move the Fabrics and Colors palette, click on the blue bar
  at the top and, holding down the mouse button, drag the
  palette to a new location on the screen.

- To resize the Fabrics and Colors palette, move the cursor to
  the edge of the palette until it changes to a two-headed
  arrow. Click and drag this arrow to stretch or shrink the
  palette in any direction.

- You will learn how to change the default palette to your
  own selection of fabrics and colors later in this tutorial.

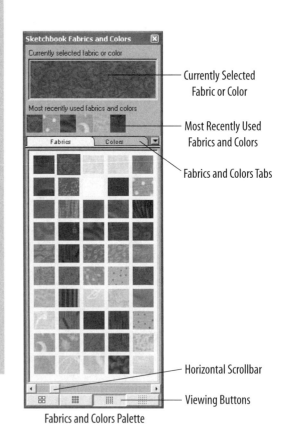

Currently Selected
Fabric or Color

Most Recently Used
Fabrics and Colors

Fabrics and Colors Tabs

Horizontal Scrollbar

Viewing Buttons

Fabrics and Colors Palette

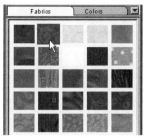

Step 2

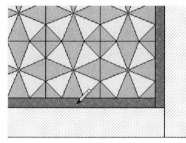

Step 3
CTRL+click

Step 4
CTRL+click

QUILT > Add Quilt to Sketchbook

Step 5
Add to Sketchbook

2 Click the sample in the Fabrics and Colors palette that you want to use to color the first border.

Notes
In EQ6, the borders are always numbered from the center of the quilt on outward. The innermost border is the first border or Border 1.

3 **Click each side of the first border** to color them individually or use **CTRL+click** to color the entire border simultaneously.

Notes
To change your fabric selection, choose a new sample in the palette and repeat step 3. The new color will replace the previous color.

4 Select a fabric in the palette for the second border and then **CTRL+click** to color all sides of the border simultaneously.

5 Click **QUILT > Add Quilt to Sketchbook** or click the **Add to Sketchbook** button on the Project toolbar to save this first version of your *Kaleidoscope* quilt. You will use this design to create a new quilt later in this lesson.

Notes

- You will find it very helpful to use the Zoom tools when working in EQ6. The four Zoom tools are in the Project toolbar at the top of the screen and are all represented by various symbols contained within a magnifying glass: Zoom In (+), Zoom Out (-), Refresh (=), and Fit to Worktable (square). You will learn to use these tools as you work through this tutorial.

- To zoom in to a quilt, click the Zoom In (+) button and then click and hold as you drag the cursor diagonally across the area that you want to enlarge. When you release the mouse button, the magnified area will fill the screen and the Zoom In tool will disengage.

- To navigate on the magnified worktable, use the vertical and horizontal scrollbars on the screen.

- To return to the previous view, click the Zoom Out (-) button.

- To redraw the screen, click the Refresh Screen (=) button. This will redraw the lines and refresh the colors, erasing debris from the screen.

- To return to normal viewing, click the Fit to Worktable (square) button.

- Remember that you can click and drag to move a palette if it is in your way in the magnified view on the Quilt worktable. You can also close a palette by clicking the X at the top of the palette. To reopen the Blocks palette, click the Set Block tool. To reopen the Fabrics and Colors palette, click a color tool on the Quilt toolbar.

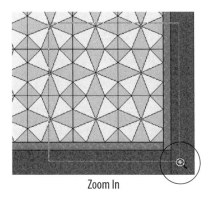

Zoom In

Zoom In   Zoom Out

Refresh Screen   Fit to Worktable

Now you will recolor the blocks in the fabrics of your choice to create the second quilt in this lesson, *Kaleidoscope Cartwheels.*

6   With the **Paintbrush** tool still engaged and the quilt displayed to fit the worktable, click a sample in the Fabrics and Color palette and then click **one patch in the quilt**, as illustrated. This selected patch will recolor with the new fabric.

Paintbrush Tool

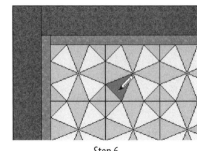

Step 6

Step 7

Spraycan Tool

Swap All Colors Tool

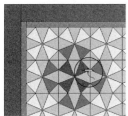

Steps 9 and 11

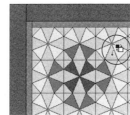

Step 13

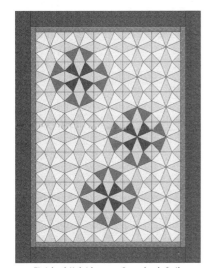

Finished *Kaleidoscope Cartwheels* Quilt

7   Click a **series of patches** to form three colored circles in the layout, as illustrated.

Notes
Remember that you can correct a mistake easily by clicking Edit > Undo or using the CTRL+Z shortcut.

8   **Add to Sketchbook.**

Notes
When you Add to Sketchbook, any block colorings that you created on the Quilt worktable are added automatically to the Blocks section of the Sketchbook.

9   Click the **Spraycan** tool and select a *different color* in the Fabrics and Colors palette. Click a *light green* patch in the blocks at the center of a circle, as illustrated in the figure. All identical, light green patches in that block will recolor with the new fabric.

10   **Add to Sketchbook.**

11   *Repeat step 9* to color the light green patches within the two remaining circles on the layout.

12   **Add to Sketchbook.**

13   Click the **Swap All Colors** tool and *select a different sample* in the Fabrics and Colors palette. Move the cursor to any *purple* patch in the layout. Click and all identically colored patches in the layout will recolor with the new fabric (currently purple). This is your *Kaleidoscope Cartwheels* quilt design.

14   **Add to Sketchbook.**

15   Click the **Eyedropper** tool and click a **fabric in the layout**. The Eyedropper tool will identify this fabric and it will appear in the large sample window. The Eyedropper tool will immediately snap back to the last color tool that you used.

Notes
You can change the Eyedropper snapping option in QUILT > Options > Tool Options > Snap Settings > Eyedropper Snapping.

Experiment with these color tools so that you are comfortable with their functions before you move on to the next part of this lesson.

Modifying a Quilt Design:
Changing the Layout and Borders

Now that you have completed and recolored a simple *Kaleidoscope* quilt in EQ6, you will modify your first completed quilt in order to create *Colliding Stars*, a more complex design. You will start designing your new quilt by making changes in the layout.

1   Click the **View Sketchbook** button to open the Project Sketchbook or use the **F8** function key shortcut.

2   Click the **Quilts** button to open the Quilts section of the Sketchbook. Use the horizontal scrollbar to view the *first completed version of your Kaleidoscope quilt*.

3   Click the **Edit** button at the bottom of the Quilts section of the Sketchbook or **double-click the quilt** to place it on the worktable.

4   Click the **Layout** tab on the lower-left of the screen. The Horizontal Layout box will open.

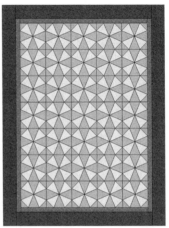

First Version of the *Kaleidoscope* Quilt

Notes

• Notice that the *Size of quilt's center layout* is displayed at the top of the Layout box. This is the measurement of the quilt without the borders.

• To move the Horizontal Layout box, click on the blue bar at the top and, holding down the mouse button, drag the box to a new location on the screen.

• To move from option to option in the Horizontal Layout box, use the keyboard TAB key. To move through the options in reverse order, use SHIFT+TAB.

Step 2 ——
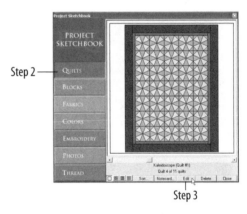
Step 3

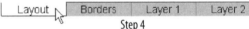
Step 4

Moving the Horizontal Layout Box

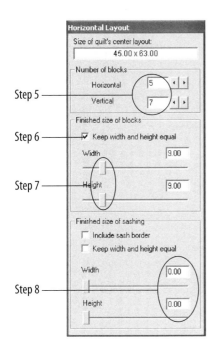

Step 5
Step 6
Step 7
Step 8

| Layout | Borders | Layer 1 | Layer 2 | Layer 3 |

Step 9

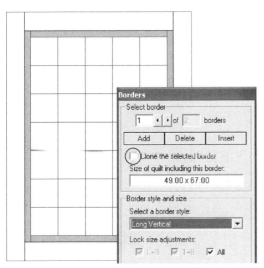

Borders Box

5 Leave the number of horizontal and vertical blocks set to **5 x 7.**

6 Under *Finished size of blocks,* click to put a check in **Keep width and height equal.**

7 Change the *Finished size of blocks* to **9.00** with the palette slider.

Notes

There are three ways to change a palette slider setting:

- **Click to the left or to the right of a palette slider button to move it in 0.25″ increments.**

- **Click directly on the palette slider button or to the left or right of it and then use the keyboard arrow keys to move it in 0.25″ increments.**

- **Highlight the current value and type in the new value. The palette slider button will move to the new setting.**

- **The default value for a palette slider jump is 0.25″ or 0.5 cm. You can change this setting under QUILT > Options > Snap Settings > Nudge Settings.**

8 Leave the width and height settings under *Finished size of sashing* set to **0.00.** Since the width and height of the sashing are set to 0.00, it does not matter if the two boxes in this section are checked or unchecked.

Now you will change the borders

9 Click the **Borders** tab. The first border is selected automatically.

10 Be sure that *Clone the selected border* at the top of the Borders box is **unchecked.**

Notes

Notice that the *Size of quilt including this border* is displayed at the top of the box.

Lesson 1

11 Click the down arrow next to *Select a border style* to drop down a list of border styles. Use the vertical scrollbar in the drop-down list to find the **Big & Little Points In** style and then click to select it.

12 Click **All** under *Lock size adjustments*. This convenient feature ensures that all borders will be sized simultaneously.

Notes
You can also lock together the top and bottom borders or left and right borders for resizing. If all of these options are unchecked, each border side can be sized separately.

13 With all sides locked, adjust the value for one side of the first border to **4.50** on the palette slider.

Notes
If you change one border and the other sides of that border do not change, click directly on the palette slider button for the changed side. The other sides of that border will immediately resize to the width of the changed side.

14 Change the *Horizontal Blocks in border* setting to **10** and the *Vertical Blocks in border* setting to **14**.

15 **Add to Sketchbook.**

16 Click the **second border** or use the arrow key in the *Select border* section at the top of the Borders box to select the second border.

17 Click the arrow next to *Select a border style* and then click **Mitered** in the drop-down list.

18 Set the border size to **1.00**.

19 **Add to Sketchbook.**

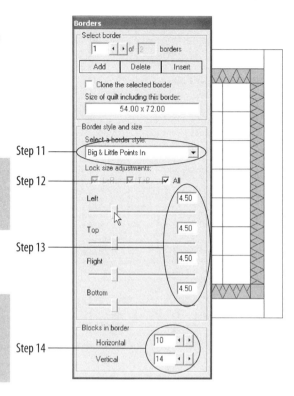

Step 11

Step 12

Step 13

Step 14

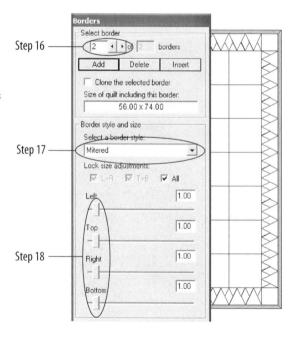

Step 16

Step 17

Step 18

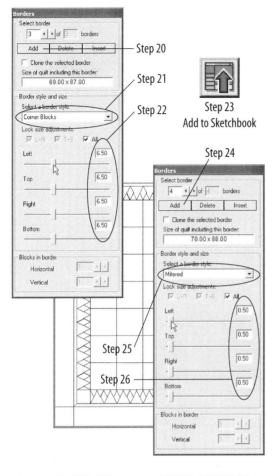

Step 20

Step 21

Step 22

Step 23
Add to Sketchbook

Step 24

Step 25

Step 26

Step 28

Step 1

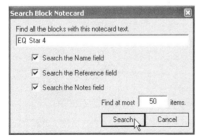
Steps 2 and 3

20 Click the **Add** button at the top of the Borders box to add a third border.

21 Click the arrow next to *Select a border style* and then click **Corner Blocks** in the drop-down list.

22 Set the border size to **6.50**.

23 **Add to Sketchbook.**

24 Click the **Add** button at the top of the Borders box to add a fourth border.

25 Click the arrow next to *Select a border style* and then click **Mitered** in the drop-down list.

26 Use the palette slider button to set the border size to **0.50**. This border represents the quilt binding.

27 **Add to Sketchbook.**

28 Click the **Layer 1** tab to return to the Quilt worktable. The Layer 1 tab is the base layer that contains the quilt's blocks and borders.

Notes
It is easy to adjust a border even after you have set designs into the quilt layout. With the quilt on the worktable, click on the Borders tab, and then click on the border that you want to change. The selected border will be shaded and the box for that border will open. Change the settings in the Borders box. Add to Sketchbook.

Modifying a Quilt Design:
Changing a Block in the Layout
You will need a new block and a striped fabric for your *Colliding Stars* quilt so you will add these designs from the EQ6 Libraries.

1 Click **LIBRARIES > Block Library > Search > By Notecard**.

2 Type *EQ Star 4* in the Search Block Notecard box.

3 Click the **Search** button at the bottom of the Search Block Notecard box. EQ6 will tell you how many block notecards contain these words.

Lesson 1

4   Click **OK** and the Search Results section will open with this design selected.

5   Click the **Add to Sketchbook** button at the bottom of the Block Library. The design will disappear from the Search Results section when it is added to the Blocks section of the current Sketchbook, but it is still in the library.

6   Click **Close** to close the Block Library.

7   Click **LIBRARIES > Fabric Library > EQ Libraries > EQ6 Libraries > by Category > 23 Geometric – Stripes**.

Step 5   Step 6

8   Use **CTRL+A** to select all samples in this library style.

9   Click the **Add to Sketchbook** button at the bottom of the Fabric Library. All of the designs will disappear from the library style when they are added to the Fabrics section of the current Sketchbook, but they are still in the library.

10 Click **Close** to close the Fabric Library.

11 With your modified *Kaleidoscope* quilt still on the worktable, click the **Set Block** tool and the Blocks palette will open.

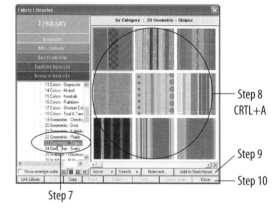

Step 8
CRTL+A

Step 9

Step 10

Step 7

Step 11
Set Block

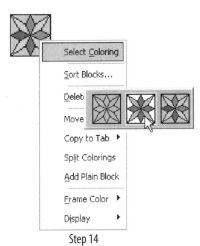

Step 14

Step 15
Alt+click

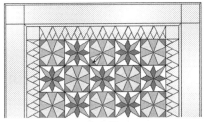

Step 17
Paintbrush

12 Click the *EQ Star 4* block to select it.

13 Right-click on the mouse to open the Blocks, Motifs & Stencils Palette Context Menu.

14 Click on **Select Coloring** in the context menu to view all colorings of the *EQ Star 4* block simultaneously. Click the **grayscale** coloring to display this coloring in the Blocks palette.

Notes
The default coloring of the *EQ Star 4* block uses several different colors. It will be easier to recolor it on the Quilt worktable if you set the grayscale coloring in the layout.

15 Place the cursor over the second *Kaleidoscope* block in the first row of the quilt layout. **ALT+click**. The *EQ Star 4* block will replace alternate *Kaleidoscope* blocks in the layout.

Notes
CTRL+click sets designs in all spaces in a horizontal quilt layout. ALT+click sets designs in alternate spaces in a horizontal layout.

16 Add to Sketchbook.

17 Click the **Paintbrush** tool.

18 Click a sample in the Fabrics and Colors palette. **CTRL+click** on each of the four *small corner triangles* in the *Kaleidoscope* block, to recolor as illustrated.

Notes
• Use the Paintbrush tool in combination with CTRL+click to recolor a specific patch in all identical blocks in the layout.

• Remember that you can undo a series of actions by clicking EDIT > Undo or using the CTRL+Z shortcut.

19 Add to Sketchbook.

Step 18
CTRL+click

Lesson 1

20 Click the **Swap All Colors** tool and then click a sample in the Fabrics and Colors palette. Click to recolor the *diagonal star points* in all of the *EQ Star 4* blocks.

21 **Add to Sketchbook.**

22 Click **another sample in the Fabrics and Colors palette** and click the *straight points* in all of the *EQ Star 4* blocks, to recolor.

23 **Add to Sketchbook.**

24 Click another sample in the Fabrics and Colors palette. With the **Swap All Colors** tool still engaged, click the *four green patches* in the *Kaleidoscope* block, to recolor.

25 **Add to Sketchbook.**

26 Click another sample in the Fabrics and Colors palette and click to recolor the *purple patches* in the *Kaleidoscope* blocks and the white background in the *EQ Star 4* blocks.

27 **Add to Sketchbook.**

> **Notes**
> The colors that you just used will be displayed under the *Most recently used fabrics and colors* in the Fabrics and Colors palette. Click on a color to use it again.

28 To color the first series of triangles in Border 1, click the **Paintbrush** tool and then click a sample in the Fabrics and Colors palette. **CTRL+click** one of the smaller triangles to recolor this series of triangles in Border 1.

29 **Add to Sketchbook.**

30 Select another sample with the **Paintbrush** tool and **CTRL+click** to color the next series of triangles in Border 1.

31 **Add to Sketchbook.**

32 Select another sample with the **Paintbrush** tool and **CTRL+click** to color the series of background triangles in Border 1.

Swap All Colors Tool

Step 20

Step 22   Step 24

Step 26

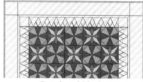

Recolored Blocks

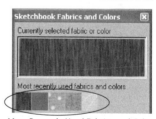

Step 28 Paintbrush

Most Recently Used Fabrics and Colors

Step 28

Step 30

Step 32

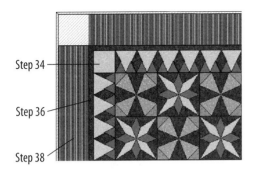

Step 34

Step 36

Step 38

Step 39
Add to Sketchbook

Step 40
Set Block

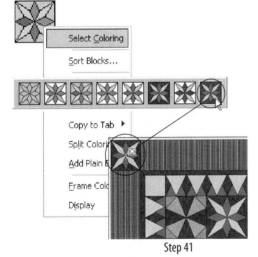

Step 41

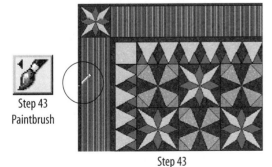

Step 43
Paintbrush

Step 43

33 **Add to Sketchbook.**

34 **CTRL+click** to color the corner squares in Border 1, to color them.

35 **Add to Sketchbook.**

36 With the **Paintbrush** tool still engaged, click a sample for Border 2 in the Fabrics and Colors palette. **CTRL+click** to color all sides of this border simultaneously.

37 **Add to Sketchbook.**

38 Click the **Fabric** tab and click one of the *striped fabrics* in the palette to color Border 3. With the **Paintbrush** tool still engaged, **CTRL+click** the border to color all sides of this border simultaneously. You will rotate this striped fabric in the next section.

39 **Add to Sketchbook.**

40 Click the **Set Block** tool and then click the *EQ Star 4* block to select it.

41 Right-click on the mouse to open the Blocks, Motifs & Stencils Palette Context Menu. Click **Select Coloring**. Click the *final coloring of this block* in the sequence and **CTRL+click** a *border corner* to set it in all corners of Border 3.

42 **Add to Sketchbook.**

43 Click the **Paintbrush** tool, click a sample in the Fabrics and Colors palette and then **CTRL+click** to color all sides of the binding.

44 **Add to Sketchbook.**

Rotating Directional Fabrics

Many fabrics contain patterns that are printed or woven in horizontal, vertical, or diagonal orientations. EQ6 gives you the option to rotate directional fabrics to a specific orientation in the layout. This feature is available through **Customize Toolbar**, the last button on the Quilt toolbar, the vertical toolbar on the right. The icon is a small black arrow and a horizontal bar.

1   With the quilt on the worktable, click the **Customize Toolbar** button to open the extended menu.

2   Click **Add/Remove Buttons**.

3   Click to put a check next to **Rotate Fabric** in the list of tools so that it will appear on the Quilt toolbar. The icon is two directional fabric samples and a curved arrow. Click anywhere away from the list to close it.

4   Find the **Rotate Fabric** tool on the Quilt toolbar and click to open the Rotate Fabric box.

5   The *Simple* option is selected automatically. Click the **striped border fabric** that you want to rotate on two opposite sides in Border 3. Each click of the mouse will rotate the fabric 90 degrees.

6   **Add to Sketchbook.**

Excellent work! Your *Colliding Stars* quilt design is complete!

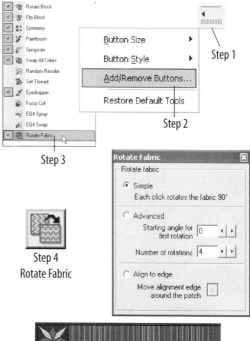

Step 1

Step 2

Step 3

Step 4
Rotate Fabric

Step 5

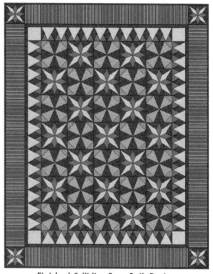

Click on two opposite borders to rotate

Finished *Colliding Stars* Quilt Design

Step 1
View Sketchbook

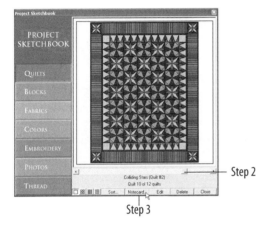

Step 2

Step 3

Completing Quilt Notecards

The notecard feature is a convenient tool that makes it easy for you to add documentation and construction notes for your quilts. Also, if you have named your final designs in Notecards, it will be much easier to recognize unwanted designs and delete them from the Sketchbook.

1   Click the **View Sketchbook** button to open the Project Sketchbook or use the **F8** function key shortcut.

2   Open the **Quilts** section of the Sketchbook and click and drag the horizontal scrollbar at the bottom of the Sketchbook to view your completed *Colliding Stars* quilt.

3   Click the **Notecard** button and the cursor will be positioned automatically on the *Name* line of the notecard, ready for you to type.

4   Type *Colliding Stars* on the *Name* line of the notecard.

5   Use the keyboard **TAB** key to move to the *Reference* section. Type **EQ6 Simplified** on the Reference line.

6   Use the **TAB** key to move to the *Notes* section. Type **Lesson 1** here.

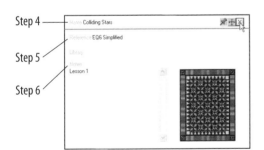

Step 4

Step 5

Step 6

Notes
Be sure to note the source or inspiration and any other pertinent information for designs that you create in EQ6. If you are recreating a design from a magazine, for example, you should record the designer, the publication, the date, and the page number for future reference.

7   Notice the symbols in the upper-right corner of the notecard: the *push pin*, the *four-headed arrows*, and the *X*. The push pin allows you to pin the notecard to the worktable. The four-headed arrow allows you to move the notecard on the worktable. The X closes the notecard. Click on the **four-headed arrow** button at the top of the notecard and, holding down the mouse button, drag the notecard to another location on the worktable.

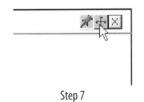

Step 7

8   Click the **X** in the upper-right corner of the notecard to close it.

9   With the **Quilts** section of the Sketchbook still open, use the horizontal scrollbar to view your *Kaleidoscope* quilt. Click the **Notecard** button and complete the notecard for this design.

10   Click the **X** to close the notecard.

11   With the Quilts section of the Sketchbook still open, scroll to view your *Kaleidoscope Cartwheels* quilt. Click the **Notecard** button and complete the notecard for this design. Click **X** to close the notecard.

12   *Repeat step 11* for each finished quilt design that you want to keep in the Sketchbook.

Deleting and Sorting Layouts

After your have named all of the designs in the Sketchbook that you want to keep, it is easy to delete the remaining designs.

1   To delete a layout, use the **horizontal scrollbar** in the Quilts section of the Sketchbook to display the design that you want to delete.

2   Click the **Delete** button at the bottom of the Sketchbook.

3   The program will ask if you want to delete this design. Click **Yes**.

4   To sort layouts, click the **Sort** button at the bottom of the Quilts section of the Sketchbook. The Sort Layouts box will open. Notice that you have several viewing options in this box.

5   In the Sort Layouts box, click the quilt layouts *in the order in which you want them to appear* in the Quilts section of the Sketchbook. You can click the first few that you want to sort and then click **Close**. Any unsorted designs will follow the sorted layouts automatically. At any point, you can click the **Start Over** button to resort.

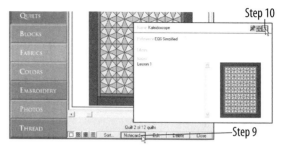

Step 10

Step 9

Step 11

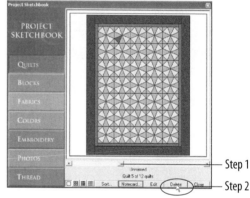

Step 1

Step 2

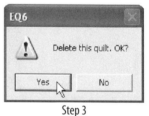

Step 3

Step 4

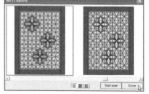

Step 5

Step 2

Step 3

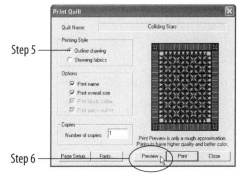

Step 5

Step 6

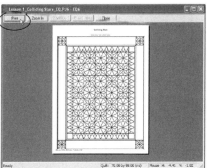

Step 7

Printing a Quilt

As you work your way thought this tutorial, you will explore EQ6's wide variety of printing options. In this lesson, you will focus on printing a quilt.

1   With the **Quilts** section of the Sketchbook still open, double-click to place your finished *Colliding Stars* quilt on the worktable.

2   Click **FILE > Print > Quilt**. The Print Quilt box will open. Click the **Page Setup** button at the bottom of the Print Quilt box. The Page Setup dialog box will open and you can **choose paper characteristics, page orientation, and page margins**.

3   Click the **Printer** button in the Page Setup dialog box to access printer information and properties. Click **OK**, **Cancel**, or click the **X** in the upper-right corner to close this dialog box.

4   Click **OK**, **Cancel**, or click the **X** in the upper-right corner to close the Page Setup dialog box

5   Under *Printing style* in the Print Quilt box, click **Outline drawing**.

6   Click **Preview**.

Notes

To zoom in on the Print Preview screen, click the Zoom In button at the top of the screen and then click and hold as you drag the cursor diagonally to frame the area that you want to enlarge. When you release the mouse button, the magnified area will fill the screen and the Zoom In tool will disengage. Click the Zoom Out button to return to the previous view or click the Fit to Screen button to return to the normal view.

7   Click the **Print** button to print the quilt outline. After printing, EQ6 will return to the Quilt worktable.

Notes

Notice that the information on the notecard *Name* line and the overall quilt size appears at the top of the quilt printout. There is also a footer that displays the quilt size and identifies EQ6 as the source of the printout.

Lesson 1

Now you will print your quilt showing fabrics

8   Click **FILE > Print > Quilt**. The Print Quilt box will open.

9   Under *Printing style*, click **Showing fabrics**.

10   Click **Preview** and **Print**. EQ6 will print your quilt in the fabrics that you have chosen. After printing, EQ6 will return to the Quilt worktable.

Step 8

Calculating Fabric Yardage

EQ6 will calculate the amount of fabric yardage that you will need for a quilt design.

1   With your *Colliding Stars* quilt on the worktable, click **FILE > Print > Fabric Yardage**. The Print Fabric Yardage box will open.

2   Click the down arrow under *Fabric Width* to display the available options and select the width upon which you want the calculations to be based.

3   Type the desired **Width** under *Seam Allowance*.

4   Click **Preview**. EQ6 will show you the number of patches and the required yardage for each fabric in your quilt, based on the fabric width and seam allowance that you specified.

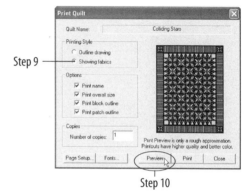

Step 9

Step 10

Notes

To zoom in on the Print Preview screen, click the Zoom In button at the top of the screen and then click and hold as you drag the cursor diagonally to frame the area that you want to enlarge. When you release the mouse button, the magnified area will fill the screen and the Zoom In tool will disengage. Click the Zoom Out button to return to the previous view or click the Fit to Screen button to return to the normal view.

5   Click **Print**.

Step 1

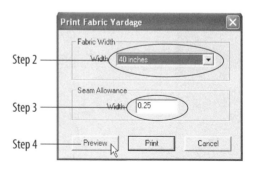

Step 2

Step 3

Step 4

Lesson 1

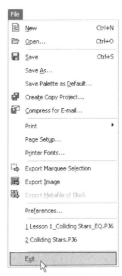

FILE > Exit

Notes
Be sure to read the information in the HELP file about how EQ6 calculates fabric yardage. The information in the HELP file is more accurate than the information in the *EQ6 User Manual*.

Exiting EQ6

Click **FILE > Exit**. Your project will close automatically when you exit the program.

CONGRATULATIONS! You have completed Lesson 1 and have learned the basic skills needed to design, document, and print a quilt in EQ6. You have also discovered the HELP file and other valuable resources that will help you to master this exciting software. You are well on your way to becoming an experienced EQ6 user!

Kaleidoscope

Kaleidoscope Cartwheels

Colliding Stars

Starting with a Quick-Quilt

EQ6 contains a collection of finished quilt designs called "quick-quilts" that you can use just as they are or change to meet your particular specifications. In this lesson, you will modify a "quick-quilt" to create two new on-point designs: *Celtic Crossroads North* and *Celtic Crossroads South*. My inspiration for these quilts is the Celtic cross, which is part of my strong Irish heritage. While designing these quilts, you will review basic skills from Lesson 1 (denoted by *) and you will also:

- Start with a quick-quilt project
- Save your project file *
- Compress for E-mail
- Add designs from the Fabric Library *
- Add designs from the Block Library *
- Color on the Block worktable
- Switch between worktables
- Change the default border style
- Adjust a quick-quilt layout
    - Add sashing
    - Set blocks in sashing
    - Rotate blocks on the layout
- Create an on-point variation
- Complete notecards *
- Print blocks and templates
- Print clipped blocks
- Save the current palette as the default

Starting with a Quick-Quilt Project

1 Run EQ6. When the Project Helper opens, click the **Start with a quick-quilt project** tab. The list of completed quick-quilts will open.

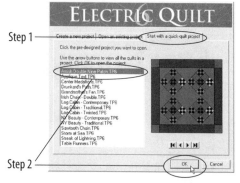

Step 1

Step 2

2 Click the first design in the list, **Amish Double Nine Patch.TP6**, and then click **OK** at the bottom of the Project Helper box. The Quilts section of the Project Sketchbook will open to the collection of *Amish Double Nine Patch* layouts.

In order to navigate more easily through the Quilts section of the Sketchbook, you will delete all except the first layout in this collection. The first quilt is a 2 block by 2 block on-point layout that is identified as *Wall Quilt - Amish Double Nine Patch, Quilt 1 of 8 quilts*. This is the layout that you should keep.

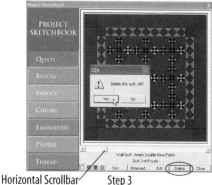

3 Click the horizontal scrollbar under the quilt display to view the *second* quick-quilt in the collection. Click the **Delete** button at the bottom of the Sketchbook. When EQ6 asks if you want to delete this quilt, click **Yes**.

Horizontal Scrollbar   Step 3

4 Using this method, **delete all layouts except the first one** in the Quilts section of the Sketchbook. Stop when the countdown at the bottom reads: "Quilt 1 of 1 quilts."

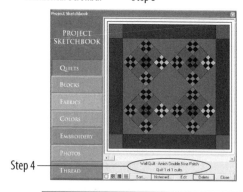

Step 4

5 Double-click on the only remaining layout, the 2 block by 2 block **Wall Quilt - Amish Double Nine Patch** to place it on the Quilt worktable.

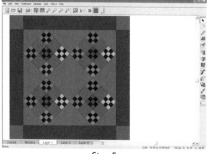

Step 5

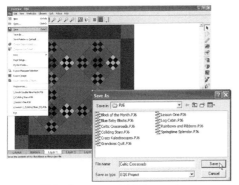

FILE > Save > type *Celtic Crossroads*

Step 1
Close

Saving your Project File

Notice that your project file is labeled "Untitled - EQ6" in the upper-left corner of the screen. To name this project file, click **FILE > Save > type** *Celtic Crossroads*. Click the **Save** button at the bottom of the Save As box. Your project file is named now and has the proper extension (.PJ6).

Compressing for E-mail

1 Open the **Project Sketchbook** (F8) and click the **Blocks** button to open the Blocks section of the Sketchbook. You will notice that there are many *Double Nine Patch* blocks here. Only one of these blocks is in the *Amish Double Nine Patch* layout in the Quilts section of the Sketchbook. The extra blocks were used in the layouts that you just deleted. As you can see, deleting a quilt from the Sketchbook does not delete the designs that were used in it. **Close** the Sketchbook.

The *Compress for E-mail* feature in EQ6 makes it easy to remove unused designs like these from the Sketchbook with just a few clicks. This feature also reduces the size of the project file so that it is easier to e-mail.

An *unused design* is defined as any block, fabric, embroidery, picture, or thread that is not used in a quilt in the Sketchbook. DO NOT use the Compress for E-mail feature if you have any designs in the file that you want to keep but have not used in a quilt!

As a safety precaution, you should *always save a copy of a project file* under a different name before compressing it. In this particular case, however, you have only one quick-quilt in the Sketchbook and you have not yet collected any designs for your new quilts. You can use the Compress for E-mail feature now without risk. Compressing this file will delete the default palette because none of these fabrics were used in the quilt. This won't be a problem because you are going to create your own palette in the next section of this lesson.

2   Click **FILE > Compress for E-mail**. The Compress for E-mail box will open with two options. You can delete all unused designs or you can delete only unused fabrics. The first option is selected by default. Click **OK**. Any unused blocks, fabrics, embroidery designs, pictures, or thread that are not used in a quilt in the Sketchbook will be deleted.

3   Open the **Sketchbook** (F8) and click the **Blocks** button to open the Blocks section of the Sketchbook. The only remaining block is the design that is used in the *Amish Double Nine Patch* quilt that is in your Sketchbook.

4   Click the **Fabrics** button to open the Fabric section of the Sketchbook. As you can see, the default palette has been deleted. You will select your own fabrics palette in the next section and save it as the default at the end of this lesson. **Close** the Sketchbook.

Adding Designs from the Fabric Library

As you know, the first step in building a quilt is to collect the elements that you need to create it. In Lesson 1, you browsed library styles by category to find striped fabrics for your *Colliding Stars* quilt. In this lesson, you will browse library styles by color to select fabrics for your *Celtic Crossroads* quilts.

1   Click **LIBRARIES > Fabric Library > EQ Libraries > EQ6 Libraries > by Color**.

2   Use the vertical scrollbar to view the library styles. Click any library style to open it.

3   Place your cursor, without clicking, over any fabric in the selected library style. A tooltip will appear that identifies the collection name and the designer of this fabric.

4   Click the fabric sample to select it and then click the **Notecard** button at the bottom of the Fabric Library box. The notecard will provide detailed information about this fabric that includes the name of the collection, the designer, the manufacturer's reference number, the EQ library location, and the copyright.

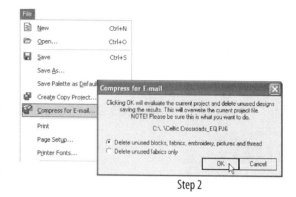

Step 2

Step 3

Step 4

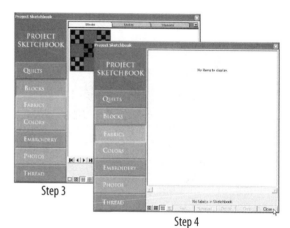

Step 1   Step 2   Step 3   Step 4

Step 5

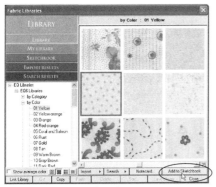

Step 6

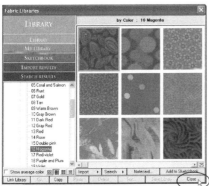

Step 7

Notes
Notice the buttons in the upper-right corner of the notecard: the push pin (pin), the four-headed arrows (move), and the X (close). These buttons function the same way as the quilt notecard buttons that you used in Lesson 1.

5   Click **X** to close the notecard.

6   Browse through the library styles *by Color* to find fabrics for your new quilts. When you find a sample that appeals to you, click the fabric to select it and then click **Add to Sketchbook**. Samples will disappear temporarily from the library when they are added to the Fabrics and Colors section of the Sketchbook. They are still in the library and you will see them the next time that you open that library.

Notes

- To add one sample within a collection, click the sample and then click Add to Sketchbook in the Fabric Libraries box.

- To add multiple samples scattered throughout a collection, hold down the CTRL key as you click the individual samples that you want. Click Add to Sketchbook in the Fabric Libraries box.

- To add a series of sequential samples within a collection, click the first sample and then, holding down the SHIFT key, click the last sample in the sequence. The first and last samples will be selected, as well as all of the samples in between. Click Add to Sketchbook in the Fabric Libraries box.

- To add all of the samples within a collection, CTRL+A to select all. Click Add to Sketchbook in the Fabric Libraries box.

- To deselect a selected sample, hold down the CTRL key as you click on it.

7   When you have added all the fabric samples that you want to use in your quilt, click **Close** in the Fabric Libraries box.

Lesson 2

Adding Designs from the Block Library

Now you will search the EQ6 Block Library for the block designs that you need for these *Celtic Crossroads* quilts.

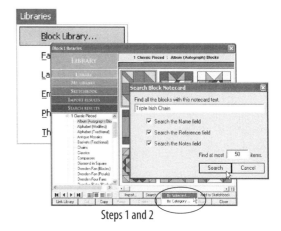

1 Click **LIBRARIES > Block Library > Search > By Notecard >** type *Triple Irish Chain*.

2 Click the **Search** button in the Search Blocks Notecard box or press the **ENTER** key on your keyboard. EQ6 will perform the search and then tell you how many block notecards contain these words. Click **OK** and the Search Results section will open with these designs displayed.

Steps 1 and 2

3 Click the *Triple Irish Chain*. **Add to Sketchbook**.

Notes

Search results are dependent upon the content of your My Library collection, as well as any add-on collections that you have linked to EQ6.

4 Click **Search > by Notecard >** type *Rose of Sharon* **> ENTER**. EQ6 will perform the search and then tell you how many block notecards contain these words. Click **OK** and the Search Results section will open.

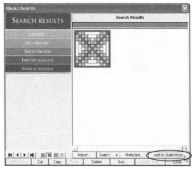

Step 3

5 Click the *Rose of Sharon* block that is illustrated in the figure. **Add to Sketchbook**.

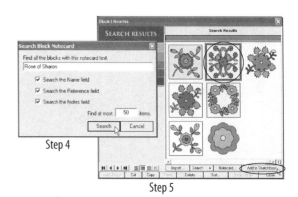

Step 4

Step 5

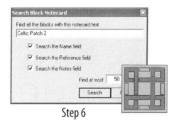

Step 6

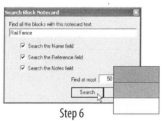

Step 6

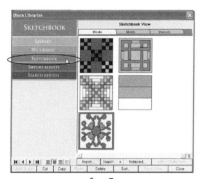

Step 7

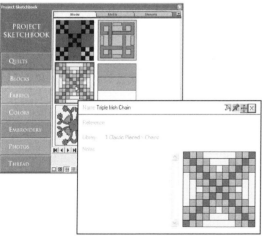

Step 1

6   Use the same procedure to add the **Celtic Patch 2** and **Rail Fence** blocks to the Blocks section of your Sketchbook. Be sure to select the *Rail Fence* design that has three rails.

Notes

- Searching the EQ6 Libraries on broad terms such as *chain*, *rose*, *patch*, or *rail* will yield many results. Searching on less common words such as *triple*, *sharon*, *celtic*, or *fence* will narrow your search and yield fewer results. Searching on several words such as *triple irish*, *rose of sharon*, *celtic patch*, or *rail fence* will narrow your search further and yield even fewer results.

- You can search the EQ6 Libraries on part of a word. Capitalization is not necessary.

- The *EQ6 Block Book* is an excellent visual reference for all of the designs in the EQ6 Block Library. It is available from The Electric Quilt Company.

7   When you have finished adding these library designs, click the **Sketchbook** button on the left side of the **Block Library** box and use the horizontal scrollbar to check that all four blocks have been added to the Blocks section. **Close** the Block Library box.

Discovering the Block Notecards

1   Open the **Project Sketchbook** (F8) and click the **Blocks** button to open the Blocks section of the Sketchbook. Click the *Triple Irish Chain* block and then click the **Notecard** button. The notecard will open and you will see the block name on the *Name* line and the library location on the *Library* line. The block will display in the default coloring on the notecard.

Notes

- Designs added from the Libraries or from other EQ software are named. Each block that you create in EQ6 will have a notecard that you can use to document the design. All notecard information is transferred automatically when designs are added to a Project Sketchbook.

- Notice the four buttons in the upper-right corner of the Block notecard. The first button flips the notecard over to reveal the categories into which EQ6 sorts this design.

- The last three buttons should be familiar because they are the same buttons that are on the quilt and fabric notecards: the push pin (pin), the four-headed arrows (move), and the X (close). These buttons have the same functions on all notecards.

- You can add, change, or delete text on notecards by using the TAB key or the mouse button to position the cursor before typing. You should always record the source of a new design on the notecard for future reference.

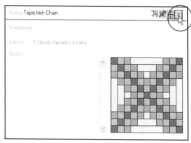

Step 2

2   Click the **X** in the upper-right corner to close the notecard.

Coloring on the Block Worktable

1   With the Blocks Section of the Sketchbook still open, select the **default coloring** of the *Triple Irish Chain* block. Double-click to place it on the EasyDraw™ worktable.

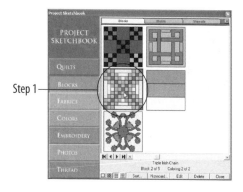

Step 1

Step 2

Notes

Use the Coloring Arrows ▶◀▶▶ in the Block Library to display the line drawing, grayscale coloring, and default coloring of all of the designs in the selected library style.

2   Click the **Color** tab. The Fabrics and Colors palette will open with the **Paintbrush** tool already engaged.

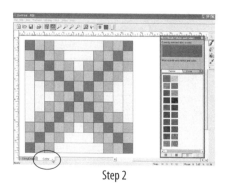

Step 2

Paintbrush Tool

Spraycan Tool

Eyedropper Tool

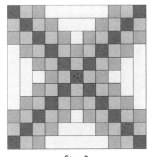

Step 3

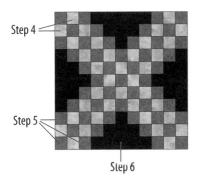

Step 4 —

Step 5 —

Step 6

Step 7
Add to Sketchbook

Notes

The color tools on the Block worktable function the same way that they do on the Quilt worktable:

- The *Paintbrush* tool recolors individual patches within a single design.

- The *Spraycan* tool recolors all identically colored patches within a single design.

- The *Eyedropper* tool finds fabrics in the Fabrics and Colors palette that have been used already in the design.

It will be easier to recolor this block using the Spraycan tool because you can recolor all identically colored patches with one click.

3   Click the **Spraycan** tool and click the color in the Fabric and Colors palette that you want to use to recolor the center chain. Click **one of the patches** to recolor all patches in the *center chain*.

4   Click the color that you want to use to recolor the *chains on either side of the center chain*. Click **one of the patches** to recolor all of the patches in these chains.

Notes

- Remember that you can undo a single action or a series of actions with EDIT > Undo or CTRL+Z.

- To find previously used colors, use the Eyedropper tool or see the *Most recently used fabrics and colors* section at the top of the Fabrics and Colors palette.

5   Click the color that you want to use to recolor the *outer chains* in the block. Click **one of the patches** to recolor all of the patches in these chains.

6   Click the color that you want to use to recolor the *background patches*. Click **one of these patches** to recolor all of the patches in the background.

7   Your *Triple Irish Chain* block is now recolored. **Add to Sketchbook**.

Lesson 2

8   Open the **Project Sketchbook** (F8) and then open the **Blocks** section of the Sketchbook. Select the **default coloring** of the *Rose of Sharon* block. Double-click to place it on the PatchDraw worktable.

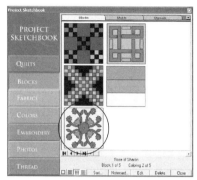

Step 8

Notes
If you can't open the Project Sketchbook using F8, click on the worktable, away from the Fabrics and Colors palette to deactivate it and then press F8 again.

9   Click the **Color** tab. Use the **Spraycan** tool to recolor this *Rose of Sharon* block, just as you recolored the *Triple Irish Chain* block. **Add to Sketchbook**.

It will be easier to choose the appropriate colors for the *Celtic Patch 2* and *Rail Fence* blocks *after* they are set into the layout later in this lesson.

Switching Between Worktables
You can switch between the Block and Quilt worktables by clicking **WORKTABLE > Work on Block** or **WORKTABLE > Work on Quilt**.

There are also two buttons on the right end of the Project toolbar that provide an easy shortcut between the Block and Quilt worktables. They are the **Work on Block** button and the **Work on Quilt** button. The *Work on Block* icon is a single colored block and the *Work on Quilt* icon is the same block design set into a 2 x 2 layout.

Click the **Work on Quilt** button on the Project toolbar to open the Quilt worktable. The Quilt worktable will open to the *Amish Double Nine Patch* design.

Notes
When the Quilt worktable opens, the word QUILT replaces the word BLOCK on the main menu. The options and tools available under these two main menu items change to accommodate the type of worktable that is open.

Step 9
Add to Sketchbook

Work on Block   Work on Quilt
Button   Button

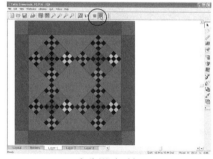

Quilt Worktable

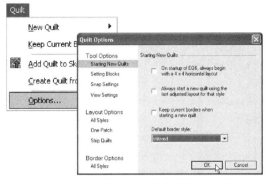

Change the Default Border Style

Changing the Default Border Style

You will use mitered borders often in this tutorial, so you will change the default border to this style now.

Click **QUILT > Options > Starting New Quilts**. Click on the arrow next to **Default border style** to open the drop-down list. Click **Mitered > OK**.

Now when you start a new quilt or add a border to a layout, the border will be in the mitered style.

Adjusting a Quick-Quilt Layout

You are ready to adjust your quick-quilt layout in preparation for setting the blocks into the quilt.

1   Click the **Layout** tab on the lower-left of the screen. Notice that under *Select a style*, there are options for two different layouts in the On-point Layout box. The layout for the *Amish Double Nine Patch* is based on the first on-point style. The quilt that you will design later in this lesson will be based on the second on-point style.

  • Leave the *Number of blocks* set to **2 x 2**.

  • Change the *Finished size of blocks* to **9**.

  • Change the *Finished size of sashing* to **3.00**.

2   Click the **Borders** tab. Change the border style to **Mitered** in the drop-down list.

  • Under *Lock size adjustments*, click **ALL** and change the size to **0.50**.

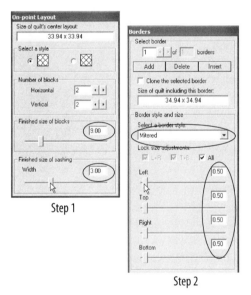

Step 1

Step 2

> **Notes**
> If all sides of this border do not change, click directly on the palette slider button for the changed side of the border. The other sides of that border will immediately adjust to the width of this side.

3   Click the **Add** button in the Borders box to add the second border. Change this second border to **Corner Blocks** style in the drop-down list. Change the size to **4.00**.

Step 3

Step 3

4 Click the **Add** button to add a third border. This third border style is **Mitered**, which is the default style. Change the size to **0.50**.

5 Click the **Add** button to add a fourth border. This fourth border style is **Mitered**. Change the size to **4.00**.

6 Click the **Add** button to add a fifth border. This fifth border style is **Mitered**. Change the size to **0.50**. This border represents the quilt binding.

7 **Add to Sketchbook.**

Your borders are now established and you are ready to set your blocks into the layout!

8 Click the **Layer 1** tab.

When replacing blocks in a layout, one option is to use the *Set Block* tool to place the new blocks over the old ones. The second option is to erase the old designs with the *Erase Block* tool and then set new blocks with the Set Block tool. For this quilt, you will use the Erase Block tool before setting the new blocks in the adjusted layout. As you learned in Lesson 1, the Erase Block tool is the fifth tool on the Quilt toolbar. The icon is a pencil eraser superimposed on a blank block.

9 Click the **Erase Block** tool on the Quilt toolbar and then **CTRL+click** a *Double Nine Patch* block in the quilt. All of the blocks in this series are now erased from the layout. Move your cursor to one of the *plain triangles* and **CTRL+click**. All of the plain triangles are now erased from the layout.

Notes

Row definition is different in horizontal and diagonal quilts, so CTRL+click and ALT+click function differently in these two types of layouts. Experiment with the Lesson 1 and Lesson 2 quilts to learn how to use CTRL+click and ALT+click in each of these layout styles.

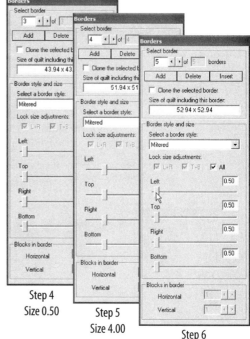

Step 4
Size 0.50

Step 5
Size 4.00

Step 6
Size 0.50

Step 7
Add to Sketchbook

Step 8

Erase Block
Tool

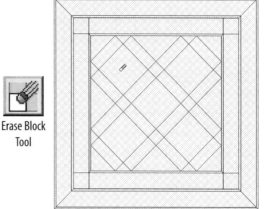

Step 9

Set Block
Tool

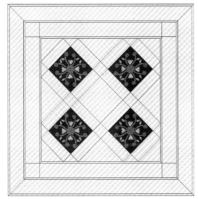

Step 10

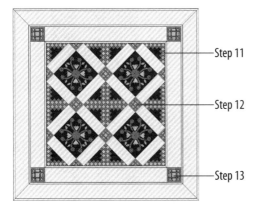

Step 11

Step 12

Step 13

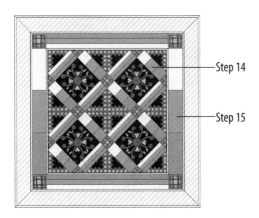

Step 14

Step 15

Step 16
Rotate Block

10 Click the **Set Block** tool, click the ***Rose of Sharon*** block in the Blocks palette, and then **CTRL+click** in the full block space in the upper-left of the layout. Four of the spaces in the layout will fill with this block. **Add to Sketchbook**.

> **Notes**
> To view the colorings of a design in the Blocks palette, click to select the block. Use the Coloring Arrows ◄◄ ◄ ► ►► to display the saved colorings or right-click to open the Blocks, Motifs & Stencils Palette Context Menu. Click Select Coloring and click the coloring that you want to set into the layout.

11 Click the ***Triple Irish Chain*** block in the Blocks palette and **CTRL+click** any other blank block space in the layout. All of the remaining spaces will fill with this block. **Add to Sketchbook**.

12 Click the ***Celtic Patch 2*** block and **CTRL+click** to set it in the sashing squares. Because row formation is different in an on-point layout, you must move your cursor to another blank sashing space and **CTRL+click** to fill the remaining sashing squares with this block. **Add to Sketchbook**.

13 **CTRL+click** the corner spaces in Border 2 to set ***Celtic Patch 2*** blocks in these spaces. **Add to Sketchbook**.

14 Click the ***Rail Fence*** block and **CTRL+click** in any sashing space to set this block in the layout. Move your cursor to another blank sashing space and **CTRL+click** to fill the remaining sashings with this block. You will rotate some of these sashings to the correct orientation within the next few steps.

15 **CTRL+click** one side of Border 2 to set the ***Rail Fence*** blocks in all sides of this border. You will rotate two of these border sides to the correct orientation in the next step. **Add to Sketchbook**.

16 Click the **Rotate Block** tool, the sixth tool on the Quilt toolbar. The icon is a sequence of rotated blocks with a curved arrow.

Lesson 2

17 **CTRL+click** one of the ***Rail Fence*** *sashing* blocks that is not in the correct orientation. All of the blocks in this series will rotate by 90 degrees. **Add to Sketchbook**.

18 With the **Rotate Block** tool still engaged, individually click the **two sides of Border 2** that need to be rotated to the correct orientation. **Add to Sketchbook**.

19 Individually click the two ***Rose of Sharon*** blocks on the right side of the layout to rotate them by 90 degrees. This is a subtle change that gives a better balance to the design. **Add to Sketchbook**.

Now you will recolor the *Rail Fence* and the *Celtic Patch 2* blocks. To achieve the "floating" effect of the *Rail Fence* sashing, you will color the two strips on the outside of this block with the same background color that you used on the *Rose of Sharon* block.

20 Click the **Eyedropper** tool and then click the **background fabric** in one of the *Rose of Sharon* blocks in the layout. This color will display in the sample window of the Fabrics and Colors palette and it will be selected in the palette.

21 Click the **Spraycan** tool and then **CTRL+click** the outside strips in one of the *Rail Fence* sashings in the layout.

22 Move your cursor to the next series of *Rail Fence* sashings and **CTRL+click** to recolor the two outside strips on these blocks. Repeat this procedure on the outside strips in the *Rail Fence* blocks in Border 2. **Add to Sketchbook**.

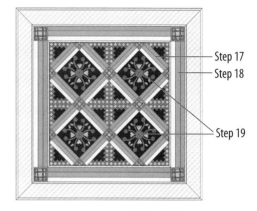

Step 17
Step 18

Step 19

Eyedropper Tool

Step 20

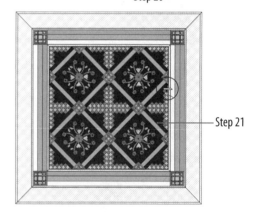

Step 21

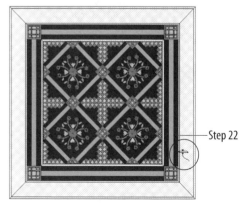

Step 22

Step 23

Spraycan
Tool

Step 23
Add to Sketchbook

Step 24
Zoom In

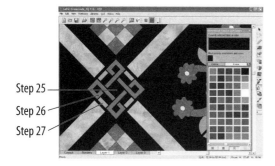

Step 25

Step 26

Step 27

Step 27
Add to Sketchbook

23 Click the color in the Fabrics and Colors palette that you want to use for the *center sashing strips*. Click the **Spraycan** tool and **CTRL+click** to recolor these center strips. Move the cursor and **repeat this action** to recolor the remaining center strips in the *sashings* and in *Border 2*. **Add to Sketchbook**.

24 Click the **Zoom In** tool and magnify one of the *Celtic Patch 2* blocks in the layout.

Notes

The Zoom In tool is on the Project toolbar and the icon is a plus (+) sign within a magnifying glass. Click the Zoom In tool and, holding down the mouse button, drag a selection box diagonally across the area that you want to enlarge. When you release the mouse button, the magnified area will fill the screen and the Zoom In tool will disengage. Use the vertical and horizontal scrollbars on the screen to navigate on the magnified worktable. Click the Fit to Worktable tool to return to a full view of the quilt. The Fit to Worktable tool is the last Zoom tool on the Project toolbar. The icon is a square within a magnifying glass.

25 Use the **Eyedropper** or the **Most recently used fabrics and colors** in the palette to find the background color that you used on the *Rose of Sharon* block. Use the **Spraycan** tool and **CTRL+click** to recolor the background of the *Celtic Patch 2* block with this fabric.

26 Select a color for the *knot* in the *Celtic Patch 2* block and use the **Spraycan** tool and **CTRL+click** to recolor.

27 Select a color for the *small rectangular* patches in this block and **CTRL+click**. **Add to Sketchbook**.

28 Repeat this procedure to recolor all of the *Celtic Patch 2* blocks in the sashing squares and borders. **Add to Sketchbook**.

29 Click the **Paintbrush** tool, select a color for each remaining border and **CTRL+click** to color. **Add to Sketchbook**.

30 Open the **Project Sketchbook** (F8) and click the **Quilts** button to open the Quilts section of the Sketchbook. Use the horizontal scrollbar to display your **Celtic Crossroads North** quilt (the last quilt in the sketchbook).

31 Click the **Notecard** button and type the quilt's name on the *Name* line. Under *Reference*, type **EQ6 Simplified** and under Notes, type **Lesson 2**.

32 **Close** the notecard and **close** the Sketchbook.

Your *Celtic Crossroads North* quilt is finished!

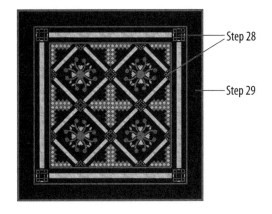

Step 28

Step 29

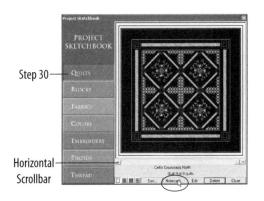

Step 30

Horizontal Scrollbar

Step 32

Step 31

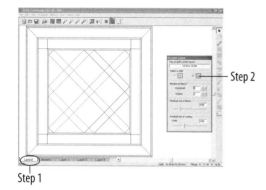

Step 2

Step 1

Creating an On-Point Variation

Now you will create *Celtic Crossroads South*, a variation of your *Celtic Crossroads North* quilt.

1   With your *Celtic Crossroads North* quilt on the worktable, click the **Layout** tab. Notice that under *Select a style*, the layout on the left has only one full block in the first diagonal row of blocks. This is the layout that you used for your *Celtic Crossroads North* quilt. The layout on the right has two full blocks in the first diagonal row of blocks. This is the layout you will use for your new *Celtic Crossroads South* quilt.

2   Click to select the **layout on the right** in the On-point Layout box. Keep all of the other settings in this box. You will not change any settings on the Borders tab because you will keep the same borders that you used in your *Celtic Crossroads North* quilt.

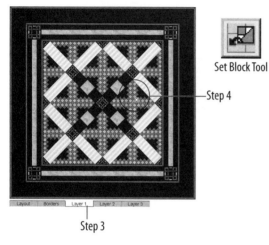

Set Block Tool

Step 4

Step 3

3   Click the **Layer 1** tab. You will notice that some of the designs in the layout were retained from the *Celtic Crossroads North* quilt.

For this particular layout, it is easier to set the same design in all block spaces in the layout and then just replace a few blocks with a different design.

4   Click the **Set Block** tool and then click the *Triple Irish Chain* in the Blocks palette. **CTRL+click** to set this design in the block spaces in the layout. Move your cursor to another block space and **CTRL+click** to fill the remaining spaces with this block. **Add to Sketchbook**.

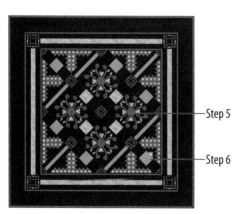

Step 5

Step 6

5   Click the *Rose of Sharon* block in the Blocks palette. Individually click the *four full Triple Irish Chain* blocks in the center of the layout to replace them with the *Rose of Sharon* block. **Add to Sketchbook**.

6   Click to select the *Rail Fence* block. **CTRL+click** to set this block in all sashing spaces in the layout. **Add to Sketchbook**.

Add to Sketchbook
Button

Lesson 2

7   Click the **Rotate Block** tool and **CTRL+click** one of the *Rail Fence* sashings to rotate it to the correct orientation. **Add to Sketchbook**.

8   Click the ***Rose of Sharon*** block on the right side of the layout to *rotate it by 90 degrees*. Rotate the ***Rose of Sharon*** block at the bottom of the layout to *rotate it by 90 degrees*. This subtle change gives better balance to the design. **Add to Sketchbook**.

9   Open the **Quilts** section of the Sketchbook and use the horizontal scrollbar to display your ***Celtic Crossroads South*** quilt. Click the **Notecard** button and type the quilt's name on the *Name line*. Under *Reference*, add **EQ6 Simplified** and under *Notes*, add **Lesson 2**. **Close** the notecard.

Isn't it amazing how quickly you created your second *Celtic Crossroads* quilt?

Printing Blocks and Templates

1   With the **Quilts** section of the Sketchbook still open, use the horizontal scrollbar to display your ***Celtic Crossroads North*** quilt. This is the first finished quilt that you designed for this lesson. Double-click to place this quilt on the worktable.

2   Click the **Select** tool, the first tool on the Quilt toolbar. The icon is an arrow. Click one of the ***Celtic Patch 2*** corner blocks in Border 2.

Your first printout of the *Celtic Patch 2* block will be in the fabrics that you selected. Your second printout of this design will be the outline drawing.

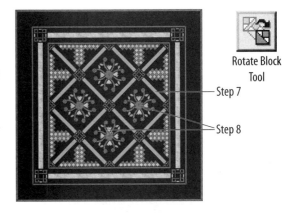

Rotate Block Tool

Step 7

Step 8

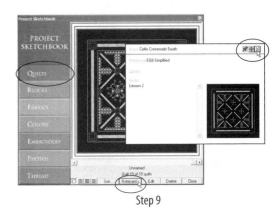

Step 9

Select Tool

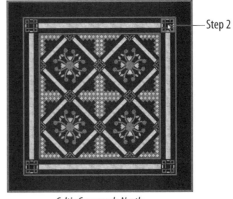

Step 2

Celtic Crossroads North

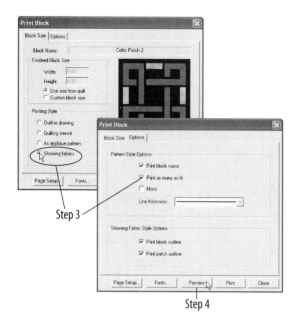

Step 3

Step 4

3   Click **FILE > Print > Block**. The Print Block box will open.

- Under *Finished Block Size*, **Use size from quilt** is selected by default. This means that the block printout will be the width of the border that you specified on the Borders tab of the Quilt worktable.

- Under *Printing Style*, click to select **Showing fabrics**. This option is available to you only if a colored version of the block is displayed in the Print Block box. You can view all versions of the selected block by using the Coloring Arrows under the block display.

- Click the **Options** tab and click to check **Print as many as fit**.

4   **Preview > Print**.

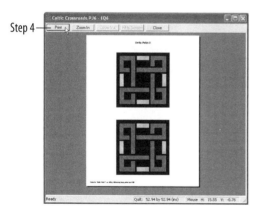

Step 4

The *Celtic Patch 2* is still selected in the corner block of Border 2. Now you will print the outline drawing of this block in a different size than you specified on the Layout tab.

5   Click **FILE > Print > Block**.

- Under *Finished Block Size*, click to check **Custom block size** and set the size to **6 x 6**.

- Under *Printing Style*, click to check **Outline drawing**.

6   **Preview > Print.**

Now you will print templates for the *Rose of Sharon* appliqué block.

7   With the **Select** tool still engaged, click one of the *Rose of Sharon* blocks in the layout.

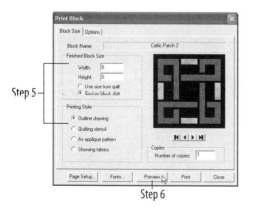

Step 5

Step 6

8 Click **FILE > Print > Templates**. The Print Template box will open.

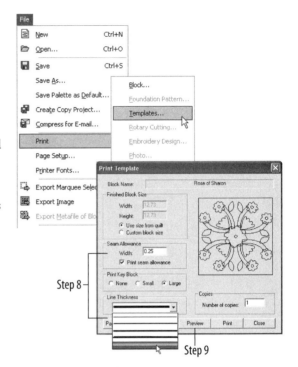

Step 8 —

Step 9

- Under *Finished Block Size*, **Use size from quilt** is selected by default. Notice that EQ6 displays the measurement of this block as 12.73". This is the diagonal measurement of this 9" block, as it appears in the layout. The printout will be 9" x 9", the size you specified on the Layout tab of the Quilt worktable.

- Under *Seam Allowance*, **Print seam allowance** is checked and **0.25"** is specified as the seam allowance width. These are the default settings.

- Under *Print Key Block*, you have the three options for the Key block: *None, Small,* and *Large*. The Key block is the diagram that maps each template to the correct position in the finished block. Click **Large** for this complicated block so that it will be easier to see.

- Under *Line Thickness*, click the **arrow** to open the drop-down list. Click the **last line** to print the template lines as thick as possible.

9 Click **Preview**.

You can move, rotate, and delete templates on the Print Preview screen.

10 Click the **Delete** button at the top of the Print Preview screen and click the background square for the *Rose of Sharon* block. The cursor will change to an "x" and the selected patch will outline in red. Press the **DELETE** key on your keyboard to remove this patch from the printout.

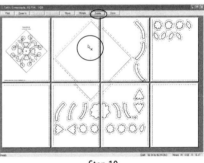

Step 10

11 Click the **Move** button at the top of the Print Preview screen and the cursor will change to a four-headed arrow. Click **any template in the printout** and it will outline in red. **Hold down the mouse button** and **drag** to move the selected template to a new location on the Print Preview screen.

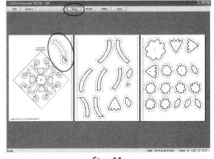

Step 11

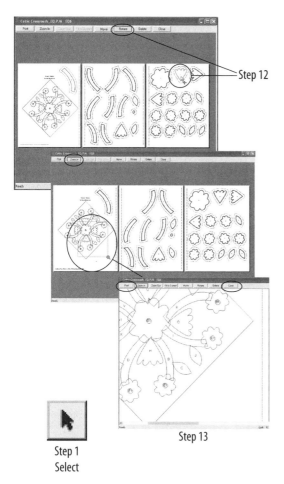

Step 12

Step 13

Step 1
Select

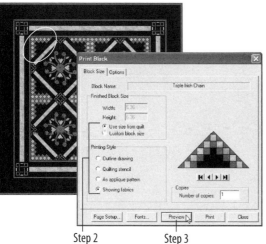

Step 2   Step 3

12   Click the **Rotate** button at the top of the Print Preview screen and then click one of the **stem or leaf** templates in the preview. The cursor will change to a curved arrow and the patch will outline in red. Each click will rotate this selected patch by 90 degrees.

Notes

To zoom in on the Print Preview screen, click the Zoom In button at the top of the screen. Click and, holding down the mouse button, drag the cursor diagonally to frame the area that you want to enlarge. When you release the mouse button, the magnified area will fill the screen and the Zoom In tool will disengage. Click the Zoom Out button to return to the previous view or click the Fit to Screen button to return to the normal view.

13   **Print** or **Close** the Print Templates box.

Printing Clipped Blocks

1   With the *Celtic Crossroads North* quilt still on the worktable, click the **Select** tool and then click one of the partial *Triple Irish Chain* blocks in a corner of the layout. This is a corner setting triangle.

Notes

In an on-point layout, all triangular blocks on the outer edges of the center design area are setting triangles. These triangles can be plain or pieced. When you place blocks in these spaces, EQ6 clips them automatically to fit. This convenient feature allows you to generate an accurate printout of a clipped block.

2   Click **FILE > Print > Block**. The Print Block box will open.

- Under *Finished Block Size*, **Use size from quilt** is checked by default.

- Under *Printing Style*, click to check **Showing fabrics**. This option is available to you only if a colored version of the block is on display in the Print Block box.

3   **Preview > Print.**

Saving the Current Palette as a Default

EQ6 allows you to designate your current palette as the new default palette.

1   Click **FILE > Save Palette as Default**. The program will ask you to verify that you want to make the current fabrics, colors, and threads your default (startup) palette in EQ6.

2   Click **OK**. Your current project's palette is now the new default fabric palette for any project that you subsequently create in EQ6. This can be changed easily at any point.

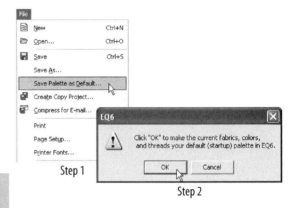

Step 1

Step 2

Notes

• To reinstall EQ6's original default palette, you must first clear the fabrics currently in your Sketchbook. Open the Fabrics section of your Sketchbook, then click Clear. Close the Sketchbook.

• Click LIBRARIES > Fabric Library > EQ Libraries > EQ6 Libraries > by Category > 01 EQ6 Default Fabrics. CTRL+A to select all fabrics and then click the Add to Sketchbook button at the bottom of the Fabric Libraries box. Click the Sketchbook button in the Fabric Libraries box to view the new default palette. Close the Fabric Libraries box.

• Follow steps 1 and 2 above to make these your default fabrics everytime you open EQ6.

Exiting EQ6

Click **FILE > Exit**. Your project will close automatically when you exit the program.

CONGRATULATIONS! You have completed Lesson 2 and have acquired many new design skills.

You have adjusted a quick-quilt, explored the Fabric and Block Libraries, colored on the Block worktable, changed a default setting, created a variation of your new quilt, printed templates and clipped blocks, and changed the default palette.

FILE > Exit

Starting from Scratch

In Lesson 1, you used block and layout designs from the EQ6 Libraries to create your quilts. In Lesson 2, you used a quick-quilt layout with block and fabric designs from the EQ6 Libraries to create your quilts. In this lesson, you will draw the blocks and define the quilt layout yourself!

I named this design *Voodoo Queen* and it was inspired by my wonderful memories of growing up in New Orleans. *Voodoo Queen* contains several elements that reflect my impressions of the music, colors, and cultural diversity of this great city. There is some discordance, but the overall design is one of intense rhythm and vitality, mixed with a warm and genuine Southern charm. In this lesson, you will learn the following new skills:

- Search the Fabric Library by Category
- Sort fabrics in the Sketchbook
- Set up the Drawing Board
- Draw with the Grid tool
- Draw with the Line tool
- Delete a line in EasyDraw™
- Sort blocks in the Sketchbook
- Discover the Fussy Cut tool
- Establish a horizontal quilt layout
- Clone a border
- Rotate fabric: Advanced
- Print a Rotary Cutting Chart
- Delete designs from the Project Sketchbook

Creating a New Project File

Run EQ6. The Project Helper will open to the **Create a new project** tab. Type *Voodoo Queen* to name your new project file. Click **OK** or press the **ENTER** key.

You will start collecting the elements that you need for your *Voodoo Queen* quilt by adding fabric designs to your Sketchbook. You will need a large-scale floral print from the EQ6 Fabric Library and a striped fabric from your Lesson 1 project file.

Searching the Fabric Library by Category

1   Click **LIBRARIES** > **Fabric Library** > **EQ Libraries** > **EQ6 Libraries** > **by Category** > **38 Nature** > **Florals, large**.

2   Browse through this library style to find a **large-scale floral print** that you want to use in your quilt.

- To add *one sample*, **click the sample** and then click **Add to Sketchbook** in the Fabric Library box.

- To *add sequential samples*, **click the first sample** and then **hold down the SHIFT key** and **click the last sample** in the sequence. The first and last samples and all samples in between will be selected. **Add to Sketchbook**.

- To *add samples that are not in sequence*, **click the first sample** and then **hold down the CTRL key** and **click to select any other samples**. **Add to Sketchbook**.

- To add *all samples* in the collection, **CTRL+A** to select all. **Add to Sketchbook**.

- To *deselect a selected sample*, **hold down the CTRL key** and **click**.

Create a New Project

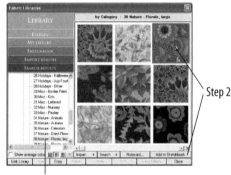

Step 2

Step 1

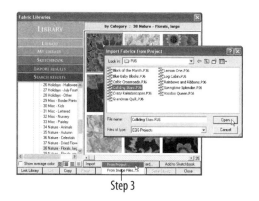

Step 3

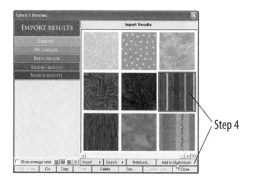

Step 4

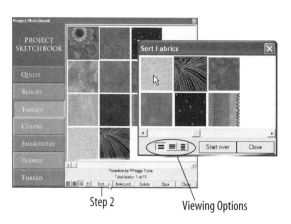

Step 2   Viewing Options

In addition to a large-scale floral print, you will need a striped fabric for the quilt binding. Since you added a collection of stripes to your Lesson 1 project file, you will use the import feature in the EQ6 Library to add these samples from that Project Sketchbook to your current Project Sketchbook.

3 With the Fabric Libraries box still open, click **Import > From Project**. The Import Fabrics from Project box will open. Navigate to the PJ6 directory (My Documents > My EQ6 > PJ6). Click **Colliding Stars.PJ6** in the list of EQ6 projects and then click **Open** or double-click the project file.

4 Scroll through the samples in the Import Results section until you find the *striped fabrics that you added in Lesson 1.* **Click the striped fabric** that you will use as the quilt binding in this new quilt. Click **Add to Sketchbook**. **Close** the Fabric Library.

> **Notes**
> You can import designs from other EQ project files into your current Project Sketchbook, including layouts, blocks, fabrics, embroidery, and photos.

Sorting Fabrics in the Sketchbook

In Lesson 1, you learned how to sort quilt layouts in the Quilts section of the Sketchbook. You can use the same procedure to sort fabrics in the Fabrics section of the Sketchbook.

1 Open the **Project Sketchbook** (F8) and click the **Fabrics** button.

2 Click the **Sort** button at the bottom of the Fabrics section. The Sort Fabrics box will open. Notice that you have several viewing options in this box.

Lesson 3

3 In the Sort Fabrics box, **click the fabric samples** *in the order in which you want them to appear* in the Fabrics section of the Sketchbook. You can click the first few that you want to sort and then click **Close**. Any unsorted designs will follow the sorted samples automatically. At any point, you can click the *Start Over* button to resort.

4 **Close** the Sketchbook.

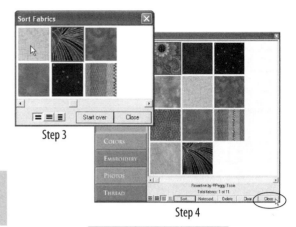
Step 3

Step 4

Notes
You can save this Fabric palette as your default by clicking FILE > Save Palette as Default.

Setting up the Drawing Board

You must determine the grid structure of a pieced block before you can draw it, whether you are using EQ6 or the old-fashioned method of graph paper and pencil. The grid structure is the pattern of evenly spaced lines upon which a block design is based.

Some block grid structures are easy to see, but many are subtle and require a little effort to recognize. In this lesson, you will learn the basic approach to block analysis by determining the grid structures of the blocks that you will use in your *Voodoo Queen* quilt. You will start with the *Nine Patch* block, a simple pieced design with an obvious grid structure. The 3 x 3 pattern of evenly spaced lines in this block is completely visible.

Once you determine the grid structure of a block, you can set up the drawing board to create the block in EQ6.

1 Click **WORKTABLE > Work on Block** or click the **Work on Block** button on the Project toolbar.

2 Click **BLOCK > New Block > EasyDraw Block**. The EasyDraw™ worktable will open to a plain block with the EasyDraw™ tools displayed on the left side of the screen. The **Line** tool will be engaged automatically. It is the third tool on the EasyDraw™ toolbar and the icon is a pencil drawing a straight line.

Nine Patch **Block**

Step 1
Work on Block

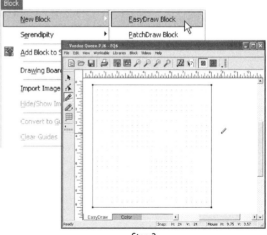
Step 2

Lesson 3

Step 3

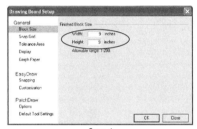

Step 4

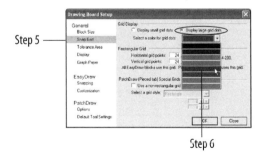

Step 5 ——

Step 6

Notes

- You are choosing EasyDraw™ Block because it is the appropriate worktable for creating pieced block designs. You will learn more about the other drawing worktables later in this tutorial.

- There is one unbreakable rule in EasyDraw™: The ends of all lines and arcs must connect to another line or arc, or to the block outline. Any unconnected ends will be trimmed automatically.

3 Click **BLOCK > Drawing Board Setup**.

Notes

Change ONLY the Drawing Board Setup values that are given in the following set of instructions. All of the other options in the Drawing Board Setup should remain set to the default values, as instructed in Lesson 1 of this tutorial.

4 Under *Finished Block Size*, set the **Width** and **Height** to **9"**.

Notes

The Finished Block Size dimensions that you specify here determine only the shape of the block, that is, whether the block will display as a square or as a rectangle on the block worktable. You can print the block in any size or set it into a quilt layout in any size, no matter what size you specify here.

5 Click **Snap Grid** in the Drawing Board Setup list.

6 Under *Grid Display*, click to check **Display large grid dots**. This will make the Rectangular Grid Points easier to see. You can also *select the color* of the grid dots by clicking the down arrow next to **Select a color for grid dots** and clicking a color.

The Rectangular Grid Points establish a network of evenly spaced dots to which your drawn lines will snap. The Rectangular Grid Points must be evenly divisible by the number of grid divisions in the block.

7 This *Nine Patch* is based on a *3 x 3 grid*, so you must set the number of grid divisions to a value that is *divisible by 3*. Set the **Horizontal grid points** and the **Vertical grid points** to **9**.

8 Under EasyDraw Snapping, be sure that *Snap to Grid* and *Snap to nodes of drawing* are checked. Click **OK**.

The Drawing Board is now set up for the *Nine Patch* block. You could have set the Rectangular Grid Points to another multiple of 3, such as 6, 12, or 15, etc., but 9 will be most useful, as you will discover when you draw the *Double Nine Patch* design in the next section.

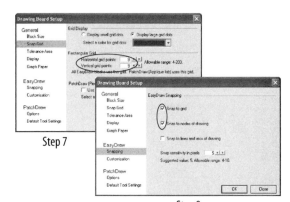
Step 7

Step 8

Notes

- The default setting for Rectangular Grid Points is 24 x 24, which is appropriate for most block designs.

- The horizontal and vertical rulers on the worktable measure 9" x 9", the size that you specified for your block. These rulers are intended to be used only as a drawing aid and do not restrict your use of this block in any way.

Drawing with the Grid Tool

You will draw the *Nine Patch* block first and then draw a series of variations until you have completed the blocks that you need for your *Voodoo Queen* quilt.

1 Click the **Grid** tool on the EasyDraw™ toolbar. The Grid tool is the fifth tool from the top and is represented by a 3 x 3 grid icon. Move the cursor to the worktable and notice that the cursor has changed to crosshairs with a small grid design.

2 Click **BLOCK > Grid Tool Setup**. The Grid Setup box will open on the worktable.

Notes

You can also open the Grid Setup box by:

- Clicking the small red square on the corner of the Grid tool.

- Clicking the Grid tool and then right-clicking on the worktable to open the EasyDraw™ Worktable Context Menu. Click Grid Setup to open the Grid Setup box.

Drawing Board

Step 1
Grid

Cursor

Step 2

Grid Tool
Setup

EasyDraw™ Worktable Context Menu

Step 3

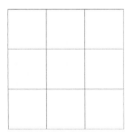

Step 4

3 Use the **arrow keys** in the Grid Setup box to set the **Columns** and **Rows** to **3**.

4 **Position the center of the crosshairs** cursor in *any corner* of the block outline. **Click** and, holding down the mouse button, **drag the cursor diagonally across the block**, releasing the button on the block outline in the *opposite corner*. This will create a *Nine Patch* block on the worktable.

> **Notes**
> If you click and release the mouse button when the crosshairs are too far from the corner of the block, the grid will not extend to the edges of the block. If this happens, undo your action with EDIT > Undo or CTRL+Z. After you undo the previous grid, redraw it, being careful to start and end on the corners of the block outline.

Step 5
Add to Sketchbook

5 When you have successfully drawn the *Nine Patch* block, **Add to Sketchbook**. There's no need to color this block at this point since you have more work to do before you are finished with it.

Now you will draw the *Double Nine Patch* block. As you can see, the *Double Nine Patch* block is just a large *Nine Patch* block with smaller *Nine Patch* designs drawn within five of the patches. You will need 3 x 3 Rectangular Grid Points within each of these smaller patches in order to accommodate the *Nine Patch* designs that you will draw there. Because you specified 9 x 9 Rectangular Grid Points when you drew the *Nine Patch* block, you already have the extra points that you need within the smaller patches.

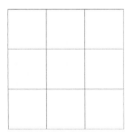 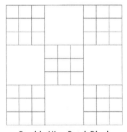

Nine Patch Block   *Double Nine Patch* Block

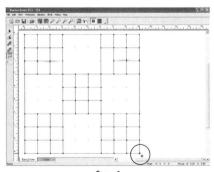

Step 6

Add to
Sketchbook
Button

6 With the *Nine Patch* block still on the worktable and the **Grid** tool still engaged, **draw a 3 x 3 grid** in *each of the five patches* of the *Nine Patch* block, as illustrated. **Add to Sketchbook**.

Lesson 3

Drawing with the Line Tool

The *Double Nine Patch* design is finished and you are ready to draw the variation of this design that you will need for your *Voodoo Queen* quilt.

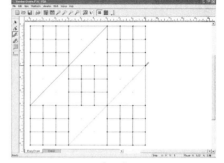

1 With the *Double Nine Patch* still on the worktable, click the **Line** tool. It is the third tool on the EasyDraw™ toolbar and the icon is a pencil drawing a straight line. **Draw diagonal lines through the plain patches in the *Double Nine Patch* block**, as illustrated. Draw the lines by clicking the point at which you want the line to begin and, dragging the cursor to the end point of the line, then releasing the mouse button. **Add to Sketchbook**.

Line Tool

Step 1

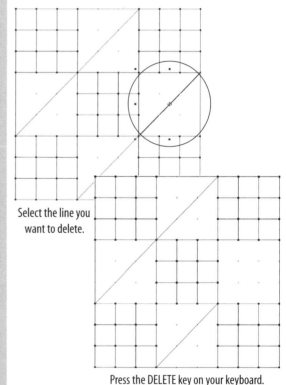

Pick Tool

Notes

• To delete a line immediately after drawing, use EDIT > Undo or CTRL+Z. You must do this before you click Add to Sketchbook. Once you have clicked Add to Sketchbook, EQ6 will place nodes at each intersection of a drawing. These nodes will define each segment of a line as a separate object.

• You will use the Pick tool to delete a selected object from the EasyDraw™ worktable. If you click the little red square on the Pick tool button, the Symmetry dialog box will open with more functions for this tool. Ignore this dialog box for now. When you choose another tool, the dialog box will disappear.

• To delete a single line in a block drawing: Click the Pick tool and then click the line to be deleted. The line will be marked with a center break and surrounded by nodes. Press the DELETE key on your keyboard.

• To delete several lines in a block drawing: Click the Pick tool and, holding down the DELETE key, click each one of the unwanted lines.

• To delete all the lines in a block: Click EDIT > Select All or use CTRL+A. The entire drawing will highlight. Press the DELETE key.

• You can also use EDIT > Cut or EDIT > Clear to delete selected lines in EQ6.

Select the line you want to delete.

Press the DELETE key on your keyboard.

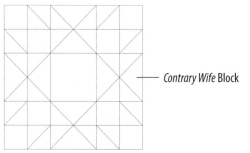

— *Contrary Wife* Block

Step 2
View Sketchbook

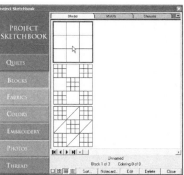

— Step 3

Precision Bar

Now you will begin the process of drawing the *Contrary Wife* block. Before drawing this design, you must analyze the block and set up the Drawing Board. As you learned with the *Nine Patch*, the easiest approach to analyzing a pieced design is to find a pattern of continuous, evenly-spaced straight lines that run through the block.

Look carefully at the *Contrary Wife* and note the *straight lines* in this block. There are *four horizontal* and *four vertical lines* that occur at regular intervals. If you envision horizontal and vertical center lines through this design, the *6 x 6 grid structure* emerges. Now that you know the grid structure of the *Contrary Wife* block, you can set up the drawing board.

Instead of starting a new block, you will use the *Nine Patch* design as the basis for this new block. The *Nine Patch* block has a 3 x 3 grid structure, which is compatible with the 6 x 6 grid structure of the *Contrary Wife* block.

2   Open the **Project Sketchbook** (F8), click the **Blocks** button to open the Blocks section of the Sketchbook, and then double-click the ***Nine Patch*** block to place it on the worktable.

You are going to use a convenient toolbar to set the parameters for your new block without opening the Drawing Board Setup.

3   Click **VIEW** and click to check **Precision Bar**. The Precision Bar will open at the top of the worktable, between the Project toolbar and the horizontal ruler. This Precision Bar contains the *main settings* in **BLOCK > Drawing Board Setup.**

This Precision Bar is labeled Drawing Setup. In this lesson, you will use the first three tools in this bar. The first tool is for *setting the block size*, the second is for *setting the rectangular grid points*, and the third is for *setting the graph paper.*

On the Precision Bar:

4   Keep the *block size* set to **9" x 9"**.

5   The *Contrary Wife* block is based on a 6 x 6 grid structure, so the rectangular grid points, **Snaps Horizontal** and **Snaps Vertical**, must be *divisible by 6*. Set these values to **12**.

6   Click the **Graph Paper** button to turn on this feature and then set the **Horizontal** and **Vertical** values to **6**.

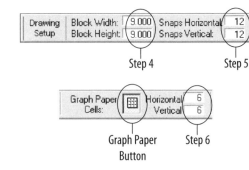

Step 4   Step 5

Graph Paper
Button   Step 6

Notes

- The graph paper is a drawing aid that is available only on the drawing worktables.

- You can change the color of the graph paper in BLOCK > Drawing Board Setup > Graph Paper by clicking the down arrow next to *Select a graph paper* color and clicking a color. Click OK.

- Clicking the Graph Paper button on the Precision Bar turns the graph paper on and off.

- Do not confuse the Graph Paper tool with the Grid tool, which is on the EasyDraw™ toolbar. The Graph Paper tool is used to establish a grid of dashed guidelines on the worktable. The Grid Tool is used to set a grid of solid, drawn lines on the worktable.

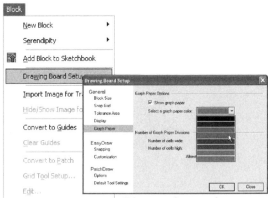

Select a graph paper color

The Drawing Board is now set up for drawing the *Contrary Wife* block.

7   Click the **Line** tool and, using the illustration as a guide, **draw the** *Contrary Wife* **block**. **Add to Sketchbook**.

Line Tool

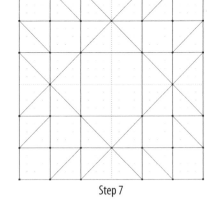

Step 7

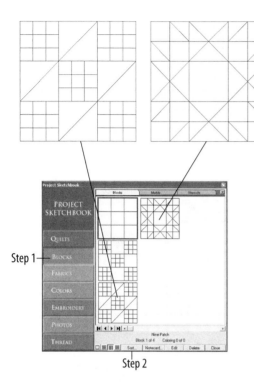

Step 1

Step 2

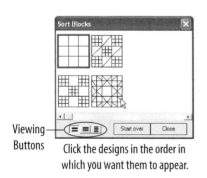

Viewing Buttons

Click the designs in the order in which you want them to appear.

You now have both of the designs that you need for your *Voodoo Queen* quilt in the Blocks section of your Sketchbook.

Sorting Blocks in the Sketchbook

You know how to sort quilt layouts and you sorted fabrics earlier in this lesson. Now you will learn how to sort designs in the Blocks section of the Sketchbook. You will use the same procedure that you used to sort fabrics in the Fabrics section of the Sketchbook.

1   Open the **Project Sketchbook** (F8) and click the **Blocks** button.

2   Click the **Sort** button at the bottom of the Blocks section. The Sort Blocks box will open. Notice that you have several viewing options in this box.

In the Sort Blocks box, click the designs in the order in which you want them to appear in the Blocks section of the Sketchbook. You can click the first few that you want to sort and then click **Close**. Any unsorted designs will follow the sorted designs automatically. At any point, you can click the **Start Over** button to resort.

Lesson 3

Coloring the Blocks

1   With the **Blocks** section of the Sketchbook still open, double-click the ***Double Nine Patch variation*** to place it on the EasyDraw™ worktable. Click the **Color** tab. The Fabrics and Colors palette will open on the Color worktable with the **Paintbrush** tool already engaged.

2   Click the fabric that you want to use for the *center chains*. Click these patches in the block to color them, as illustrated. These colored patches should form an "X" through the block design. **Add to Sketchbook**.

3   Select another color for the remaining *corner patches in the smaller Nine Patch blocks*, as illustrated. Click to color. **Add to Sketchbook**.

4   Select a color for the *half square triangle* patches, as illustrated. Click to color. **Add to Sketchbook**.

5   Select a color for the *remaining patches* in the block, click to color. **Add to Sketchbook**.

6   Open the **Project Sketchbook**, open the **Blocks** section of the Sketchbook, and double-click to place the ***Contrary Wife*** block on the EasyDraw™ worktable.

7   Click the **Color** tab. With the **Paintbrush** engaged, click the **large-scale floral print** in the Fabrics and Colors palette. Click to color the *center square* in the block design.

8   Color the rest of the patches in the block. **Add to Sketchbook**.

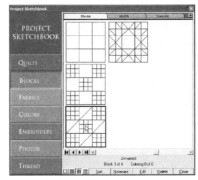

Step 1

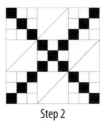

Step 2

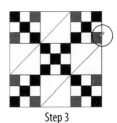

Step 3

Step 4

Step 5

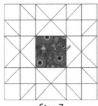

Step 7

Step 8

Add to
Sketchbook
Button

Fussy Cut Tool

Step 2

Step 3
Add to Sketchbook

Step 1
Work on Quilt

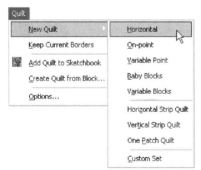

Step 2

Discovering the Fussy Cut Tool

EQ6 gives you the ability to "fussy cut" a fabric, that is, to frame a particular part of the fabric pattern, such as a flower, within a patch. The program also scales the fabric automatically, so that the view of the print is true to the actual scale of the fabric in the block and in the layout.

Notes

For best results on the Quilt worktable, set the block size on the Block worktable to the same size that it will be in the quilt layout. This will ensure that the scale and fussy cut arrangement in the block will look the same when you set this block into a quilt layout.

1   Click the **Fussy Cut** tool on the Color toolbar. The icon is a set of four way arrows over two samples of a patterned fabric in different arrangements.

2   Click the **large-scale floral print** in the *center of the Contrary Wife block* and, holding down the mouse button, **drag the fabric within the patch** so that the pattern in the fabric is displayed to your satisfaction. You can also use the keyboard arrows to move the fabric within a patch.

3   **Add to Sketchbook**. The fussy cut fabric arrangement is saved with your block and will have the same appearance when you set this block in the layout.

Establishing a Horizontal Quilt Layout

Your blocks are complete, so you are ready to create the layout for your *Voodoo Queen* quilt.

1   Click the **Work on Quilt** button on the Project toolbar to switch to the Quilt worktable.

2   Click **QUILT > New Quilt > Horizontal**.

Lesson 3

3   Click the **Layout** tab on the lower-left of the screen. Use the *arrows* and *palette sliders* to set the following values in the Horizontal Layout box:

- Number of blocks:

    Horizontal: **3**

    Vertical: **3**

- Finished size of blocks:

- Click to check **Keep width and height equal**

    Width: **9.00**

    Height will set automatically to the same value.

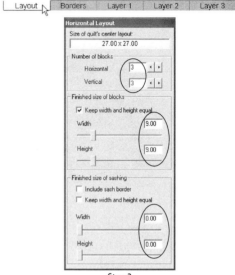

Step 3

Notes
If the Height setting does not change to 9.00 automatically, click directly on the palette slider button. This setting will immediately change to match the Width setting.

- Finished size of sashing:

    Width: **0.00**

    Height: **0.00**

Step 4

4   Click the **Borders** tab on the lower-left of the screen. A Borders box will open with the first border selected automatically.

By default, every new quilt layout has one, one-inch border that you can keep, modify, or remove. There are 11 borders in this quilt, but they will be easy to add because most of them will be in the default Mitered style that you specified in Lesson 2.

5   Under *Lock size adjustments*, click **All** so that it is checked. All sides of each border will adjust automatically now to the selected width for that border.

6   BORDER 1

    Style: **Mitered** (default)

    Size: **0.50**

Step 5 ——

Step 6

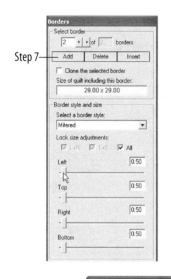

Step 7 —

Add to
Sketchbook
Button

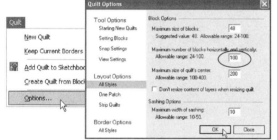

Step 9

Step 10 —

Add to
Sketchbook
Button

7   BORDER 2

   • Click the **Add** button at the top of the
      Borders box.

      Style: **Mitered** (default)

      Size: **0.50**

8   **Add to Sketchbook**.

9   Before adding the next border, you must change
     the default setting that limits the number
     of vertical and horizontal blocks in a layout.
     Click **QUILT > Options > All Styles**. Set the
     *Maximum number of blocks horizontally and
     vertically* to **100**. This is the maximum value
     allowed. Click **OK**. You will return to the
     Borders tab.

10   BORDER 3

   • Click the **Add** button at the top of the
      Borders box.

      Style: **Tile Squares**

      Blocks in border, Horizontal: **29**

   Use the arrow buttons next to Horizontal if you
   have difficulty setting the number accurately.

   The only setting that you can specify under
   this style is the number of horizontal *Blocks in
   border*. Although the block size is grayed out,
   you can read the settings and see that these
   squares will be 1.00" on all sides of Border 3.

11   **Add to Sketchbook**.

Lesson 3

Notes

There are several Tile border styles available to you in EQ6. Selecting any of these Tile styles ensures that square border blocks of the same size will be set in all sides of the selected border. For any Tile style border, you must designate the number of squares in the horizontal border. EQ6 will calculate the number of blocks that are required to construct the vertical border from the same size blocks. A spacer may be added to make the blocks fit evenly. Experiment with the tile size by changing the number of horizontal blocks in the border. Notice that as you change this setting, the tile size changes and spacers may appear to equalize the blocks. See the EQ6 Help file for more information about Tile borders.

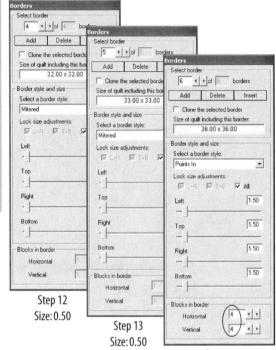

12 BORDER 4

• Click **Add**.

    Style: **Mitered** (default)

    Size: **0.50**

13 BORDER 5

• Click **Add**.

    Style: **Mitered** (default)

    Size: **0.50**

14 Add to Sketchbook.

15 BORDER 6

• Click **Add**.

    Style: **Points In**

    Size: **1.50**

    Blocks in border:

        Horizontal: **4**

        Vertical: **4**

16 Add to Sketchbook.

Step 12
Size: 0.50

Step 13
Size: 0.50

Step 15
Size: 1.50

Steps 14 and 16
Add to Sketchbook

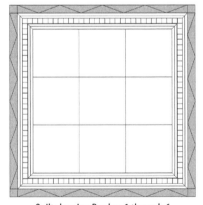

Quilt showing Borders 1 through 6

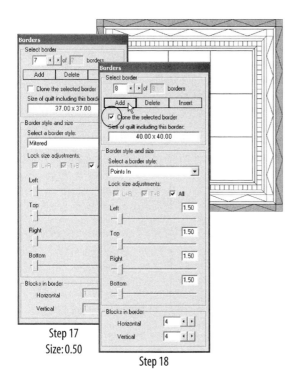

Step 17
Size: 0.50

Step 18

17 BORDER 7

- Click **Add**.

  Style: **Mitered** (default)

  Size: **0.50**

18 BORDER 8

- Click **Border 6 to select it** and click to check **Clone the selected border**. Click **Add**.

  Border 8 will be added to the layout and it will be a clone of Border 6.

19 Add to Sketchbook.

Notes
You can clone a border easily in EQ6. Click the border that you want to clone, click to check the *Clone the selected border* option, and then click the Add button at the top of the Borders box. A new border will be added to the outer edge of the quilt layout and it will be a clone of the selected border. Turn off this feature by clicking the check to remove it.

20 BORDER 9

- Click to **uncheck** *Clone the selected border.*
- Click **Add**.

  Style: **Mitered** (default)

  Size: **0.75**

21 BORDER 10

- Click **Add**.

  Style: **Mitered** (default)

  Size: **4.00**

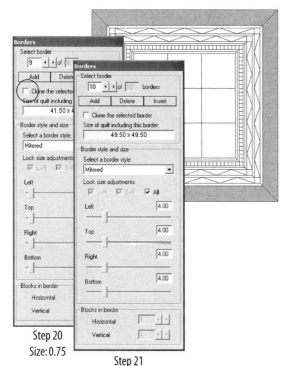

Step 20
Size: 0.75

Step 21

Lesson 3

Lesson 3

22 BORDER 11

- Click **Add**.

  Style: **Mitered** (default)

  Size: **0.50**

This border represents the quilt binding.

23 Add to Sketchbook.

Your quilt layout is now established and you are ready to set your blocks in the layout!

Setting Blocks in the Layout

1 Click **Layer 1** and click the **Set Block** tool to open the Blocks palette.

2 Click the ***Contrary Wife*** block in the Blocks palette and **ALT+click** the block space in the *upper-left corner* of the layout to set this block into alternate spaces.

3 Click the ***Double Nine Patch variation*** and move the cursor to a *blank space* in the layout. **ALT+click** to set this block in alternate spaces in the layout. **Add to Sketchbook**.

4 Click the **Rotate Block** tool and click the **two *Double Nine Patch variation* blocks** in **Row 2** to turn them by 90 degrees. **Add to Sketchbook**.

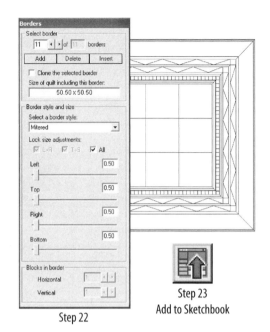

Step 22

Step 23
Add to Sketchbook

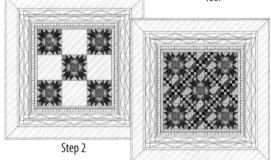

Step 1

Set Block
Tool

Step 2

Step 3

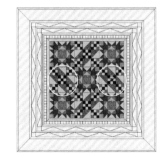

Step 4
Rotate Block

Eyedropper Tool

Customize Toolbar Button

Fussy Cut Tool

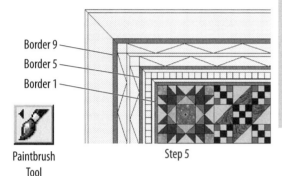

Border 9
Border 5
Border 1

Step 5

Paintbrush Tool

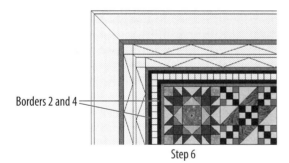

Borders 2 and 4

Step 6

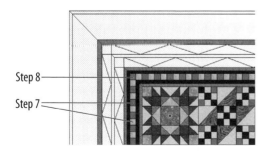

Step 8
Step 7

Notes

- Remember to use the convenient *Eyedropper* and *Most recently used fabrics and colors* feature when coloring the borders.

- Notice that the fabrics in the layout are true to scale, including the large-scale floral print in the center of the *Contrary Wife* block.

- You can also fussy cut fabrics on the Quilt worktable. Click the Customize Toolbar button at the bottom of the Quilt toolbar > Add/Remove Buttons > check Fussy Cut. Click anywhere off of the list to close it. The Fussy Cut button is now on the Quilt toolbar. You can also customize the toolbar by right-clicking anywhere on the toolbar and using the context menu to open the tool list.

- When you use the Fussy Cut tool on the Quilt worktable, it is helpful to use the Zoom In tool to get a closer view of the fabric pattern.

5   Click the **Paintbrush** tool, select a fabric in the Fabrics and Colors palette, and **CTRL+click** to color **Borders 1**, **5**, and **9**.

6   Select a sample in the Fabrics and Colors palette, and then **CTRL+click** to color **Borders 2** and **4**.

Each of the squares in Border 3 must be colored individually, but there is a way to cut the work in half. You will color all of the squares the same color and then recolor half of them individually to get the checkerboard effect.

7   Select a sample in the Fabrics and Colors palette, and then **CTRL+click** to color **Border 3**. Click another fabric and individually click alternate squares in Border 3 to recolor them. Click **Add to Sketchbook** often while coloring.

8   **CTRL+click** to color the corner squares. **Add to Sketchbook**.

Notes

- It is helpful to zoom in when recoloring the small patches in this border. Click the Zoom In (+) button and then click and hold as you drag the cursor diagonally across the area that you want to enlarge. When you release the mouse button, the magnified area will fill the screen.

  Use the horizontal and vertical scrollbars on the Quilt worktable to navigate around the magnified layout.

- To undo an action, use EDIT > Undo or CTRL+Z.

Zoom In
Button

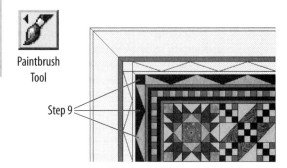

Paintbrush
Tool

Step 9

9 With the **Paintbrush** tool engaged, select a fabric in the Fabrics and Colors palette, and **CTRL+click** to color *one series of triangles* in **Border 6**. Select another color and **CTRL+click** to color *the other series of triangles* in this border. Color the *corner blocks*. **Add to Sketchbook**.

10 Select a sample in the Fabrics and Colors palette, and then **CTRL+click** to color **Border 7**. **Add to Sketchbook**.

11 *Repeat step 9* to color **Border 8**.

12 Select a sample in the Fabrics and Colors palette, and then **CTRL+click** to color **Border 10**.

13 Select the *striped fabric* and **CTRL+click** to color **Border 11**. This border represents the quilt binding.

Step 10

Step 11

Step 12

Step 13

Notes

You used the Rotate Fabric tool on the Quilt toolbar when you rotated the striped border fabric in Lesson 1. If this button is no longer on the Quilt toolbar, add it now by clicking Customize Toolbar button > Add/Remove Buttons > Rotate Fabric. Click anywhere off of the list to close it.

Customize Toolbar
Menu

Rotate Fabric
Tool

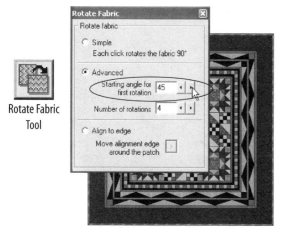

Rotate Fabric Tool

Step 15

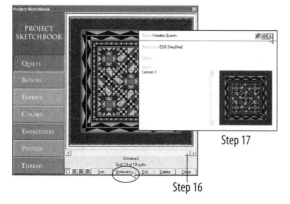

Step 17

Step 16

Select Tool

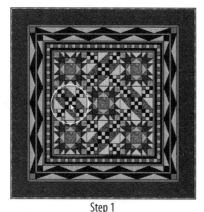

Step 1

15 Click the **Rotate Fabric** tool on the Quilt toolbar and the Rotate Fabric box will open. Click **Advanced** and use the arrow keys to set the **Starting angle for first rotation to 45**. **CTRL+click** to rotate the *striped fabric* by 45 degrees on all sides of Border 11. **Add to Sketchbook**.

16 Open the **Project Sketchbook** (F8) and click the **Quilts** button to open the Quilts section of the Sketchbook. Use the horizontal scrollbar to display the final version of your quilt.

17 Click the **Notecard** button and type **Voodoo Queen** on the *Name* line. Under *Reference*, type **EQ6 Simplified** and under *Notes*, type **Lesson 3**. **Close** the notecard and **close** the Sketchbook.

Your *Voodoo Queen* quilt is finished! Now you will explore one of EQ6's most convenient printing options.

Printing a Rotary Cutting Chart

EQ6 will create a Rotary Cutting Chart for any pieced design that can be constructed using this straight-cut method. You can print these instructions from the Block worktable or from the Quilt worktable.

1 With your *Voodoo Queen* quilt still on the worktable, click the **Select** tool and click one of the ***Double Nine Patch variation*** blocks in the layout.

2 Click **FILE > Print > Rotary Cutting**. The Print Rotary Cutting Chart box will open. By default, **Use size from quilt** is checked under *Finished Block Size*.

3 Under *Seam Allowance*, keep the **0.25"** default setting.

4 Under *Print Key Block*, click to select **Small**. The Key block is the diagram that maps each rotary cut strip to the correct position in the finished block.

5 Under *Round to Nearest*, keep the **1/16** default setting. With this option checked, EQ6 will calculate the width of the strip to the nearest 1/16".

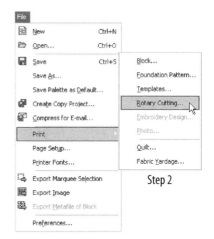

Step 2

Notes
Use the Coloring Arrows under the block to display the colored version of the block. This will ensure that your Rotary Cutting Chart will preview and print in color.

6 Click **Preview**. EQ6 will tell you how many patches to rotary cut for each fabric in the block. It will also give you the patch dimensions, including the height of the strip and the width and angle of the individual patches to be cut. The Key block identifies the location of each patch in the design.

7 **Print**.

Notes
Always check the Rotary Cutting Chart against the templates before cutting your fabric. By their nature, rotary cutting instructions are an approximation. Templates are always accurate.

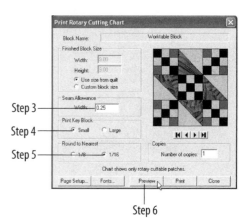

Step 3
Step 4
Step 5

Step 6

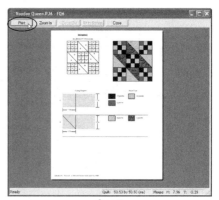

Step 7

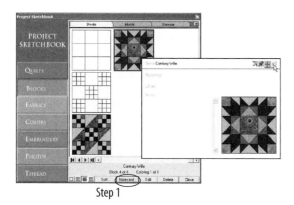

Step 1

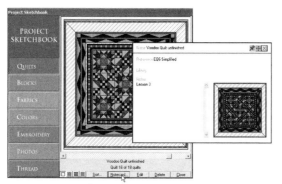

Step 2

Deleting Designs from the Project Sketchbook

You learned in Lesson 1 that it is very easy to delete unwanted designs from the Sketchbook. As you create more complex designs, you will find that it is best to delete unwanted designs right after you have finished a project, while it is still fresh in your mind.

1   Open the **Project Sketchbook** (F8) and click to open the **Blocks** section of the Sketchbook. Create notecards for the blocks that you drew for this *Voodoo Queen* quilt.

2   Click the **Quilts** button to open the **Quilts** section of the Sketchbook. Scroll through this section, creating notecards for all layouts that you want to keep.

Exiting EQ6

Click **FILE > Exit**.

CONGRATULATIONS! You are gaining confidence and experience in EQ6. You have drawn blocks, established a quilt layout, and printed a Rotary Cutting Chart. In Lesson 4, you will learn how to add appliqué and quilting stencils to your layouts.

Adding a Layer

In this lesson you will apply the techniques that you have learned so far in this tutorial to create *Wildflower Wheelies*, a new design that includes appliqué motifs and quilting stencils. This layout is based on the *Colliding Stars* quilt that you designed in Lesson 1, but as you can see, this new quilt is very different. The most obvious difference is the circular movement in this *Wildflower Wheelies* quilt, compared to the angular movement in the *Colliding Stars* quilt. This new design will help you to realize how easy it is to make each quilt very unique in EQ6, even if it is based on a previous design. In this lesson, you will:

- Clear the Fabrics section of the Sketchbook

- Learn about the drawing worktables

- Draw a block using guides

- Convert a block to a motif

- Resize a design

- Combine EasyDraw™ and PatchDraw designs

- Create quilting stencils

- Adjust a layout: Insert a border

- Work on layers

    - Set quilting stencils on Layer 3

    - Change the thread color

- Use the Tape Measure

- Turn layers on and off

- Delete blocks from the Sketchbook

- Print foundation patterns, templates & stencils

Creating a New Project File

1 Run EQ6. The Project Helper will open to the **Create a new project** tab. Type *Wildflower Wheelies* > **OK** or press the **ENTER** key.

As you know, the first step in creating a new quilt is to collect the layout, blocks, and fabrics that you will need for it. For this *Wildflower Wheelies* quilt, you will use the layout and one block design from Lesson 1. You will also copy several designs from the EQ6 Libraries.

2 Click **LIBRARIES** > **Layout Library**. Click the **Import** button at the bottom of the Layout Libraries box. The Import Layouts from Project box will open. Navigate to **My Documents > My EQ6 > PJ6 >** *Colliding Stars.PJ6* > **Open**. The Import Results section will open. Use the horizontal scrollbar to view the layout for your *Colliding Stars* quilt. Click to select it. **Add to Sketchbook** > **Close**.

3 Click **LIBRARIES** > **Block Library**. Click the **Import** button at the bottom of the Block Libraries box. The Import Blocks from Project box will open. Click the *Colliding Stars.PJ6* **file** > **Open**. The Import Results section will open. Click the *Kaleidoscope* **block** > **Add to Sketchbook**.

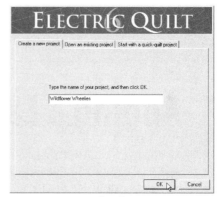

Step 1

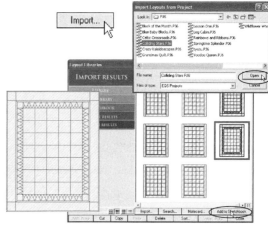

Step 2

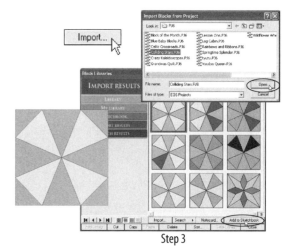

Step 3

Step 4

Topeka Rose

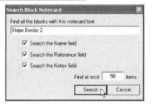

Step 5

4 With the Block Library still open, click **Search > by Notecard > type *Topeka Rose* > ENTER > OK**. In the Search Results section, select the ***Topeka Rose*** block and **Add to Sketchbook**.

5 With the Block Library still open, click **Search > by Notecard > type *Stripe Border 2* > ENTER > OK**. In the Search Results section, select the ***Stripe Border 2*** block and **Add to Sketchbook > Close**.

Now you will select fabrics for your *Wildflower Wheelies* quilt. You will need *four fabrics* for the *Kaleidoscope* and *Octagon* pieced blocks: light, light/medium, medium, and dark. You will need *five fabrics* for the *Topeka Rose* appliqué: light/medium and medium for the petals and buds, light/medium and medium for the leaves and stems, and medium for the centers.

Notes

To clear the palette completely before adding new samples, open the Project Sketchbook (F8) and click the Fabrics button to open the Fabrics section. Click the Clear button at the bottom of the Fabrics section. EQ6 will ask if you want to clear all fabrics or only unused fabrics. Unused fabrics are defined as those that are not used in a saved quilt. Since there are no quilts in your project file yet, all of the fabrics in the Sketchbook are currently unused. Click OK if you want to delete all fabrics from the Sketchbook. Click Cancel if you want to keep your current palette. Close the Sketchbook.

Stripe Border 2

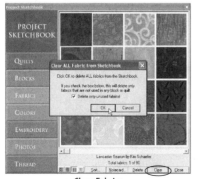

Clear Fabrics

Lesson 4

6   Click **LIBRARIES > Fabric Library**. Browse through the library and select fabrics for your new quilt.

- To *add one sample*: Click the **sample > Add to Sketchbook**.

- To *add sequential samples*: Click **the first sample > SHIFT+click the last sample in the sequence > Add to Sketchbook**.

- To *add non-sequential samples*: Click the **first sample > CTRL+click each sample > Add to Sketchbook**.

- To *add all samples* in a collection: **CTRL+A > Add to Sketchbook**.

- To *deselect* a selected sample, **CTRL+click**.

7   **Close** the Fabric Library.

Now you will choose the thread for your quilting stencils.

8   Click **LIBRARIES > Thread Library**. Browse this library to find a variety of colors that will contrast well with the values of the fabrics in your palette. **Add to Sketchbook**. **Close** the Thread Library.

9   Open the **Project Sketchbook** (F8) and click the **Quilts** button to open the Quilts section of the Sketchbook. View the *Colliding Stars* layout. You will notice that the block designs did not transfer with the layout. Only the quilt layout is saved in the Layout Library.

10 Click the **Blocks** button to open the Blocks section of the Sketchbook. There are three tabs along the top of the Sketchbook: *Blocks*, *Motifs*, and *Stencils*. All of the designs that you added from the EQ6 Library will be on the Blocks tab. You will add designs to the Motifs and Stencils tabs later in this lesson.

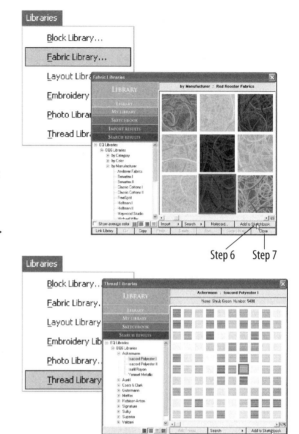

Step 6   Step 7

Step 8

Step 9

Step 10

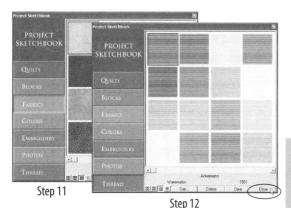

Step 11

Step 12

11 Click the **Fabrics** button to open the Fabrics section of the Sketchbook. View the fabrics that you added for your quilt.

12 Click the **Thread** button to open the Thread section of the Sketchbook. View the threads that you added for your quilting stencils. **Close** the Project Sketchbook.

Notes
- Click FILE > Save Palette as Default > OK to make this current palette your default palette. The new default palette will include the thread samples that you just selected.

- To reinstall EQ6's original default palette, clear your Sketchbook first, then click LIBRARIES > Fabric Library > EQ Libraries > EQ6 Libraries > by Category > 01 EQ6 Default Fabrics. CTRL+A to select all, then Add to Sketchbook. Close the Sketchbook. Then click FILE > Save Palette as Default > OK again.

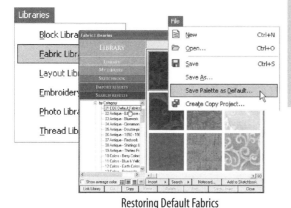

Restoring Default Fabrics

Learning about the Drawing Worktables

Before proceeding with this quilt design, you must understand the differences between EQ6's four drawing worktables: *EasyDraw Block, PatchDraw Block, PatchDraw Motif,* and *EasyDraw + PatchDraw.* By the end of this lesson, you will have used designs from all four worktables.

1 Click **WORKTABLE > Work on Block** or click the **Work on Block** button in the Project tools. Click **BLOCK > New Block**. The extended menu will open with the four drawing worktables listed.

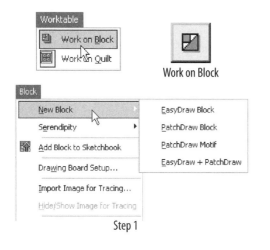

Work on Block

Step 1

Lesson 4

Lesson 4

2   Click **EasyDraw Block**. This is the appropriate worktable for drawing *pieced* designs. Pieced designs are composed of lines, arcs, or a combination of lines and arcs. All lines and arcs in an EasyDraw™ design must connect to another line or arc or to the block outline. The *Kaleidoscope* and *Stripe Border 2* blocks that you will use in this lesson are examples of EasyDraw™ designs.

There are three pieced block categories in the Block Library: *Classic Pieced*, *Contemporary Pieced*, and *Foundation Pieced*. All of the designs in these categories were created on the EasyDraw™ worktable.

3   Click **BLOCK > New Block**. PatchDraw Block and PatchDraw Motif are the next two worktables in the list. These worktables are appropriate for drawing appliqué designs. Appliqué designs are composed of closed patches that can be layered.

4   Click **PatchDraw Block**. This is the appropriate worktable for drawing an appliqué design that has a *background square*. The *Topeka Rose* block that you added from the Block Library is an example of a PatchDraw Block.

There are two appliqué block categories in the Block Library: *Classic Appliqué* and *Contemporary Appliqué*. The designs in these categories have background squares.

5   Click **BLOCK > New Block > PatchDraw Motif**. This is the appropriate worktable for drawing an appliqué design that has *no background square*. In this lesson, you will create an appliqué motif from the *Topeka Rose* block.

There is one appliqué motif category in the Block Library and it is *Motifs*. The designs in this category do not have background squares.

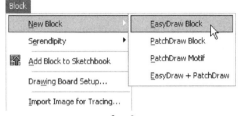

Step 2

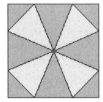 

EasyDraw™ Pieced Blocks

Steps 3 and 4

PatchDraw Appliqué Block

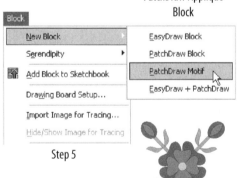

Step 5

PatchDraw Appliqué Motif

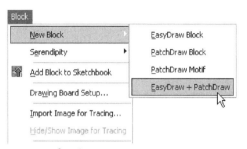

Step 6

EasyDraw + PatchDraw
Block

Notes
The designs in the Classic Appliqué and Contemporary Appliqué categories can be used as appliqué motifs if they are removed from their background squares. The designs in the Motifs category can be used as appliqué blocks if they are added to a plain or pieced background.

6 Click **BLOCK > New Block > EasyDraw + PatchDraw**. This is the appropriate worktable for combining *pieced* and *appliqué* designs in one block. You will create an EasyDraw + PatchDraw design in this lesson.

There is one EasyDraw + PatchDraw category in the Block Library and it is *Overlaid Blocks*.

Notes
• The Quilting Stencils and Border Blocks categories contain designs that were drawn on the EasyDraw Block, PatchDraw Block, or PatchDraw Motif worktables.

• The designs in the Quilting Stencils category are available only as line drawings. When you add a design from this category to your project file, it will always save on the Stencils tab in the Blocks section of the Sketchbook.

Now that you know the differences between EQ6's drawing worktables, you will create five new designs for your *Wildflower Wheelies* quilt.

The first design that you will create is the *Octagon* block. You will draw this design on the EasyDraw™ worktable, using the *Kaleidoscope* block as your guide. You are already familiar with this worktable because you created EasyDraw™ blocks for your *Voodoo Queen* quilt in Lesson 3.

You will create a second design by converting the *Topeka Rose* block to a motif.

You will create a third design by combining the *Octagon* block from EasyDraw™ with the *Topeka Rose* motif from PatchDraw to form an EasyDraw + PatchDraw block.

You will create two additional designs that you will use as quilting stencils on your *Wildflower Wheelies* quilt. One will be based on the *Kaleidoscope* block and the other will be based on the *Topeka Rose* motif.

Lesson 4

Drawing a Block Using Guides

Many quilt layouts contain a main block and an alternate block that compliments the main block. An alternate block is usually compatible with the main block's structure. The arrangement of main blocks and alternate blocks in the layout often work together to form an overall pattern in the layout. EQ6 makes it easy to use a main block as a guide for drawing an alternate block, as you will learn now when you use the *Kaleidoscope* block as a guide for drawing the *Octagon* block.

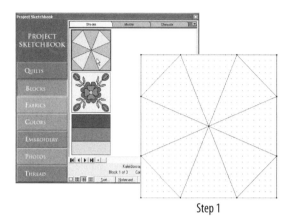

Step 1

1   Open the **Project Sketchbook** (F8) and then open the **Blocks** section of the Sketchbook. Double-click the ***Kaleidoscope*** block to place it on the worktable.

2   Click **BLOCK > Convert to Guides**. All of the solid lines in the *Kaleidoscope* block will change to dashed lines.

Notes

• You can also right-click anywhere on the worktable to open the EasyDraw™ Worktable Context Menu and then click the Convert to Guides option.

• If you have difficulty seeing the guide lines, you can change the color so that they are more visible on the worktable. Click BLOCK > Drawing Board Setup > Display > Guide Color. Click the down arrow next to *Select a color for guides*. The list of guide line colors will open. Click a color that is easy for you to see.

• Before drawing, be sure that the Snapping options are set to the default settings: Click BLOCK > Drawing Board Setup > Snapping. *Snap to grid* and *Snap to nodes of drawing* should be checked > OK.

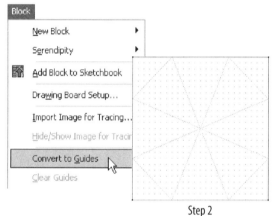

Step 2

Changing Guide Line Color

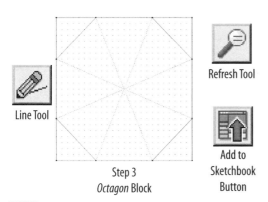

Line Tool

Refresh Tool

Add to
Sketchbook
Button

Step 3
Octagon Block

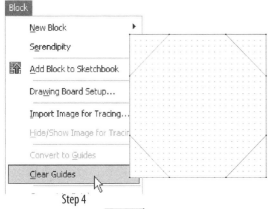

Step 4

Refresh Tool

VIEW > Precision Bar

3 Click the **Line** tool and draw *the four diagonal lines* in the corners of this block, as illustrated, to form the *Octagon* block. Click the **Refresh** tool to redraw the new lines if they are hard to see on top of the guides. You can also click the **Color** tab and then click back to the **EasyDraw** tab to refresh the screen. **Add to Sketchbook**. This is the *Octagon* block that you will use as a base to create your EasyDraw + PatchDraw block.

4 Click **BLOCK > Clear Guides** or right-click to open the EasyDraw™ Worktable Context Menu and then click the **Clear Guides** option. Click the **Refresh** tool.

Notes
Guides will remain on the worktable until you clear them, but they will not appear in the finished block, even if you do not remove them from the worktable.

Converting a Block to a Motif

Now you will remove the *Topeka Rose* motif from its background square and add it to the Sketchbook as a separate design. You will do this by selecting the *Topeka Rose* motif, copying it to the Windows® clipboard, and pasting it on the PatchDraw Motif worktable to create a new appliqué motif design. This new design will not have a background square.

Notes
Be sure that the Precision Bar is open on the worktable. You used the Precision Bar in Lesson 3 when you were drawing on the EasyDraw™ worktable. If it is not open, click VIEW and click to check Precision Bar. The Precision Bar will open at the top of the worktable, under the Project toolbar and above the rulers. It contains the main options in BLOCK > Drawing Board Setup, as well as a variety of convenient features that make it easy to edit your designs on the worktable. The Precision Bar will change, depending upon the tasks that you are performing.

Lesson 4

1 Open the **Project Sketchbook** (F8) and then open the **Blocks** section of the Sketchbook. Double-click the *Topeka Rose* block to place it on the worktable. This is the design that you copied from the library. It is a PatchDraw Block design that combines a plain block and an appliqué motif in one block.

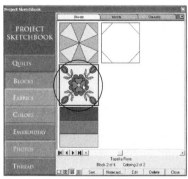

Step 1

2 Click the **Appliqué** tab. Click **EDIT > Select All** or use **CTRL+A** to select all patches in the motif.

Notes
When a patch or group of patches are selected, they are surrounded by nodes with a small four-headed arrow in the center.

3 Click **EDIT > Copy** or use **CTRL+C** to copy the motif. The design is now on the Windows® clipboard. You can't see it, but it is there and ready to paste on the new worktable.

4 Click **BLOCK > New Block > PatchDraw Motif**. When this worktable opens, click **EDIT > Paste** or use **CTRL+V** to paste the *Topeka Rose* design on the worktable.

Notes
Notice the Precision Bar. With the design selected, the bar is labeled Multiple Select. This means that the tools that are available to you right now on this bar are the ones that are appropriate for the action you are taking.

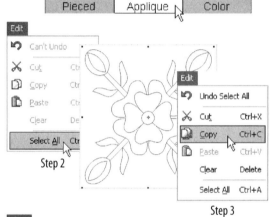

Step 2

Step 3

Step 4

Move selected segments to center of block

Step 5

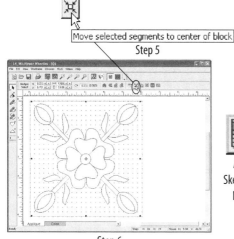

Step 6

Add to
Sketchbook
Button

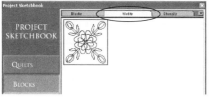

Topeka Rose Motif

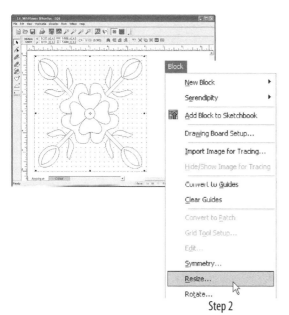

Step 2

5 Without clicking, place your cursor over the **Centering** button, the fifth button from the right on the Precision Bar. The tooltip will read *Move selected segments to center of block*. The icon is a square with four arrows on the corners.

6 Click this button and the *Topeka Rose* design will center on the PatchDraw Motif worktable. **Add to Sketchbook**. This is the *Topeka Rose* motif. It does not have a background square.

Notes
- When you click Add to Sketchbook, the motif will be deselected.

- EQ6 identifies drawn designs as either blocks or motifs. The program will save this *Topeka Rose* design on the Motifs tab in the Blocks section of the Sketchbook because it does not have a background square. You will learn how to move designs from tab to tab within the Blocks section of the Sketchbook later in this lesson.

Resizing a Design

You will resize the *Topeka Rose* motif before using it to create the new EasyDraw + PatchDraw design.

1 With the *Topeka Rose* motif still on the worktable, click **EDIT > Select All** or use **CTRL+A** to select all patches.

2 Click **BLOCK > Resize**. You can also right-click on the worktable to open the EasyDraw™ Worktable Context Menu and then click **Resize**.

Lesson 4

3   The Resize box will open with the *Horizontal* percentage setting highlighted. Type in **75** to reduce the horizontal proportion of the *Topeka Rose* to 75% of its original size. Hit the **TAB** key *twice* to move the cursor past the Horizontal scrollbar and on to the *Vertical* percentage setting. Type in **75** to reduce the vertical proportion of the *Topeka Rose* to 75% of its original size. Click **OK**.

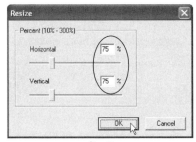

Step 3

4   **Add to Sketchbook**. This is the *Resized Topeka Rose* motif that you will use to create an EasyDraw + PatchDraw block.

Combining EasyDraw + PatchDraw Designs

Now you will create an EasyDraw + PatchDraw block for your quilt by combining the *Octagon* block from EasyDraw™ with the *Resized Topeka Rose* motif from PatchDraw. There are a number of steps in this procedure, but it's simply a matter of copying and pasting designs in the right order.

First, you will copy the *Octagon* block to the EasyDraw tab of the EasyDraw + PatchDraw block. This will establish the pieced base of the new EasyDraw + PatchDraw block. Next, you will copy the *Resized Topeka Rose* motif to the Appliqué tab of the EasyDraw + PatchDraw block. This will overlay the appliqué motif on the pieced base. Last, you will color the new *Topeka Rose Octagon* block.

1   Open the **Project Sketchbook** (F8) and then open the **Blocks** section of the Sketchbook. Double-click the ***Octagon*** block to place it on the EasyDraw™ worktable.

Step 4
Resized Topeka Rose Motif

Add to
Sketchbook
Button

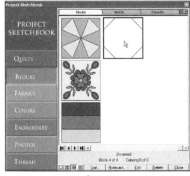

Step 1

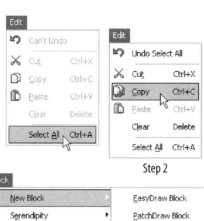

Step 2

Step 3

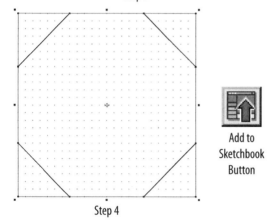

Add to
Sketchbook
Button

Step 4

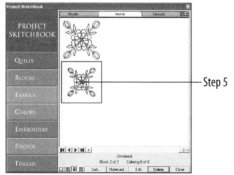

Step 5

2 Click **EDIT > Select All** or use **CTRL+A** to select all lines in the drawing. Click **EDIT > Copy** or use **CTRL+C** to copy. The *Octagon* design is now on the Windows® clipboard. You can't see it, but it is there and ready to paste on the new worktable.

3 Click **BLOCK > New Block > EasyDraw + PatchDraw**. There are three tabs on the EasyDraw + PatchDraw worktable: *EasyDraw, Appliqué,* and *Color.* The worktable will open to the EasyDraw tab.

4 **CTRL+V** to paste the *Octagon* on the worktable. Click on the **four-headed arrow** in the center of the *Octagon* design. **Drag the design to center it** on the worktable. **Add to Sketchbook**. This is the base for your new EasyDraw + PatchDraw block.

5 Now you will open and copy the *Resized Topeka Rose* motif. Open the **Project Sketchbook** (F8) and then open the **Blocks** section of the Sketchbook. Click the **Motifs** tab and double-click the ***Resized Topeka Rose*** motif to place it on the worktable.

6   Click **EDIT > Select All** or use **CTRL+A** to select all patches. Click **EDIT > Copy** or use **CTRL+C** to copy. The *Resized Topeka Rose* design is now on the Windows® clipboard. You can't see it, but it is there and ready to paste on the new worktable. Now you will reopen the new EasyDraw + PatchDraw block and paste this motif there.

7   Open the **Project Sketchbook** (F8) and then open the **Blocks** section of the Sketchbook. Double-click the *last Octagon* block to open it on the EasyDraw + PatchDraw worktable. The last *Octagon* is the EasyDraw + PatchDraw design. The block before it is the original EasyDraw™ *Octagon* design. Do not choose this design. You will know that you have the EasyDraw + PatchDraw design on the worktable if there are three tabs in the lower-left: *EasyDraw*, *Appliqué*, and *Color*.

8   Click the **Appliqué** tab in the EasyDraw + PatchDraw block and click **EDIT > Paste** or use **CTRL+V** to paste the *Resized Topeka Rose* motif on this tab.

9   With the *Resized Topeka Rose* motif still selected, click the **Centering** button, the fifth button from the right on the Precision Bar. You used this button to center the original *Topeka Rose* motif on the PatchDraw worktable. The *Resized Topeka Rose* motif will center on the Appliqué tab of the EasyDraw + PatchDraw worktable. **Add to Sketchbook**. This is the *Topeka Rose Octagon* block that you will set in your quilt layout.

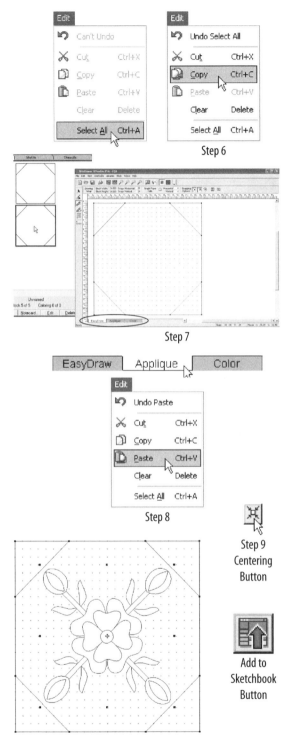

Step 6

Step 7

Step 8

Step 9
Centering
Button

Add to
Sketchbook
Button

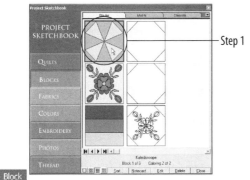

— Step 1

Creating Quilting Stencils

Now you will use the *Kaleidoscope* block as a guide to draw the stencil that you will superimpose on this design. You will also create a variation of the *Topeka Rose* motif to use as a corner stencil in your *Wildflower Wheelies* quilt.

1   Open the **Project Sketchbook** (F8) and then open the **Blocks** section of the Sketchbook. Double-click to place the ***Kaleidoscope*** block on the EasyDraw™ worktable.

2   Click **BLOCK > Convert to Guides**.

3   Click the **Line** tool and draw two diagonal lines across the block, from corner to corner, as illustrated. **Add to Sketchbook**. This is the *4X* design that you will use as a stencil on Layer 3. Click **BLOCK > Clear Guides**.

Now you will modify the *Topeka Rose* motif.

4   Open the **Project Sketchbook** (F8) and then open the **Blocks** section of the Sketchbook.

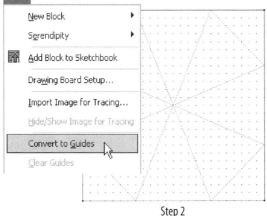

Step 2

Step 3

Notes
Notice that the *4X* design that you just created is stored on the Blocks tab. Remember that EQ6 sorts designs based on whether they are blocks or motifs, not on how you will use a design in the layout. You will move this design to the Stencil tab later in this lesson.

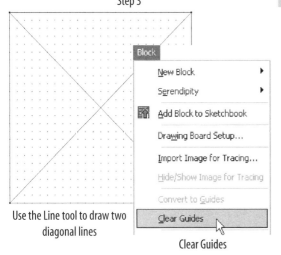

Use the Line tool to draw two diagonal lines

Clear Guides

5 Click the **Motifs** tab and double-click to place the *original* **Topeka Rose** motif, not the *Resized Topeka Rose* motif, on the PatchDraw worktable.

Now you will copy the inner petals and flower center to use as a stencil in the corners of Border 4. It will be easier to select these patches if you delete a few of the surrounding patches first.

6 Click the **Pick** tool, the first tool on the PatchDraw Motif worktable. The icon is a black arrow. Starting in the *upper-left corner* of the worktable, **click and hold** as you **drag a selection box** around the *bud, stem,* and *leaves* on this side of the design. **Release** the mouse button and this group of patches will be selected. Press the **DELETE** key to remove them from the drawing.

7 Hold down the **DELETE** key and click the large petal in this section of the drawing.

8 With the **Pick** tool still engaged, **click in the empty space to the upper-left of the inner petals**. Hold down the mouse button and **drag the cursor diagonally** to form a selection frame or marquee that includes all of the inner petals and the flower center. Be sure that the petal patches are *completely within the selection frame*. **Release** the mouse button and the patches will be selected.

Notes
Remember to use the Zoom tools whenever you need them.

Step 5

Pick Tool

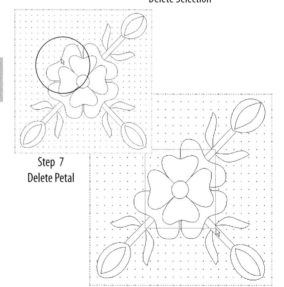

Step 6
Delete Selection

Step 7
Delete Petal

Step 8
Select Inner Flower

Step 9

9 Click **EDIT > Copy** or use **CTRL+C** to copy the patches. The design is now on the Windows® clipboard. You can't see it, but it is there and ready to paste on the new worktable.

10 Click **BLOCK > New Block > PatchDraw Motif** to open a new worktable. EQ6 will warn you that the modified *Topeka Rose* motif has not been saved and ask if you want to save this design before starting a new one. Click **No**. The new PatchDraw Motif worktable will open.

Step 10

11 Click **EDIT > Paste** or use **CTRL+V** to paste the patches on the worktable. This is the *Topeka Rose Blossom*.

12 With the *Topeka Rose Blossom* still selected, click the **Centering** button, the fifth button from the right in the Precision Bar. The *Topeka Rose Blossom* will center on the Appliqué tab of the PatchDraw Motif worktable. **Add to Sketchbook**.

Now you will resize the *Topeka Rose Blossom*. Enlarging this design to fill the PatchDraw Motif worktable will make it easier to set it on Layer 3 because it will be large enough that you won't have to resize it there.

13 **CTRL+A** to select all the patches, then click **BLOCK > Resize** or right-click on the worktable to open the PatchDraw Block & Motif Worktable Context Menu. Click **Resize**.

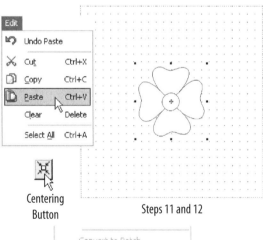

Centering Button

Steps 11 and 12

Step 13

Lesson 4

14 In the Resize box, set the *Horizontal* and *Vertical* percentages to **250**. Click **OK**. The inner petals and flower center will now fill the worktable area. **Add to Sketchbook**. This is the *Topeka Rose Blossom* motif that you will use as a quilting stencil for the corners of Border 4.

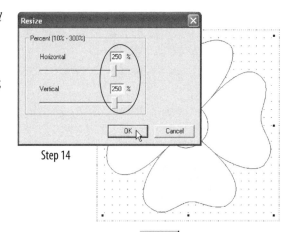

Step 14

Coloring the Designs

1 Open the **Project Sketchbook** (F8) and then open the **Blocks** section of the Sketchbook. Double-click to place the *Kaleidoscope* block on the EasyDraw™ worktable.

2 Click the **Color** tab and the Fabrics and Colors palette will open with the **Paintbrush** tool engaged. **Color the *Kaleidoscope*. Add to Sketchbook**.

Add to Sketchbook Button

3 Open the **Project Sketchbook** (F8) and then open the **Blocks** section of the Sketchbook. Double-click to place the *Topeka Rose Octagon* block on the worktable.

4 Click the **Color** tab and color this block. **Add to Sketchbook**.

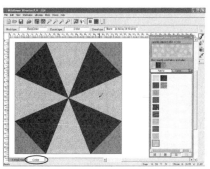

Step 2

Add to Sketchbook Button

Step 4

Add to Sketchbook Button

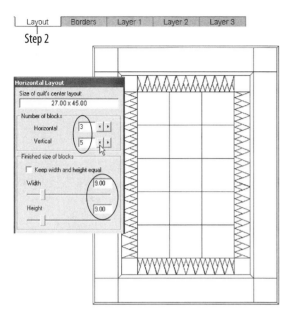

Step 2

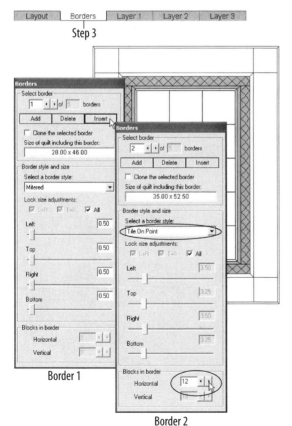

Step 3

Border 1

Border 2

Adjusting a Layout

All of the designs that you will use in the layout are ready. Now you will adjust the *Colliding Stars* layout for your new *Wildflower Wheelies* quilt.

1　Open the **Project Sketchbook** and click the **Quilts** button to open the Quilts section of the Sketchbook. Double-click the ***Colliding Stars*** layout to place it on the worktable.

2　Click the **Layout** tab and make this change:

- Number of blocks:

    Horizontal: **3**

    Vertical: **5**

- Keep the *Finished size of blocks* set to **9" x 9"**.

3　Click the **Borders** tab. Under *Lock size adjustments*, click to check **All**.

4　Border 1 is automatically selected. Set and adjust the borders to the following specifications.

BORDER 1

- Click the **Insert** button at the top of the Borders box. A new border will be added before Border 1 and it will be Mitered, the default style that you set in Lesson 2.

    Size: **0.50**.

BORDER 2

　　Style: **Tile On Point**

　　Blocks in border, Horizontal: **12**

　　Use the arrow buttons next to Horizontal if you have difficulty setting the number accurately.

Lesson 4

Notes

In a Tile style border, you specify only the horizontal number of blocks. EQ6 determines the size of these horizontal blocks and the number of identical vertical blocks that are required to form the border. A spacer may be added to make the blocks fit evenly around the layout. The spacer widths for the horizontal and vertical sides of a Tile style border can be different.

BORDER 3

Style: **Mitered** (default)

Size: **1.00**

BORDER 4

Style: **Corner Blocks**

Size: **4.00**

BORDER 5

Style: **Mitered** (default)

Size: **0.50**

5   Click **Add to Sketchbook**.

Setting Blocks in the Layout

1   Click **Layer 1**. Click the **Set Block** tool and the Blocks palette will open.

2   Right-click the ***Topeka Rose Octagon*** block, click **Select Coloring**, and then click the coloring that you want to use in your quilt. **ALT+click** the block space in the *upper-left corner of the layout* to set this block into alternate spaces.

Notes

• You can use the Erase Block tool to remove a block from the layout. You can use ALT+click with the Erase Block tool to erase alternate blocks in the layout. You can use CTRL+click with the Erase Block tool to erase all blocks in the layout.

• You can use EDIT > Undo or CTRL+Z to undo an action.

• You can use the Set Block tool to replace a previously set block in the layout with another block.

• You can sort designs in the Blocks section of the Sketchbook, as described in Lesson 3, Sorting Blocks in the Sketchbook.

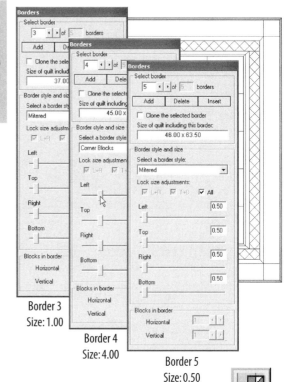

Border 3
Size: 1.00

Border 4
Size: 4.00

Border 5
Size: 0.50

Layout | Borders | Layer 1 | Layer 2

Step 1
Set Block

Select Coloring

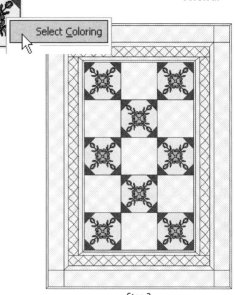

Step 2

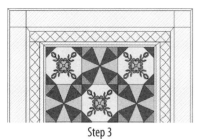

Add to
Sketchbook
Button

Step 3

Paintbrush
Tool

Step 4
Step 5
Step 6
Step 7

Add to
Sketchbook
Button

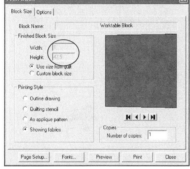

Select Tool

Size of Spacer

3 Click the *Kaleidoscope* block in the Blocks palette. Move the cursor to a blank space in the layout. **ALT+click** to set this block in alternate spaces in the layout. **Add to Sketchbook**.

4 Click the **Paintbrush** tool, select a sample in the Fabrics and Colors palette, and **CTRL+click** to color Border 1.

5 Select a sample in the Fabrics and Colors palette, and then **CTRL+click** to color the spacer on Border 2.

6 Select another color and **CTRL+click** to color the on-point squares in this border.

7 Select another color and **CTRL+click** to color the border background. **Add to Sketchbook**.

Notes
To find the size of a spacer in a Tile style border, click the Select tool and click a horizontal or vertical border spacer in the layout. Click FILE > Print > Block > Use size from quilt. The Width and Height values will be grayed out, but you can still see them. In Border 2, the vertical spacers measure 1.00" x 47.50" and the horizontal spacers measure 30.00" x 0.75".

8 Color **Borders 3, 4,** and **5. Add to Sketchbook**.

The basic design layer of your quilt is finished but you still have work to do on Layer 3!

Lesson 4

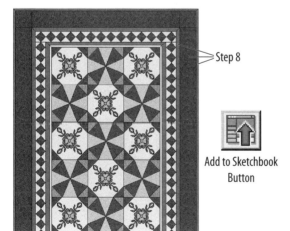

Step 8

Add to Sketchbook
Button

Step 8

Working on Layers

The Layers feature in EQ6 defines three distinct layers in a quilt:

Layer 1 is the *basic design layer of the quilt* and is composed of pieced blocks and/or appliqué blocks and borders. Layer 1 also includes the Custom Set layout, which you will explore later in this tutorial. The Custom Set layout allows you to set blocks of different sizes together in one quilt layout.

| Layer 1 | Basic design layer of the quilt. Composed of pieced blocks and/or appliqué blocks and borders. Includes the Custom Set layout.

Layer 2 consists of *appliqué motifs and blocks that "float" over the basic design layer.* An appliqué motif is an appliqué design that has no background square. The *Topeka Rose* motif that you created earlier in this lesson is an example of an appliqué motif that can be used on Layer 2.

| Layer 2 | Consists of appliqué motifs and blocks that "float" over the basic design layer.

Layer 3 contains *quilting stencils and embroidery designs* that are superimposed on Layers 1 and 2. Any block or motif can be used as a stencil because Layer 3 will display only the outline of the design. Embroidery designs can also be set on this layer.

| Layer 3 | Contains quilting stencils and embroidery designs that are superimposed on Layers 1 and 2.

You learned in previous lessons that multiple blocks can be set simultaneously on Layer 1, the basic design layer. Designs on Layer 1 (Custom Set only), Layer 2 (appliqué) and Layer 3 (quilting stencils and embroidery) must be set individually. The procedure is the same for all layers. EQ6 provides several tools that make this process fast, efficient, and precise: the Graph Pad, the Adjust tool, and the Zoom tools.

The Graph Pad

The Graph Pad is a powerful EQ6 feature that allows you to accurately size and position individual designs on layers. This feature contains advanced tools for block placement, block rotation, block size, layering order, border constraints, and centering. Alignment and resizing tools are available to you when you adjust multiple designs on layers. You will explore several of these tools in this lesson.

To place the Graph Pad on the worktable, click **VIEW**. Click to check **Graph Pad**.

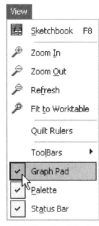

VIEW > Graph Pad

Adjust Tool

This is the left side of the Graph Pad.

This is what you will see on the right side of your Graph Pad when only one design is selected.

Align [icons] Size [icons]

This is what you will see on the right side of your Graph Pad when multiple designs are selected. The left side of the Graph Pad will be grayed out.

Adjust Tool

Zoom In Tool

Zoom Out Tool

Refresh Tool

Fit to Worktable Tool

The Graph Pad is activated only when a design has been selected with the **Adjust** tool.

When designs are selected, the Graph Pad looks like the illustration on the left.

In this lesson, you will use these Graph Pad tools: *Block Size, Rotation, Centering,* and *Align.*

The Adjust Tool

The **Adjust** tool is the primary editing tool for designs on layers. It is the second tool on the Quilt toolbar and the icon is a skewed block outline with a white arrow. With the Adjust tool, you can *move, resize* and *delete* designs on Layer 1 (Custom Set only), Layer 2 (appliqué), and Layer 3 (quilting stencils and embroidery). You will learn more about this tool in the following sections as you set designs on layers.

Notes
The Quilt Tools that are available on Layers 2 and 3 function the same way that they do on Layer 1, the basic design layer.

The Zoom Tools

You are already familiar with the Zoom tools because you have been using them since Lesson 1. These four tools are on the Project toolbar at the top of the screen and are represented by various symbols within a magnifying glass: *Zoom In* (+), *Zoom Out* (-), *Refresh* (=), and *Fit to Worktable* (square).

- Click the **Zoom In (+)** tool and then **click and hold, dragging the cursor diagonally across an area** to enlarge it. Release the mouse button and the magnified area will fill the screen. Navigate on the magnified worktable by using the vertical and horizontal scrollbars on the right and bottom of the screen, respectively.

- Click the **Zoom Out (-)** tool to return to the previous view.

- Click the **Refresh (=)** tool to redraw the design and eliminate debris from the screen.

- Click the **Fit to Worktable (square)** tool to return to normal viewing.

Setting Quilting Stencils on Layer 3

It's time to start setting your quilting stencils on Layer 3! This process might seem complicated, but it is actually very easy. To learn this technique, you will set a stencil over each of the *Kaleidoscope* blocks in the *Wildflower Wheelies* layout. You will also set stencils in one of the quilt borders.

1 With your *Wildflower Wheelies* quilt on the worktable, click the **Layer 3** tab.

2 Click the **Zoom In** tool and **click and drag** to form a selection box around **Row 3**, the center row of the quilt layout. When you release the mouse button, this portion of the quilt will be magnified.

3 Click the **Set Block** tool and the Blocks palette will open. Click the **Blocks** tab and click the *4X* block.

Notes

• You can use any design as a stencil, even if it is colored. Any block or motif design set on Layer 3 will display as an outline drawing.

• A design does not have to be stored on the Stencils tab in the Blocks section of the Sketchbook in order for you to be able to use it as a stencil.

• You can copy or move designs to the Stencils tab.

4 To copy this design to the Stencils tab, right-click on the **Blocks** palette and the Blocks, Motifs & Stencils Palette Context Menu will open. Move your cursor to **Copy to Tab**. The extended menu will open. Click **Stencil Tab** and the *4X* block will copy to the Stencils tab in the Blocks section of the Sketchbook. The Blocks, Motifs & Stencils Palette Context Menu will close. Click the **Stencils** tab at the top of the Sketchbook Blocks palette and click the *4X* block to select it.

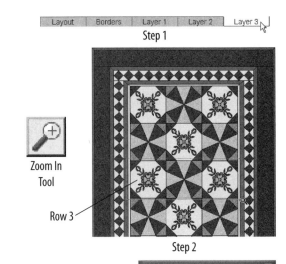

Step 1

Zoom In
Tool

Row 3

Step 2

Set Block
Tool

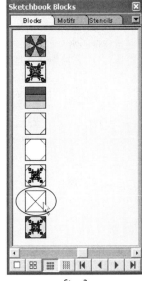

Step 3

Step 4

Row 3

Step 5

Add to
Sketchbook
Button

Step 6
Adjust

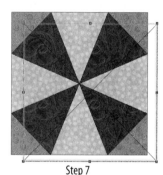

Step 7

Step 8

Step 9

5 Position the cursor over the *upper-left corner of the **Kaleidoscope** block in Row 3*, the center block in the quilt layout. Hold down the **SHIFT** key and the cursor will change to crosshairs. **Click and drag diagonally to the lower-right corner of the *Kaleidoscope* block** to form a frame over the block. When you release the mouse button, the *4X* stencil will appear in the frame. **Add to Sketchbook**. Don't worry about exact size and placement at this point.

Notes

• Use EDIT > Undo or CTRL+Z when necessary.

• Add to Sketchbook often when working on layers!

• You can easily replace a design with the Set Block tool.

• You can click and drag to move the Blocks palette on the worktable.

6 Now you will adjust the size and location of the *4X* stencil. Click the **Adjust** tool, the second tool on the Quilt toolbar. The icon is a skewed block outline with a white arrow.

7 Click the *4X* stencil. Notice that the Graph Pad is now activated. The Block Size tool will display the design dimensions. The Block Size tool is the third tool from the left on the Graph Pad.

8 Use the **arrow keys** on the Block Size section to set the size of the stencil to **9.00 x 9.00**. The *4X* stencil is now accurately sized on the layout.

9 With the *4X* stencil still selected, click the *vertical* **Center** button on the Graph Pad. This is the second to last button on the end of the Graph Pad. The icon is a square between two vertical arrows. The *4X* stencil will center vertically in the quilt layout.

Lesson 4

Lesson 4

10 Click the *horizontal* **Center** button on the Graph Pad. This is the last button on the end of the Graph Pad. The icon is a square between two horizontal arrows. The *4X* stencil will center horizontally in the quilt layout. The *4X* stencil is now accurately positioned on the layout. Click the **Fit to Worktable** button on the Project toolbar to return to normal viewing. **Add to Sketchbook**.

Step 10

Add to Sketchbook Button

Notes

The Adjust tool allows you to resize, move, and delete designs on layers.

There are three ways to *resize* a design on layers. Click the Adjust tool and then:

• Use the Block Size tool on the Graph Pad to set the size of the selected design.

• Use the Same Size tools on the Graph Pad to resize the selected design relative to a reference design. You will find information about this tool in the *EQ6 User Manual*.

• Click and drag the nodes on the selected design to shrink or enlarge it.

There are four ways to *move* a design on layers. Click the design with the Adjust tool and then:

• Click and hold as you drag the design into position on the layout.

• Use the keyboard arrow keys to move a selected design.

• Use the Align tools to position a design relative to a reference design.

• Use the Selected Block coordinates on the Graph Pad to position the design. You will learn this method later in this tutorial.

To *delete* a design on layers, click the design with the Adjust tool and then press the DELETE key.

To select all designs on a Layer, click the Adjust tool and, holding down the CTRL key, click on any design in that layer. All of the designs on that layer will be selected and highlighted. This is especially helpful when you want to find a design on a busy worktable.

Use the Adjust Tool to resize blocks.

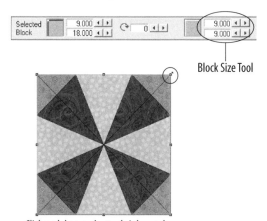

Block Size Tool

Click and drag nodes to shrink or enlarge.

Use the Adjust Tool to move blocks.

Selected Block Coordinates

Use the Adjust Tool to delete, select, and align blocks.

Align and Size Tools

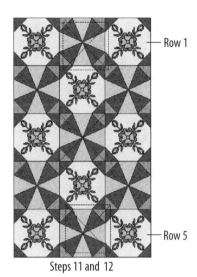

Row 1

Row 5

Steps 11 and 12

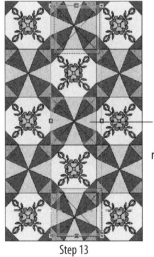

Use central *4X*
stencil as
reference block.

Step 13

11 Select the *4X* stencil with the **Adjust** tool, then **CTRL+C** to copy and **CTRL+V** to paste a second copy of the stencil on the worktable. Move this second stencil over the *Kaleidoscope* block in Row 1. Don't worry about exact placement at this point.

Notes

- The settings in QUILT > Options > Snap Settings make it easier to set and adjust designs on layers. The Nudge Settings control the distance that the Adjust tool moves a design when you use the arrows on the Graph Pad or on the keyboard. The default Nudge Setting of ¼" is recommended for this particular layout.

- The Grid Settings control the size and position to which a design will snap on the layout when you set it or adjust it manually. Specifically, the *Snap block position to grid* setting controls the increment to which a design will snap into position when you set it on the layout or when you click and drag to move it.

- The *Snap block size to grid* setting controls the increment to which a design will resize when you use the nodes to adjust the size. The default Grid Setting of 1" is recommended for setting the *4X* stencils on this layout.

12 **CTRL+V** to paste a third copy of the *4X* stencil on the worktable. Move this third stencil over the *Kaleidoscope* block in Row 5. Don't worry about exact placement at this point.

13 Using the centered *4X* stencil as a reference, you will align the Row 1 and Row 5 stencils horizontally. Click the centered *4X* stencil in Row 3. Hold down the **SHIFT** key and click the stencils in Rows 1 and 5.

Lesson 4

Notes

- As soon as you select multiple designs with the Adjust tool, the Align and Size tools will become available to you. The Align tools help you to position your designs on that layer, relative to the design that you choose as the reference. The Size tools allow you to change the size of your designs, relative to the design that you choose as the reference.

- The Align tools are: Align Left, Align Right, Align Top, and Align Bottom. These tools line up the selected designs with the designated side of the reference design.

- It doesn't matter which design you choose as your reference in a quilt layout, as long as it is correctly sized and/or positioned and you select it first with the Adjust tool.

14 With the three *4X* stencils selected, click **Align Left** or **Align Right**. The stencils in Rows 1 and 5 are now aligned horizontally with the centered stencil in Row 3. Click off the stencils to deselect them.

15 Zoom in, click the *4X* stencil in Row 1, and use the arrow keys to fine tune its vertical position, if necessary. Fine tune the vertical position of the stencil in Row 5, if necessary. **Add to Sketchbook**.

16 **CTRL+V** to paste another copy of the *4X* stencil on the worktable. Zoom in and adjust the position of the stencil so that it is positioned accurately over the left *Kaleidoscope* block in Row 2. **Add to Sketchbook**.

Notes
Remember to use the Zoom tools when working on layers.

17 **CTRL+V** to paste another copy of the *4X* stencil on the worktable. Zoom in and adjust the position of the stencil so that it is positioned accurately over the right *Kaleidoscope* block in Row 2. **Add to Sketchbook**.

18 Hold down the **SHIFT** key and click the two *4X* stencils in Row 2. **CTRL+C** to copy and **CTRL+V** to paste another row on the worktable.

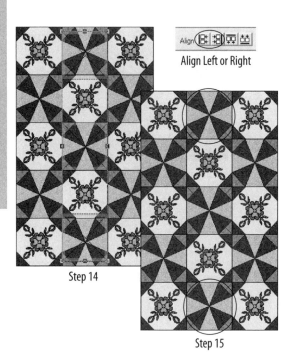

Align Left or Right

Step 14

Step 15

Row 2

Step 16   Step 17

Add to Sketchbook
Button

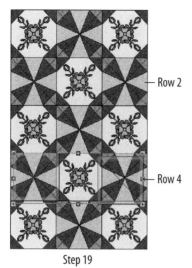

Row 2

Row 4

Step 19

Align Left or Right

Step 20

19 Click and drag the copy of the Row 2 stencils into position over Row 4. Click anywhere off of the stencils to deselect them. **Add to Sketchbook**.

20 Using the left stencil in Row 2 as a reference, click the left stencil in Row 4 and **Align Left** or **Align Right**. Using the right stencil in Row 2 as a reference, click the right stencil in Row 4 and **Align Left** or **Align Right**. **Add to Sketchbook**.

Changing the Thread Color

Black is the default color of quilting stencils in EQ6, but black stencils can be difficult to see on a dark quilt. The Set Thread tool gives you the option to choose the color, style, and weight of your quilting stencils.

The Set Thread tool is available on the Quilt worktable through the Customize Toolbar button, the last button on the Quilt toolbar. The Customize Toolbar icon is a small black arrow and a horizontal bar.

21 With the quilt on the worktable, click the **Customize Toolbar** button to open the extended menu. Click **Add/Remove Buttons**. Click to check the **Set Thread** tool in the list of tools. The icon is a spool of thread. Click anywhere off of the list to close it.

22 Find the **Set Thread** tool on the Quilt toolbar. **Click and hold down** the button or click the **little black arrow** on the button to open the **Set Thread flyout bar**. There are three tools available here: *Brush Thread*, *Spray Thread*, and *Swap Thread*.

- The **Brush Thread** tool recolors the thread in a *single patch*.

- The **Spray Thread** tool recolors *identical thread in all patches* within a single design.

- The **Swap Thread** tool recolors *all identical thread* in all layers of the quilt.

Step 22

Brush Thread   Spray Thread   Swap Thread

Step 21

23 Click the **Spray Thread** tool and the Thread palette will open. Under *Quilting Thread Properties*, click to check **Color, Style, and Weight**. Click the **thread sample** that you want to use in the layout. This color will display in the Color box. Click the **solid line** under *Style*. Click the last **line style** under *weight*. This is the thickest, most visible stitching line. This option will make it much easier for you to see the stencils that you set on the quilt layout. The cursor will change to a needle and thread on the worktable.

24 You can extend the function of the Brush Thread and Spray Thread tools with the CTRL key. With the **Spray Thread** tool engaged, **CTRL+click** any stencil on Layer 3. All of the stencils will change to the color, style, and weight that you selected. **Add to Sketchbook**.

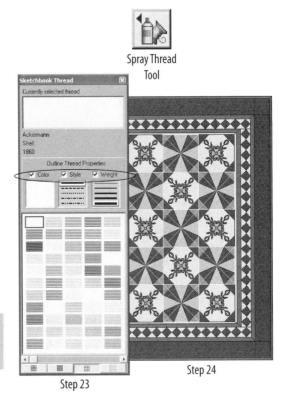

Spray Thread Tool

Step 24

Step 23

> **Notes**
> The Spray Thread tool and CTRL+click recolors all identical thread on the layer.

Now you will set the quilting stencils in the borders of this layout. You will set the corner designs in Border 4 first and then set the stencils on the sides of the quilt.

25 Click the **Set Block** tool, click the **Motifs** tab, and click the *Large Topeka Rose Blossom* design.

26 To move this design to the Stencils tab, right-click on the **Blocks** palette and the Blocks, Motifs & Stencils Palette Context Menu will open. Move your cursor to **Move to Tab**. The extended menu will open. Click **Stencil Tab**. The *Large Topeka Rose Blossom* design is now on the Stencils tab in the Blocks section of the Sketchbook.

27 Click the **Stencils** tab and click the *Large Topeka Rose Blossom*. Hold down the **SHIFT** key and **click and drag** to set the stencil in the *upper-left corner of Border 4*.

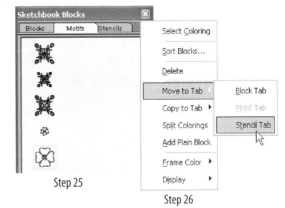

Step 25

Step 26

Step 27

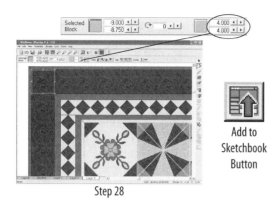

Step 28

Add to
Sketchbook
Button

Step 29
Spray Thread

Copy, paste and align three more *Topeka Rose Blossom*
stencils for the other three corners

Step 32
Tape Measure

28 Click the **Adjust** tool, click this **stencil** and set the size to **4.00 x 4.00** on the Graph Pad. Fine tune the position of the stencil with the **Adjust** tool and the **keyboard arrow keys** or **click and drag** with the mouse. **Add to Sketchbook**.

29 At this point, you can change the color, style, and weight of this stencil with the **Spray Thread** tool on the Quilt toolbar, as described in steps 23 and 24. Be sure to check the options that you want to change under *Quilting Thread Properties* in the Thread palette. **Add to Sketchbook.**

To change the thread color in this design only, use the **Spray Thread** tool *without* holding down the CTRL key.

> **Notes**
> After you click Add to Sketchbook, the copies that you make of this stencil will be in the new color.

30 Click the **Adjust** tool and use **CTRL+C** to copy to copy the stencil. **CTRL+V** *three times* to paste three more *Large Topeka Rose Blossom* stencils on the worktable.

31 Use the **Adjust** tool and the **keyboard arrow keys** or the mouse to fine tune the positions of the individual stencils in the corners of Border 4. Use a *correctly positioned corner stencil* as a reference to line up individual stencils with the appropriate **Align** button. **Add to Sketchbook**.

> **Notes**
> Remember to use the Zoom tools when working on layers.

Using the Tape Measure Tool

Before setting the long stencils on Border 4, you will learn how to use the Tape Measure tool. The Tape Measure tool is a very convenient feature that can be used on all layers and tabs of the Quilt worktable. With this tool, you can measure between any two points on the Quilt worktable. Now you will measure the vertical and horizontal sides of Border 4, between the corner blocks.

32 Click the **Tape Measure** tool.

Lesson 4

33 Position the cursor at the *right seam line on the upper-left corner block in Border 4*. **Hold down the mouse button** as you **click and drag** the cursor to the *left seam line of the upper-right corner block*. The horizontal measurement between the two top blocks is **37.00"**. This measurement will display on the screen until you release the mouse button.

34 Position the cursor at the *bottom seam of the upper-left corner block in Border 4*. **Hold down the mouse button** as you **click and drag** the cursor to *the top seam of the lower-left corner block*. The vertical measurement between the corner blocks is **54.50"**. This measurement will display on the screen until you release the mouse button.

Now you will use these measurements to set *Stripe Border 2* stencils in the horizontal and vertical sides of Border 4.

35 Click the **Set Block** tool, click the **Blocks** tab, and then click the *Stripe Border 2* design.

36 To move this design to the Stencils tab, right-click on the **Blocks** palette and the Blocks, Motifs & Stencils Palette Context Menu will open. Move your cursor to **Move to Tab**. The extended menu will open. Click **Stencil Tab**. The *Stripe Border 2* block is now on the Stencils tab in the Blocks section of the Sketchbook.

37 Click the **Stencils** tab and click the *Stripe Border 2* stencil. It doesn't matter if you select the colored version to set on Layer 3 since only the line drawing will display on this layer. Hold down the **SHIFT** key and draw this design near the top horizontal side of Border 4.

38 Click the **Adjust** tool and click the **stencil**. Set the size on the Graph Pad to the length of the border (between corner blocks) and the width: **37.00 x 4.00**. Click the *horizontal* **Center** button on the Graph Pad and the stencil will be centered horizontally on the layout.

Measure the Horizontal Border- 37.00"

Step 33

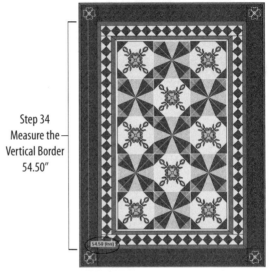

Step 34
Measure the
Vertical Border
54.50"

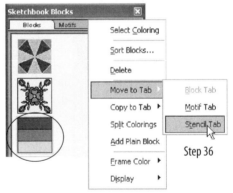

Step 36

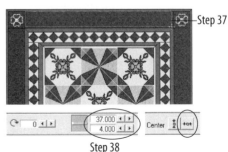

Step 37

Step 38

Step 39

Step 40
Spray Thread
Tool

Steps 41 and 42

Horizontal Center
Button

Align Top or
Align Bottom

Add to
Sketchbook
Button

Step 44   Step 45

Step 46

39 Use *one of the upper corner* stencils as a reference to **Align Top** or **Align Bottom**. **Add to Sketchbook**.

40 At this point, you can change the color, style, and weight of this stencil with the **Spray Thread** tool on the Quilt toolbar, as described in steps 23 and 24. Be sure to check the options that you want to change under *Quilting Thread Properties* in the Thread palette. **Add to Sketchbook**.

To change the thread color in this design only, use the **Spray Thread** tool *without* holding down the CTRL key.

> **Notes**
> After you click Add to Sketchbook, the copies that you make of this stencil will be in the new color.

41 Click the **Adjust** tool and click the stencil. **EDIT > Copy** or **CTRL+C** to copy the *Stripe Border 2* stencil.

42 Click **EDIT > Paste** or use **CTRL+V** to set another horizontal stencil on the worktable. With this stencil still selected, click the *horizontal* **Center** button on the Graph Pad and the stencil will be centered on the layout. Use *one of the lower corner stencils* as a reference to **Align Top** or **Align Bottom**. **Add to Sketchbook**.

43 **CTRL+C** and **CTRL+V** to copy and set another horizontal stencil on the worktable. You will resize and rotate this stencil and place it on the left vertical side of Border 4.

44 Rotate this design by **90 degrees** with the Graph Pad Rotation tool, the second tool from the left. The icon is a curved arrow.

45 You measured the distance between the vertical corner blocks as **54.50"**. Set the size of this stencil to **54.50 x 4.00** on the Graph Pad.

46 With this stencil still selected, click the *vertical* **Center** button in the Graph Pad. Use *one of the left corner stencils* as a reference to **Align Left** or **Align Right**. **Add to Sketchbook**.

Lesson 4

47 Select the **left vertical stencil** with the **Adjust** tool and **CTRL+C** and **CTRL+V** to copy and set another copy on the worktable.

48 With this stencil still selected, click the *vertical* **Center** button on the Graph Pad. Use *one of the right corner stencils* as a reference to **Align Left** or **Align Right**. **Add to Sketchbook**.

Your *Wildflower Wheelies* quilt is finished!

Notes
You can still change the color, style, and weight of the quilting thread on your layout with CTRL+Spray Thread tool. If you use the Swap Thread tool, all identically colored thread and outline colors will change on all layers of the quilt.

Turning Layers On and Off
You can turn layers on and off on the Quilt worktable in order to see the individual design layers more clearly.

49 Click **QUILT > Options > View Settings > Layer Icons**. Click to check *Provide icons to show and hide quilt layers* > **OK**.

50 You will notice that there are now light bulb icons on the three layer tabs on the Quilt worktable. Click the **yellow light bulb on Layer 3** and the quilting stencils will be hidden. Click the **grayed out light bulb** to restore the stencils. Click the **yellow light bulb on Layer 1** and the pieced designs in your quilt layout will be hidden. Click the **grayed out light bulb** to restore the pieced designs.

51 Open the **Quilts** section of the Sketchbook and use the arrows to display the final version of your new quilt. Click the **Notecard** button and name your *Wildflower Wheelies* design. **Close** the Notecard.

Vertical Center Button

Align Left or Right

Steps 47 and 48

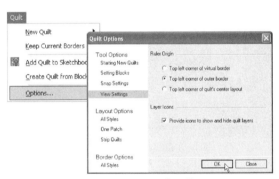

Step 49

Step 50

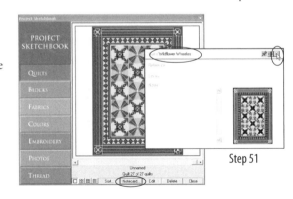

Step 51

Lesson 4

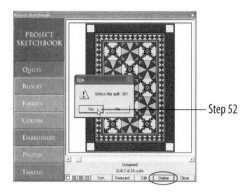

Step 52

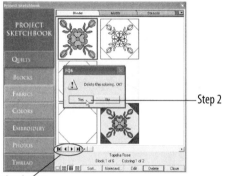

Step 2

Coloring Arrows

Select Tool

Step 2

52 **Delete** the unfinished designs in the Quilts section of the Sketchbook, using the instructions in Lesson 1: Deleting and Sorting Layouts.

Deleting Blocks from the Sketchbook

1 Before deleting any designs from the Blocks sections of the Sketchbook, you should complete **notecards** for any unnamed designs that you want to keep.

2 To *delete individual colorings* of a selected design from the Sketchbook, use the **Coloring Arrows** to display the coloring that you want to delete. Click the **Delete** button at the bottom of the Sketchbook. EQ6 will ask if you want to delete this coloring. Click **Yes**.

3 To *delete the line drawing and all colorings* of a selected design from the Sketchbook, use the **Coloring Arrow** on the *far left* to display the line drawing. Click the **Delete** button in the Sketchbook. EQ6 will ask if you want to delete this design and all colorings. Click **Yes**.

Printing Foundation Patterns

EQ6 offers a wide range of printing options for your block and appliqué designs.

1 Open the **Quilts** section of the Sketchbook and double-click to put your *Wildflower Wheelies* quilt on the worktable.

2 Click the **Select** tool and click any *Kaleidoscope* block on Layer 1.

3 Click **FILE > Print > Foundation Pattern**. The Print Foundation Pattern box will open. There are three tabs in this box: *Sections, Numbering,* and *Options*.

Notes
You can also use the Print button in the Project toolbar to generate a printout. Click the Print button and then click Foundation Pattern in the drop-down menu.

On the **Sections** tab of the Print Foundation Pattern box, EQ6 automatically divides the foundation pattern into sections in preparation for construction. You can change this sectioning and divide a block into the construction units that you prefer. For this lesson, you will use the sectioning recommended by EQ6.

On the **Numbering** tab, EQ6 automatically numbers the construction sequence for a foundation pattern. You can change the numbering sequence on this tab by clicking *Change Numbers*, then clicking the patches in the sequence that you prefer. For this lesson, you will use the numbering recommended by EQ6.

The **Options** tab contains the basic options for your foundation pattern. Under *Block Size*, keep **Use size from quilt** checked. Under *Seam Allowance*, click to check **Print seam allowance**. Under *Line Thickness*, click **the last option in the drop-down box**. Click to check these options: **Print numbering**, **Separate units**, **Grayscale**, and **Print block name**.

4   On the **Sections** tab, the *Kaleidoscope* foundation pattern will be divided into two sections by a dark blue line, split diagonally into top and bottom halves or left and right halves.

If your *Kaleidoscope* foundation pattern is split into *top and bottom halves* (see illustration), you must print it in **Landscape** orientation to fit each half onto a standard 8.5" x 11" page. Click the **Page Setup** button at the bottom of the Print Foundation Pattern box. Under *Orientation*, click to check **Landscape > OK > Preview**.

If your *Kaleidoscope* foundation pattern is split into left and right halves, you must print it in **Portrait** orientation to fit each half onto a standard 8.5" x 11" page. Click the **Page Setup** button at the bottom of the Print Foundation Pattern box. Under *Orientation*, click to check **Portrait > OK > Preview**.

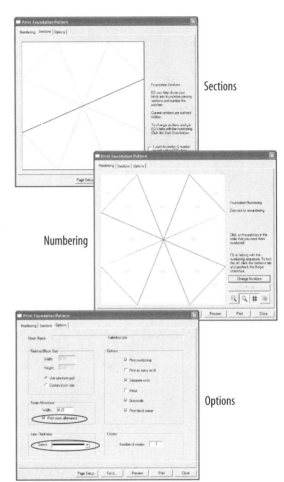

Sections

Numbering

Options

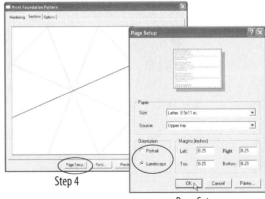

Step 4

Page Setup
Change Orientation

Lesson 4

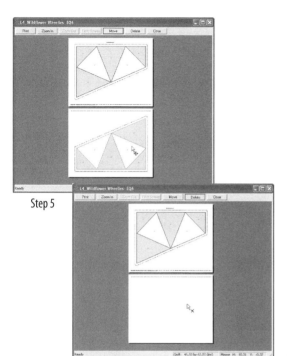

Step 5

Step 6

EQ6 allows you to move and delete foundation patterns.

5   Click the **Move** button at the top of the Print Preview page and **click half of the foundation pattern**. The section will highlight in red and the cursor will change to a four-headed arrow. Hold down the mouse button and move this section to the second page.

6   Click the **Delete** button at the top of the Print Preview page and **click one of the foundation pattern sections**. This section will be highlighted in red and the cursor will change to an *X*. Press the **DELETE** key on your keyboard and this section will be deleted. **Print**.

Printing Templates

In Lesson 2, you learned that you can move, rotate, and delete templates in EQ6. You will practice those skills now.

7   With your *Wildflower Wheelies* quilt still on the worktable, click the **Select** tool, and then click the ***Topeka Rose Octagon*** block in the layout. Click **FILE > Print > Templates**. The Print Template box will open. Under *Finished Block Size*, keep **Use size from quilt** checked. Under *Seam Allowance*, set the value to **0.25** and click to check **Print seam allowance**. Under *Print Key Block*, click to check **Small**. Under *Line Thickness*, click the **last option in the drop-down box**. **Preview**.

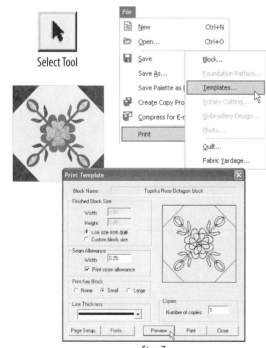

Select Tool

Step 7

> **Notes**
>
> If you changed your page orientation setting to Landscape when printing your *Kaleidoscope* block, your *Topeka Rose Octagon* print preview will still be in the same orientation. To change it back to Portrait, click Close on the Print Preview page and then click Page Setup at the bottom of the Print Template box. Under Orientation, click Portrait > OK.

8 In Print Preview, click the **Delete** button, click the *large Octagon patch*, and click the **DELETE** key on your keyboard.

9 Click the **Move** button, click a *triangle and move it next to the Key block*. Notice that EQ6 has already trimmed the corners of the triangle template.

10 Click the **Rotate** button, click the *triangle and it will rotate 90 degrees* with each click.

11 **Print**.

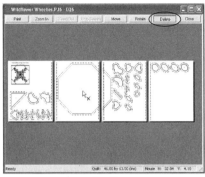

Step 8

Printing Stencils

12 With the *Wildflower Wheelies* quilt still on the worktable, click **Layer 3**.

13 Click the **Select** tool and click one of the *Large Topeka Rose Blossom* stencils in a *corner of Border 4*. Click **FILE > Print > Block**. Under *Finished Block Size*, keep **Use size from quilt** checked. Under *Printing Style*, click **Outline Drawing**. **Preview**. The stencil is drawn in solid lines. **Print**.

14 Click **FILE > Print > Block**. Under *Printing Style*, click **Quilting Stencil**. **Preview**. The stencil is displayed in dashed lines that resemble quilting stitches. **Print**.

Exiting EQ6

Click **FILE > Exit**.

CONGRATULATIONS! You can now design, color, edit, save, and print your own quilt designs in EQ6! There is still a lot to learn, so continue on to Lesson 5.

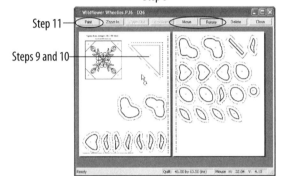

Step 11 —

Steps 9 and 10 —

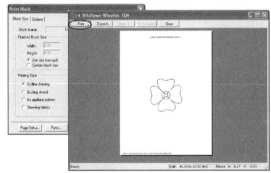

Step 13

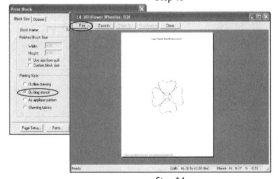

Step 14

Exploring Serendipity and Symmetry

Now that you have a firm foundation in EQ6, you are ready to start exploring the program's more advanced features. In this lesson, you will learn about the Symmetry and Serendipity tools and how they will significantly expand your creativity and productivity. In fact, you will generate more than 64 different layouts when you apply these tools to the four quilt designs that you will create in this lesson!

I named this collection of quilts *Beaucoup Begonias*. (Beaucoup is pronounced "bow-KOO" and that's Cajun French for "a lot.") You will learn many new EQ skills in this lesson as you strengthen the skills that you have developed in previous lessons. You will:

- Convert a motif to a block

- Rotate in PatchDraw

- Set Auto Borders

- Edit in EasyDraw™

- Maintain block rotation

- Experiment with the Symmetry tool

- Experiment with the Rotate & Flip Block tools

- Experiment with the Serendipity tool

    - Merge blocks

    - Tilt a block

    - Frame a block

- Print appliqué blocks

- Remove outlines from quilts

- Export images

- Add designs to My Library

Lesson 5

Creating a New Project

Run EQ6 and create a new project file with the name *Beaucoup Begonias*.

Adding Designs from the Block Library

As usual, your first task is to collect the designs that you will use in your quilts. For this collection of quilts, you will need three blocks from the EQ6 Block Library: *Flower from the 30s*, *Hovering Hawks*, and *Four X Variation*.

1 Click **LIBRARIES > Block Library > Search > By Notecard > type in:** *Flower from* **> Search > OK**. In the Search Results section, click the *Flower from the 30s* motif. **Add to Sketchbook**.

Step 1

Notes

The three search fields in the Search Block Notecard box are checked by default. Change any of these options by clicking to uncheck. *Find at most 50 items* is set by default. Change this option by highlighting the number and typing in a new value.

2 Click **Search > by Notecard > type in:** *Hovering Hawks* **> ENTER > OK**. Click the *Hovering Hawks* block. **Add to Sketchbook**.

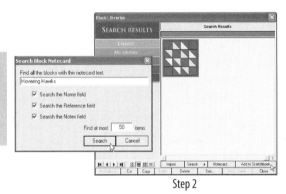

Step 2

3 Click **Search > by Notecard > type in:** *Four X* **> ENTER > OK**. Click the *Four X Variation* block. **Add to Sketchbook**.

4 **Close** the Block Library.

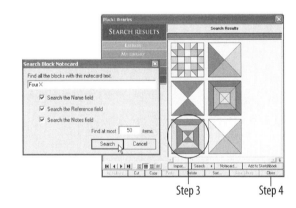

Step 3   Step 4

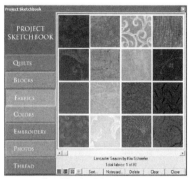

Sketchbook - Fabrics Section

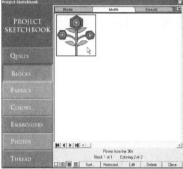

Step 1

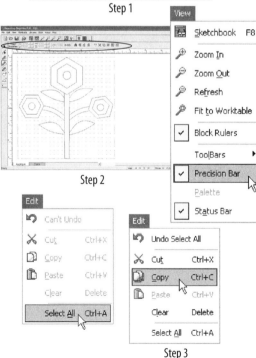

Step 2

Step 3

Adding Designs from the Fabric Library

You will need a range of light, light/medium, medium, medium/dark, and dark fabrics for your *Beaucoup Begonia* quilt series. You have enough coloring experience by now to know that you have several options for preparing your palette for a new project. You can:

- Keep your default palette.

- Supplement your default palette with additional samples from the Fabric Library, as described in Lessons 1 through 4.

- Clear the default palette and select new fabrics from the Fabric Library, as described in Lesson 4.

Make any changes that you wish to your palette and then proceed to the next section.

Converting a Motif to a Block

In Lesson 4, you converted the *Topeka Rose* block to a motif. In this lesson, you will convert a motif to a block. You will use this new block in all of the quilts in this lesson.

1 Open the **Blocks** section of the Sketchbook, click the **Motifs** tab, and double-click the *Flower from the 30s* to place it on the worktable. This is an appliqué design with no background square so it will open on the Appliqué tab of the PatchDraw Motif worktable.

2 Make sure that the Precision Bar is open on the worktable. If it is not, click **VIEW**, then click to check **Precision Bar**.

3 Click **EDIT > Select All** or use **CTRL+A** to select all patches. Click **EDIT > Copy** or use **CTRL+C** to copy all patches. The *Flower from the 30s* design is now on the Windows® clipboard. You can't see it, but it is there, ready to be pasted onto the new worktable.

4 Click **BLOCK > New Block > PatchDraw Block**. Click the **Appliqué** tab. Click **EDIT > Paste** or use **CTRL+V** to paste the *Flower from the 30s* design on the worktable.

5 With the design still selected, click **BLOCK > Rotate**. In the Rotate box, type in: **45**, then click **OK**. This is your *Button Begonia* block.

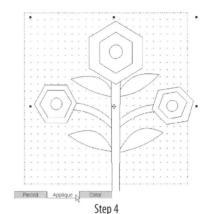

Step 4

> **Notes**
> With the design selected, you can also right-click anywhere on the worktable to open the PatchDraw Block & Motif Worktable Context Menu and then click Rotate. In the Rotate box, type in: 45, then click OK.

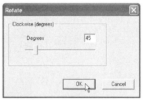

Step 5

Step 6
Centering

6 Center the design with the **Centering** button on the Precision Bar.

7 Color the *Button Begonia* block. **Add to Sketchbook**.

Adjusting a Layout

You will start your *Beaucoup Begonia* series by establishing a simple 4 x 4 horizontal layout. You will adjust this layout to create the first of four new quilt designs in this lesson. I named the first quilt in the *Beaucoup Begonia* series "*Button Begonia*" because the flower centers are the perfect showcase for some antique buttons from my Grandma Flo.

Add to Sketchbook
Button

Step 7

1 Click the **Work on Quilt** button on the project toolbar to switch to the Quilt worktable.

> **Notes**
> You can set the 4 x 4 horizontal layout as the default for future quilt layouts in QUILT > Options > Starting New Quilts. Notice the other options that are available to you here, including the default border style that you changed to Mitered in Lesson 2. Click to check *On startup of EQ6, always begin with a 4 x 4 horizontal layout*, then click OK.

2 Click **QUILT > New Quilt > Horizontal**.

Step 1
Work on Quilt

Step 2

Lesson 5

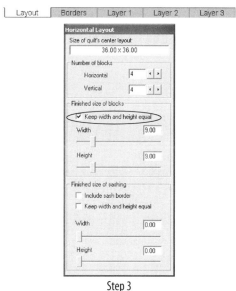

Step 3

Step 4

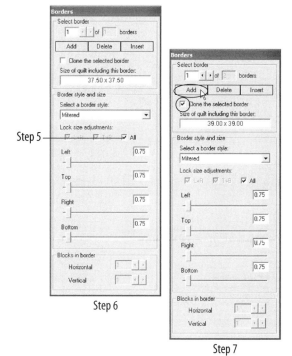

Step 5

Step 6

Step 7

3 Click the **Layout** tab on the lower-left of the screen. Use the arrows and palette sliders to set the following values in the Horizontal Layout box:

- Number of blocks:

    Horizontal: **4**

    Vertical: **4**

- Finished size of blocks: Click to check **Keep width and height equal**.

    Width: **9.00**

    Height will set automatically to the same value.

- Finished size of sashing:

    Width: **0.00**

    Height: **0.00**

4 Click the **Borders** tab on the lower-left of the screen. A Borders box will open with the first border selected automatically.

5 Under *Lock size adjustments*, click **All** so that it is checked. All sides of each border will adjust automatically now to the selected width for that border.

6 BORDER 1

    Style: **Mitered** (default)

    Size: **0.75**

7 BORDER 2

- Border 1 is still selected. Click to check **Clone the selected border**. Click **Add**.

    Border 2 will be added and it will be a clone of Border 1.

Lesson 5

8   BORDER 3

- Border 2 is still selected. **Clone the selected border** is still checked. Click **Add**.

  Border 3 will be added and it will be a clone of Border 2.

9   BORDER 4

- Border 3 is still selected. **Clone the selected border** is still checked. Click **Add**.

  Border 4 will be added and it will be a clone of Border 3.

- Change the size to **1.50**.

10   BORDER 5

- Click **Border 3** and click **Add**. Border 5 will be added and it will be a clone of Border 3.

11   BORDER 6

- Border 5 is still selected. Click **Add**.

  Border 6 will be added and it will be a clone of Border 5. You will change this border to an Auto Borders in the next section.

12   BORDER 7

- Border 6 is still selected. Click **Add**. Border 7 will be added.

- Change the size to **1.00**.

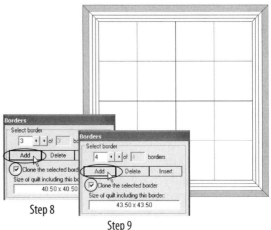

Step 8

Step 9
Size: 1.50

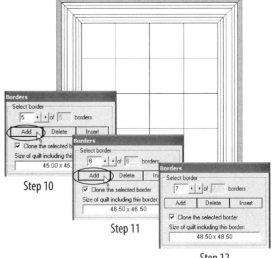

Step 10

Step 11

Step 12
Size: 1.00

Setting Auto Borders

With the Set Auto Borders feature, EQ6 has made complex borders easy to achieve with just a few clicks!

1   Click the **Layer 1** tab. Click **Customize Toolbars**, the last button on the Quilt toolbar. Click **Add/Remove Buttons > Set Auto Borders**. Click anywhere off of the list to close it. The Set Auto Borders tool is now on the Quilt toolbar. The icon is a *Nine Patch* corner block in a quilt border.

Step 1
Set Auto Borders

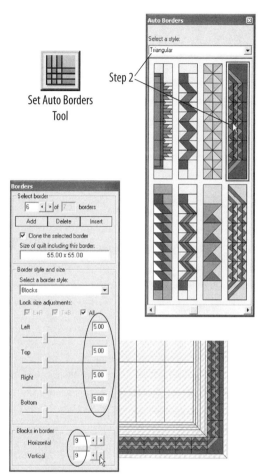

Set Auto Borders Tool

Step 2

Step 3

Step 4

Graph Paper Cells: Horizontal 4 Vertical 4

Step 5

Notes
- You can also customize the toolbar by right-clicking anywhere on the toolbar to open the tool list.

- You cannot use the Auto Borders feature on a quilt without borders.

2 Click the **Set Auto Borders** tool on the Quilt toolbar to open the Auto Borders box. Click the down arrow under *Select a style* and scroll down to **Triangular**. Click the *Double Zig Zag* design. It is the border style in the upper-right of the Auto Borders box.

3 Click **Border 6** on the quilt layout and the Triangular Auto Border will be set in the layout. Click the **Borders** tab and change *all sides of Border 6* to **5.00**. Set the number of *Horizontal and Vertical Blocks in border* to **9**. **Add to Sketchbook**.

4 Open the **Blocks** section of the Sketchbook and notice that with the addition of the Auto Border on your layout, there are now two border blocks in the Blocks section of the Sketchbook: the *Double Zig Zag* and the *Double Zig Zag Corner*. Before you color the Auto Border on the layout, you will modify the *Double Zig Zag Corner* block to add more visual interest.

5 Double-click to place the ***Double Zig Zag Corner*** block on the EasyDraw™ worktable. You will find it helpful to have *4 x 4 graph paper* on the worktable when you make modifications to this block. To display graph paper on the worktable, click the **Graph Paper** button on the Precision Bar to turn it on and change the *Horizontal* and *Vertical* settings to **4**.

Notes
Before drawing, be sure that the Snapping options are set to the default settings: Click BLOCK > Drawing Board Setup > Snapping > *Snap to grid* and *Snap to nodes of drawing* should be checked. Click Options under PatchDraw. *Snap to node of drawing* should be checked > OK.

Lesson 5

6 Draw a **diagonal line** from the *upper-right corner* to the *lower-left corner*. Complete the drawing by adding **horizontal** and **vertical** lines, as illustrated. **Add to Sketchbook**.

7 Click the **Work on Quilt** button in the Project tools to return to the Quilt worktable. Click the **Layer 1** tab.

Notice that the corner blocks in the Triangle Auto Border are rotated to the appropriate orientation in the layout. EQ6 gives you the option to maintain the specific rotation for designs in the layout when you replace them with other designs. The new designs will be set to the same rotation as the previous designs. This feature works on all layers and will save you a lot of time and effort when you are replacing rotated blocks in a layout! You will activate this setting before you replace the rotated corner blocks in Border 6.

8 Click **QUILT > Options > Setting Blocks > Setting Options**. Click to check **Maintain the block rotation from the current quilt when replacing blocks,** then click **OK**.

9 Click to select the **Set Block** tool, then click the *Modified Double Zig Zag Corner* block, and **CTRL+click** to set it into Border 6. Notice that these modified corner blocks are in the correct orientation. **Add to Sketchbook**.

10 With the **Set Block** tool still engaged, click the *Button Begonia* block in the Blocks palette. **CTRL+click** to set this block in every space in the layout. We will color these blocks in the next couple of steps. **Add to Sketchbook**.

11 Use the **Paintbrush** tool to color Borders 1, 2, 3, 4, 5, and 7. Use **CTRL+click** with the **Paintbrush** to color the *Double Zig Zag Corner* blocks in Border 6. Use the **Swap All Colors** tool to recolor the *Double Zig Zag* blocks in Border 6. **Add to Sketchbook**.

Your *Button Begonia* quilt is now finished and ready for experimentation!

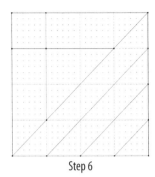

Step 6

Step 7

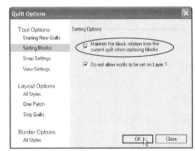

Step 8

Set Block Tool

Step 9

Step 10

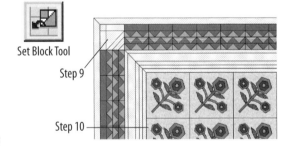

Paintbrush Tool

Swap All Colors Tool

Step 11

Flip Block Tool

Symmetry Tool

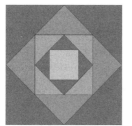

Square in a Square
Symmetrical Design

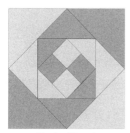

Monkey Wrench
Asymmetrical by Color

Alphabet Letter *"P"*
Asymmetrical by Design

Step 1
Rotate Block

Experimenting with the Symmetry Tool

You learned in Lessons 2 and 3 that it's very easy to rotate designs in 90 degree increments on the quilt layout in EQ6. It's also very easy to flip designs in EQ6. The **Flip Block** tool enables you to reverse or mirror image a design on the worktable with just one click.

With the **Symmetry** tool, EQ6 takes rotating and flipping one giant step further by combining these functions in a specific sequence that enables you to create 16 different layout variations from one quilt! To fully appreciate this powerful and convenient tool, you will practice briefly with the Rotate Block and Flip Block tools before progressing to the Symmetry tool.

When rotating or flipping, you must use a block that is *asymmetrical* by color or design in order to be able to see a difference in the design's orientation. The *Square in a Square* block illustrated at the left is symmetrical by color and design. You would see no difference if you rotated or flipped it. The *Monkey Wrench* block is asymmetrical by color and the Alphabet letter *"P"* block is asymmetrical by design, so you would see a difference if you rotated or flipped these designs. Now you will use your *Button Begonia* block to experiment with the Rotate Block, Flip Block, and Symmetry tools on your quilt layout.

The Rotate Block Tool

1   With the *Button Begonia* quilt on the worktable, click the **Rotate Block** tool on the Quilt toolbar. The icon is a sequence of rotated blocks with a curved arrow.

Lesson 5

2 Click the ***Button Begonia*** block in the upper-left corner of the layout. The block will rotate 90 degrees. Click *three more times* and the block will complete a 360 degree rotation, returning to its original orientation.

Step 2

3 Hold down the **ALT** key and click the same block. Every alternate block in the layout will rotate 90 degrees. Hold down the **ALT** key again and click *three more times*, until the Begonias return to their original orientation.

4 Hold down the **CTRL** key and click the same block. Every block in the layout will rotate 90 degrees. Hold down the **CTRL** key again and click *three more times*, until the Begonias return to their original orientation.

Step 3
ALT+click

Step 4
CTRL+click

The Flip Block Tool

5 Now, click the **Flip Block** tool on the Quilt toolbar, right below the **Rotate Block** tool. The icon is a mirror image of a block with a curved arrow.

Flip Block
Tool

6 Click the ***Button Begonia*** block in the upper-left corner of the layout. The block will flip to a mirror image of itself. Click again to return the *Button Begonia* block to its original orientation.

Step 6

7 Hold down the **ALT** key and click the same block. Every alternate block in the layout will flip to a mirror image of itself. Hold down the **ALT** key again and click to return the *Button Begonia* blocks to their original orientation.

8 Hold down the **CTRL** key and click the same block. Every block in the layout will flip to a mirror image of itself. Hold down the **CTRL** key again and click to return the *Button Begonia* blocks to their original orientation.

Step 7

Step 8

Lesson 5

Step 9
Symmetry

Step 10

Add to
Sketchbook
Button

Symmetry Tool Variations

The Symmetry Tool

Now, imagine a tool that can perform a combination of 16 rotations and flips in a systematic series of steps. That is exactly what the Symmetry tool does!

9 With the *Button Begonia* quilt on the worktable, click the **Symmetry** tool on the Quilt toolbar. The icon is four "P" blocks in a series of rotations and flips. **Be sure to have returned your *Button Begonia* blocks to their original orientation.**

10 **CTRL+click** on the block in the upper-left corner of the layout. The new layout is the first of 16 symmetrical variations. With each successive **CTRL+click** of the Symmetry tool, you will create another symmetrical layout. Click **Add to Sketchbook** for any layouts that you want to keep.

11 Continue to hold down the **CTRL** key and click the block with the **Symmetry** tool until you have completed the series of 16 different symmetries. To return to the original quilt layout, open the **Quilts** section of the Sketchbook and double-click to place it on the worktable.

Notes

- The Symmetry tool works best in horizontal quilt layouts with no sashing. EQ6 will rotate and flip each set of four blocks within the quilt for a total of 16 different symmetrical layouts. Be sure to add your original layout to the Sketchbook before experimenting with the Symmetry tool.

- You can use the same asymmetrical design throughout the quilt or use a combination of asymmetrical blocks.

Lesson 5

Experimenting with the Serendipity Tool

Webster's *New World Dictionary* defines serendipity as "an apparent aptitude for making accidental fortunate discoveries." There is nothing accidental about EQ6's Serendipity tool! With this feature, the program gives you the opportunity to make many fortunate design discoveries by merging, tilting, and framing your existing block designs.

You used the *Button Begonia* quilt to demonstrate the Symmetry tool. Now you will explore the Serendipity options by creating three more block and quilt variations in your *Beaucoup Begonia* series.

Busby Begonias is the second quilt that you will design in this series and you will use it to demonstrate the Merge Blocks feature. I named this quilt after Busby Berkeley, the famous movie director and choreographer from the 1930's. If you have ever seen any of Busby Berkeley's elaborately choreographed musicals such as *Gold Diggers of 1933*, you will notice the similarity of movement in EQ6's precise and sequential rearrangement of blocks in a quilt layout.

You will start by modifying the *Hovering Hawks* block to create the base for your new merged design.

1   Open the **Blocks** section of the Sketchbook and double-click to place the *Hovering Hawks* block on the EasyDraw™ worktable. With the **Line** tool, draw a diagonal line in the upper-right corner patch and in the lower-left corner patch, as illustrated. **Add to Sketchbook**.

2   Click the **Pick** tool, the first tool on the EasyDraw™ toolbar. The icon is a black arrow. Hold down the **DELETE** key and click the *six line segments* in the center square of the block. **Add to Sketchbook**. This is the *Modified Hovering Hawks* block that you will use in your merged design.

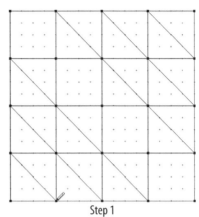

Step 1

Add to Sketchbook Button

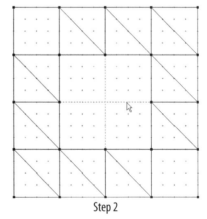

Step 2

Pick Tool

Add to Sketchbook Button

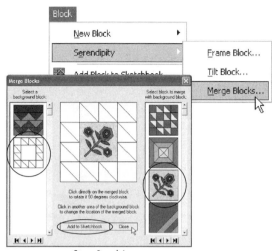

Steps 3 and 4

Step 5

Add to Sketchbook
Button

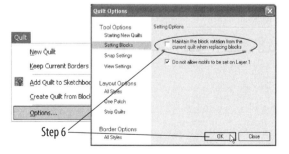

Step 6

Merging Blocks

3   Click **BLOCK > Serendipity > Merge Blocks**. The Merge Blocks box will open. Select the ***Modified Hovering Hawks*** block in the left column and it will appear as the background block in the Merge Blocks box.

Notes
EQ6 determines which characteristics a block must have to be used as a background block, so be willing to experiment when using the Serendipity tool.

4   Select the ***Button Begonia*** block in the right column and it will appear in the center of the *Modified Hovering Hawks* block. **Add to Sketchbook**. You now have a merged design, the *Busby Begonia* block.

Notes
There are several options available to you in the Merge Blocks box:

- You can click the inset design to rotate it in 90 degrees increments.

- You can click a different square or rectangle within the background block to move the inset design to that space.

- You can use the Coloring Arrows at the bottom of the left and right columns to view the colorings of the selected blocks in each column.

5   **Close** the Merge Blocks box. Open the **Blocks** section of the Sketchbook and double-click the *Busby Begonia* block. **Color** the block. **Add to Sketchbook**.

Before you set the *Busby Begonia* block into your *Button Begonia* layout, you will turn off the option to maintain the block rotation. This means that your blocks will be in the initial orientation in the layout, with no rotation. This will make it easy for you to see the effect of the Symmetry tool on this layout.

6   Click the **Work on Quilt** button. Click **QUILT > Options > Setting Blocks > Setting Options**. Click to uncheck **Maintain the block rotation from the current quilt when replacing blocks**. Click **OK**.

Lesson 5

7   Click the **Set Block** tool. Click the *Busby Begonia* block and **CTRL+click** to set this block in all spaces in the layout. This is your *Busby Begonia* quilt design. **Add to Sketchbook**.

8   Now, click the **Symmetry** tool and **CTRL+click** on the block in the upper-left corner of the layout. The new layout is the first of 16 symmetrical variations. With each successive CTRL+click of the Symmetry tool, you will create another symmetrical layout. Click **Add to Sketchbook** for any layouts that you want to keep.

Tilting a Block

Now you will create a tilted block and then make small modifications to it to enhance the design in the layout.

9   Click the **Work on Block** button on the Project toolbar. Click **BLOCK > Serendipity > Tilt Block**. Scroll down the left column to find the *Busby Begonia* block.

10 In the Tilt a Block box, click the slider button on the horizontal scrollbar and then use the keyboard arrow keys to move it to a **10 degree tilt**. This is your *Tipsy Begonia* block. **Add to Sketchbook**. **Close**.

11 Open the **Blocks** section of the Sketchbook and double-click the *Tipsy Begonia* block to place it on the worktable. The **Line** tool is engaged automatically. Draw lines to the corners of the block, as illustrated. This is your *Begonia Boogie* block. **Color** the block. **Add to Sketchbook**.

12 Click the **Work on Quilt** button in the Project toolbar. The Quilt worktable will open with one of the *Busby Begonia* quilt layouts. Remember that you turned off the option to maintain block rotation. When you set the *Begonia Boogie* block in this layout, the blocks will be in the initial orientation, with no rotation.

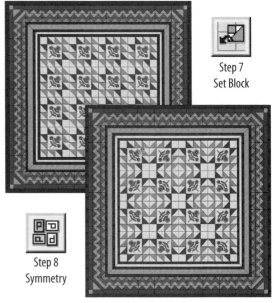

Step 7
Set Block

Step 8
Symmetry

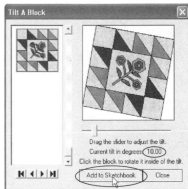

Step 10

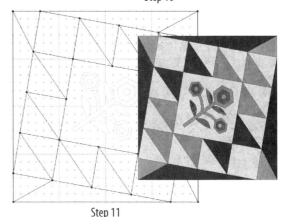

Step 11

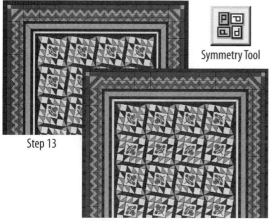

Symmetry Tool

Step 13

Step 14

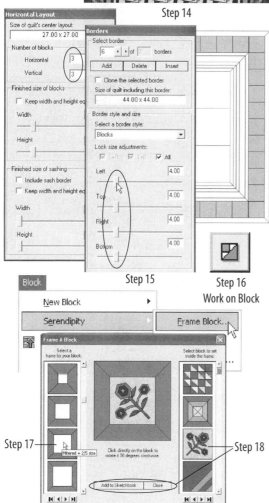

Step 15

Step 16
Work on Block

Step 17

Step 18

13 Click the **Layer 1** tab. Click the **Set Block** tool, click the ***Begonia Boogie*** block and **CTRL+click** to set it in all spaces in the layout. This is your *Begonia Boogie* quilt design. **Add to Sketchbook**.

14 Now, click the **Symmetry** tool and **CTRL+click** on the block in the upper-left corner of the layout. The new layout is the first of 16 symmetrical variations. With each successive **CTRL+click** of the Symmetry tool, you will create another symmetrical layout. Click **Add to Sketchbook** for any layouts that you want to keep.

Framing a Block

15 You will make a few minor adjustments in the layout for the last quilt in your *Beaucoup Begonia* series. With your *Begonia Boogie* quilt still on the worktable, click the **Layout** tab. Change the number of *horizontal* and *vertical* blocks to **3**. Click the **Borders** tab and change the width of *Border 6* to **4.00**. **Add to Sketchbook**.

16 Click the **Work on Block** button on the Project toolbar.

17 Click **BLOCK > Serendipity > Frame Block**. Use the left vertical scrollbar to view the series of mitered frames. Find the *four-sided mitered* frames in the left column and hold your cursor over each until the tooltip displays the **Mitered + 2/5 size**. Click this design to select it as the frame.

18 Use the right vertical scrollbar to view the ***Button Begonia*** block. Click to select it. Use the Coloring Arrows to display the coloring that you want to use. This is your *Boxed Begonia* block. **Add to Sketchbook**. **Close**. Open the **Blocks** section of the Sketchbook and double-click the ***Boxed Begonia*** block to place it on the worktable.

Lesson 5

Lesson 5

19 Create *two colorings* of this block, as illustrated. In one block, use a medium color on opposite sides of the frame. Color the remaining two sides of the frame with a medium/dark color. Change the color and create another block with the same values, reversing the value placement in the second block frame, as illustrated.

20 Click the **Work on Quilt** button on the Project toolbar. The Quilt worktable will open with one of the *Begonia Boogie* quilt layouts. Remember that you turned off the option to maintain block rotation. When you set the *Boxed Begonia* block in this layout, it will be in the initial orientation, with no rotation.

21 Click the **Layer 1** tab. Click the **Set Block** tool then use the coloring arrows to select the *first coloring* of the **Boxed Begonia** block. Place your cursor over the upper-left block space in the layout and **ALT+click** to set it in alternate spaces in the layout.

22 Click the *second coloring* of the **Boxed Begonia** block. Place your cursor over the adjacent block space and **ALT+click** to set it in alternate spaces in the layout.

23 Click the **Four X Variation** in the Blocks palette and click the **center block** in the layout, replacing one of the *Boxed Begonia* blocks. **Add to Sketchbook**.

24 Use the **Eyedropper** tool to find previously used colors in the Fabrics and Colors palette. Use the **Paintbrush** tool to color the **Four X Variation** block with these fabric samples. This is your *Boxed Begonia* quilt design. **Add to Sketchbook**.

25 Use the **Symmetry** tool or the **Rotate Block** and **Flip Block** tools to experiment with variations of this layout. Click **Add to Sketchbook** for any layouts that you want to keep. Be sure to name the designs that you want to keep before you clean out your Sketchbook. It is best to do these organizational tasks before you print your designs.

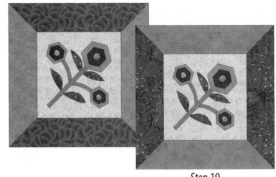

Step 19

Step 20
Work on Quilt

Coloring Arrows

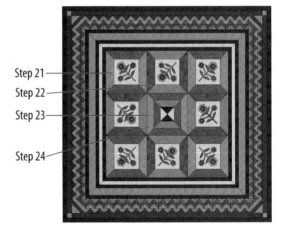

Step 21

Step 22

Step 23

Step 24

Add to Sketchbook
Button

Symmetry

Rotate Block

Flip Block

Step 25

Select Tool

Step 1

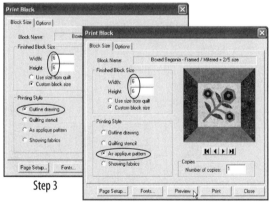

Step 2

Step 3

Step 4

Print Appliqué Blocks

In EQ6, you can print appliqué blocks as outline drawings and as appliqué patterns.

1   Click the **Select** tool and click one of the ***Boxed Begonia*** blocks in your ***Boxed Begonia*** quilt on the worktable.

2   Click **FILE > Print > Block** or click the **Print** button on the Project toolbar and click **Block**.

3   On the Block Size tab, click **Custom block size** under *Finished Block Size*. Set the *Width* and *Height* to **6 x 6**. Under *Printing Style*, click to check **Outline drawing**. **Preview** and **Print**. Notice that all of the patch outlines are visible in this drawing, including the outlines of overlapping patches.

4   Click **FILE > Print > Block** or click the **Print** button on the Project toolbar and click **Block**. Click **Custom block size** under *Finished Block Size* on the Block Size tab. Set the *Width* and *Height* to **6 x 6**. Under *Printing Style*, click to check **As appliqué pattern**. **Preview** and **Print**. Notice that the design is layered realistically in this printout so that overlapping patch outlines are not visible.

Removing Outlines from Quilts

In EQ6, you can display your designs on the Quilt worktable without patch or block outlines. Removing the patch or block outlines will give your quilts a softer, more realistic appearance.

1   With your *Boxed Begonia* quilt on the worktable, right-click to open the Quilt Worktable Context Menu. Click to uncheck **Outline Patches**. The context menu will close automatically. EQ6 will display your quilt without patch outlines. Right-click to open the Quilt Worktable Context Menu again and click to uncheck **Outline Blocks**. EQ6 will display your quilt without block outlines.

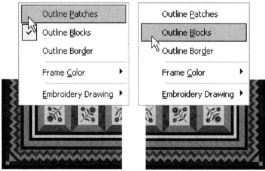

Step 1

Lesson 5

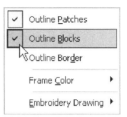

Step 2

2   The patch and block outlines will not display on the Quilt worktable until you reverse these settings. Right-click on the worktable to open the Quilt Worktable Context menu. Click to check **Outline Patches**. The context menu will close automatically. Right-click to open the context menu again and click to check **Outline Blocks**. The context menu will close automatically. EQ6 will now display your quilt with patch and block outlines.

You can print your quilts without patch or block outlines.

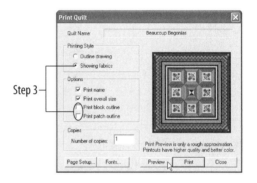

Step 3

3   Click **FILE > Print > Quilt** or click the **Print** button on the Project toolbar and click **Quilt**. The Print Quilt box will open. Under *Printing Style*, click **Showing fabrics**. Under *Options*, click to uncheck **Print block outline** and **Print patch outline**. Click **Preview** and **Print**.

You can also export a design without patch or block outlines. In the next section, you will learn how to export high-quality images in your choice of file formats.

Notes
Any quilt design that you Add to Sketchbook will have patch and block outlines.

Exporting Images

There are two ways to export images from the quilt worktable. You can export a selected area of the quilt worktable or you can export the entire image.

1   To export a *selected area* of a quilt layout, click **FILE > Export Marquee Selection**. The cursor will change to crosshairs within a magnifying glass. Click and drag a selection frame around the area in the layout that you want to export. When you release the mouse button, an Export Selection box will appear with three choices: *Save a file*, *Copy to Windows clipboard*, and *Print*.

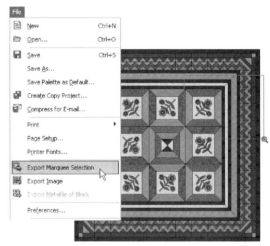

Step 1

Step 2

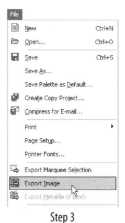

Step 3

Save Box

Export Image File of Quilt Box

2   If you click the **Save a file** button, the Export Selection box will open. Navigate to the directory in which you want to save this snapshot. Type a file name and click the **Save** button at the bottom of the Export Image box.

If you click the **Copy to Windows clipboard** button, the selection is copied and is ready to be pasted into any Windows® application with **CTRL+V**.

If you click the **Print** button, the selection will go directly to your default printer.

Notes
You can export a marquee (framed) selection only as a bitmap file.

3   To export the whole image, click **FILE > Export Image**. The Export Image box will open. Navigate to the folder in which you want to save this image. Type in a file name and use the down arrow to select the file type. Click **Save**. An Export Image File of Quilt box will open giving you more options, depending upon the file format that you selected. See **HELP > Search > type in** *export* **> List Topics button > Exporting > Display button** for more information about the options and advantages when using the various file types for exporting.

Lesson 5

Adding Designs to My Library

EQ6 provides space for your own personal library within each of the main libraries in the program. These My Library sections allow you to organize your designs in any way that you wish. They also serve as a convenient and safe storage location in the event that you lose a project file.

Now you will add your EQ6 Simplified blocks to My Library in the Block Library.

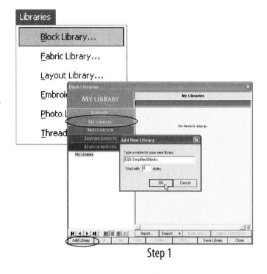

1   Click **LIBRARIES > Block Library**. Click **My Library** in the upper-left of the Block Libraries box. Click the **Add Library** button in the lower-left corner of the Block Libraries box. The Add New Library box will open. Type in *EQ6 Simplified Blocks* for your new library and change the number of styles to **8**. You will establish a library style for each of the eight lessons in this book. Click **OK**. Your new EQ6 Simplified Blocks library will be listed under My Custom Libraries in the My Libraries list.

Step 1

Notes
Click the plus (+) sign next to EQ6 Simplified Blocks to expand the list. Click the minus (-) sign next to EQ6 Simplified Blocks to collapse the list.

2   Under EQ6 Simplified Blocks, click to select **Style 5**. Right-click in the Libraries list in the Block Libraries box to open the My Library Context Menu. You can use this menu to add a new library to the list, to rename a library or style, or to change the number of styles in a library. Click **Modify Style** and type in: *Lesson 5*. Click **OK**. Rename the rest of the library styles in numerical sequence from **Lesson 1** to **Lesson 8**.

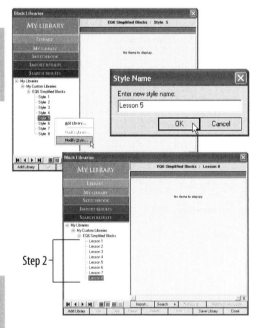

Step 2

Notes
You can add designs to My Library from any of the sections in the Block Libraries box. These sections are: Library, Sketchbook, Import Results, and Search Results.

Lesson 5

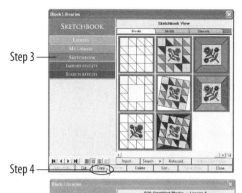

Step 3

Step 4

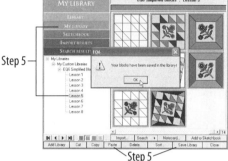

Step 5

Step 5

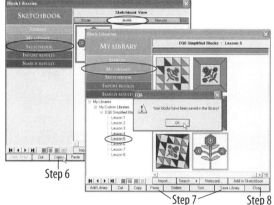

Step 6

Step 7   Step 8

Step 9

3   In the Block Library, click the **Sketchbook** button on the left to view the blocks currently in the Sketchbook. The Blocks section of Lesson 5, the current Sketchbook, will open.

4   **CTRL+A** to select all of the designs in the Blocks section. Click **Copy** at the bottom of the Block Libraries box. The designs are all on the Windows® clipboard, ready to be pasted into your new library style.

Notes

Click to select one design. SHIFT+click on first and last designs to select multiple designs in a sequence. CTRL+click to select multiple designs that are not in a sequence. CTRL+A to select all designs. CTRL+click to deselect a selected design.

5   Click **My Library > EQ6 Simplified Blocks > Lesson 5**. Click the **Paste** button at the bottom of the Block Libraries box. Click **Save Library > OK**.

6   Click the **Sketchbook** button and then click the **Motifs** tab at the top of the Sketchbook. The *Flower from the 30s* motif is selected. Click **Copy**.

7   Click **My Library > EQ6 Simplified Blocks > Lesson 5 > Paste > Save Library > OK**.

8   **Close** the Block Library.

You can use this procedure to establish a My Library for each of the project files in this tutorial.

Now you will add your EQ6 Simplified fabrics to My Library in the Fabric Library.

9   Click **LIBRARIES > Fabric Library > My Library**. Click the **Add Library** button in the lower-left corner of the Fabric Libraries box. The Add New Library box will open. Type in *EQ6 Simplified Fabrics* for your new library and change the number of styles to **8**. You will establish one library style for each of the eight lessons in this book. Click **OK**. Your new EQ6 Simplified Fabrics library will be listed under My Custom Libraries in the My Libraries list.

Lesson 5

Notes
If you get a message saying "No library files found," just click OK and continue.

10 Click to select **Style 5**. Right-click to open the My Library Context Menu. Click **Modify Style** and type in: *Lesson 5*. Click **OK**. Rename the rest of the library styles in numerical sequence from **Lesson 1** to **Lesson 8**.

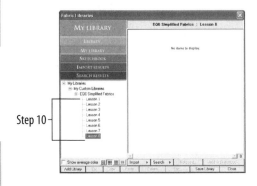

Step 10

Notes
You can add designs to My Library from any of the sections listed under My Library in the Fabric Libraries box. These sections are: Library, Sketchbook, Import Results, and Search Results.

11 Click the **Sketchbook** button on the left to open the current Sketchbook.

12 **CTRL+A** to select all of the samples in the Fabrics section. Click **Copy** at the bottom of the Fabric Libraries box to copy the designs to the Windows® clipboard.

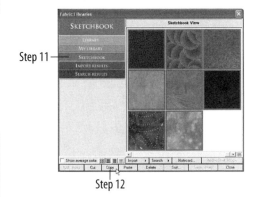

Step 11

Step 12

Notes
Click to select one design. SHIFT+click on first and last designs to select multiple designs in a sequence. CTRL+click to select multiple designs that are not in a sequence. CTRL+A to select all designs. CTRL+click to deselect a selected design.

13 Click **My Library > EQ6 Simplified Fabrics > Lesson 5**. Click the **Paste** button at the bottom of the Fabric Libraries box. Click **Save Library > OK**.

14 **Close** the Fabric Library.

Now you will add your EQ6 Simplified layouts to My Library in the Layout Library.

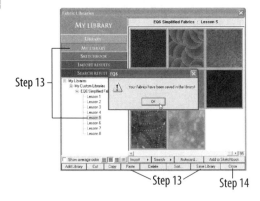

Step 13

Step 13

Step 14

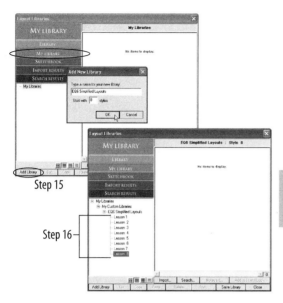

Step 15

Step 16

15 Click **LIBRARIES > Layout Library > My Library**. Click the **Add Library** button in the lower-left corner of the Layout Libraries box. The Add New Library box will open. Type in *EQ6 Simplified Layouts* for your new library and change the number of styles to **8**. You will establish one library style for each of the eight lessons in this book. Click **OK**. Your new EQ6 Simplified Layouts library will be listed under My Custom Libraries in the My Libraries list.

Notes
If you get a message saying "No library files found," just click OK and continue.

16 Click to select **Style 5**. Right-click to open the My Library Context Menu. Click **Modify Style** and type in: *Lesson 5*. Click **OK**. Rename the rest of the library styles in numerical sequence from **Lesson 1** to **Lesson 8**.

Notes
You can add designs to My Library from any of the sections listed under My Library in the Layout Libraries box. These sections are: Library, Sketchbook, Import Results, and Search Results.

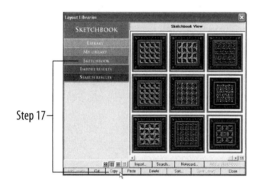

Step 17

17 Click the **Sketchbook** button on the left to open the current Sketchbook. **CTRL+A** to select all of the designs in the Layouts section. Click **Copy** at the bottom of the Layout Libraries box to copy the designs to the Windows® clipboard.

18 Click **My Library > EQ6 Simplified Layouts > Lesson 5 > Paste > Save Library > OK**.

19 Close the Layout Library.

The block, motif, fabric, and layout designs in this project file are now saved in the appropriate sections of My Library.

Exiting EQ6
Click **FILE > Exit**.

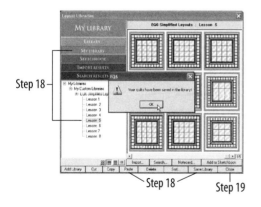

Step 18

Step 18

Step 19

Customizing with EasyDraw™

In this lesson, you will design *Nebraska Sunrise*, a quilt that reflects the warmth and welcome that Nebraska State Quilt Guild members extended to me when I taught at QuiltNebraska for two consecutive years. This quilt will give you more opportunities to practice your EasyDraw™ skills as you create an original pieced design and customize an existing design. You will:

- Create a complex design in EasyDraw™
- Design a quilt backing
- Design a quilt label
- Design with WreathMaker
- Draw with the Shape tools
- Add text with the Set Appliqué Text tool
- Install rulers on the Quilt worktable
- Print complex foundation patterns
- Print quilt backing information
- Print a quilt label

Creating a New Project

Run EQ6 and create a new project with the file name *Nebraska Sunrise*.

Adding Designs from the Libraries

1   Open the **Block Library** and search for the word **sunflower**. In the Search Results section, click the *Sunflowers* block. This design is an EasyDraw + PatchDraw block. **Add to Sketchbook**.

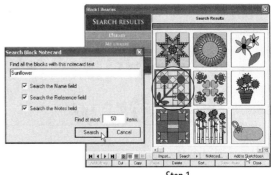

Step 1

2   In the Search Results section, click *Dean's Sunflower Sun* block. **Add to Sketchbook**.

3   Click **Library** on the left side of the Block Libraries box, then open **3 Foundation Pieced**. Open the **New York Beauties** library style. Find the *Radiant Beauty* block and **Add to Sketchbook**.

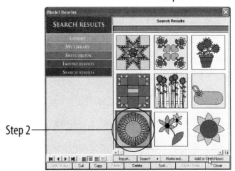

Step 2

Notes
A few blocks in the EQ6 Block Library, such as *Radiant Beauty*, are not indexed so they will not be found in a word search. You will have to find these blocks by viewing the library or by using the *EQ6 Block Book*.

4   **Close** the Block Library.

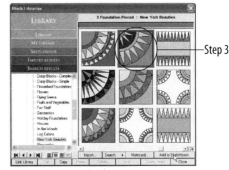

Step 3

5   Open the **Fabric Library** and find several fabrics that range from golden yellow to deep bronze, as well as a dark fabric for the sky, a light color for the fence, and a variety of green samples for the leaves and stems. **Add to Sketchbook**. **Close** the Fabric Library.

6   Open the **Thread Library** and select a thread color that will contrast well with the fabrics that you will use in Border 4. I've chosen yellow and orange fabric for my Border 4, so a dark thread works best here. You will use this thread for your quilting stencil. **Add to Sketchbook**. **Close** the Thread Library.

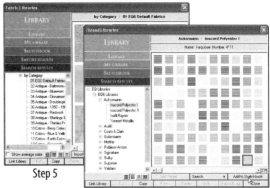

Step 5

Step 6

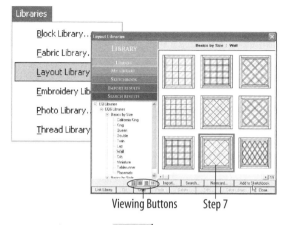

Viewing Buttons   Step 7

Work on Block
Button

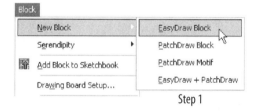

Step 1

Step 3

Line Tool

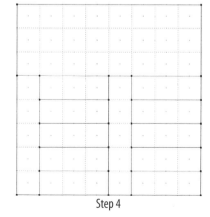

Step 4

7   Open the **Layout Library > Basics by Size > Wall**. Use the viewing button at the bottom of the Layout Libraries box to display nine layouts simultaneously. Click the last layout in the second column, the on-point layout that is **9" Blocks - 9 Total. Add to Sketchbook. Close** the Layout Library.

Creating a Complex Design in EasyDraw™

You will draw the *Pasture Fence* block for your *Nebraska Sunrise* quilt, so you will set up the drawing board in preparation for creating this EasyDraw™ design.

1   Click the **Work on Block** button on the Project toolbar. Click **BLOCK > New Block > EasyDraw Block**.

2   The EasyDraw™ worktable will open. If the Precision Bar is not open at the top of the worktable, click **VIEW > click to check** *Precision Bar*.

Notes
Before drawing, be sure that the Snapping options are set to the default settings: Click BLOCK > Drawing Board Setup > Snapping > *Snap to grid* and *Snap to nodes of drawing* should be checked. Click Options under PatchDraw. *Snap to node of drawing* should be checked > OK.

3   The *Pasture Fence* block is based on an 8 x 8 grid structure. Set these values on the Precision Bar:

   • Block Width and Height: **6.00**

   • Snaps Horizontal and Vertical: **16**

   • Graph Paper: **ON**, Horizontal and Vertical: **8**

4   The **Line** tool is engaged automatically. Draw the block as illustrated. **Add to Sketchbook**.

5   Open the **Blocks** section of the Sketchbook and double-click to place the *Radiant Beauty* on the EasyDraw™ worktable.

6   Click the **Pick** tool, the first tool on the EasyDraw™ toolbar. Hold down the **DELETE** key and click *all of the lines and arcs* that form the smaller sun and rays. **Add to Sketchbook**. This is the *Modified Radiant Beauty* block that you will use as a stencil in the corners of Border 4.

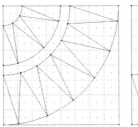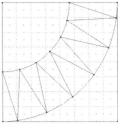

Step 6

7   Open the **Blocks** section of the Sketchbook and click the ***Modified Radiant Beauty*** block. Right-click on the display area of the Sketchbook to open the Blocks, Motifs & Stencils Palette and Sketchbook Context Menu. Click **Move to Tab > Stencil Tab**.

8   Color the ***Sunflowers*** block, ***Dean's Sunflower Sun*** block, and the ***Pasture Fence***. Use the same dark blue fabric for the background of all 3 blocks. **Add to Sketchbook**.

Step 7

Adjusting a Layout

1   Open the **Quilts** section of the Project Sketchbook and double-click the **9" Blocks - 9 Total Wall** layout that you added from the Layout Library.

2   Click the **Layout** tab and change the *Finished size of sashing* to **0.50**.

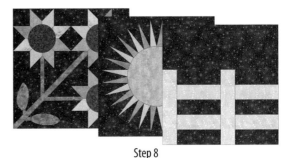

Step 8

3   Click the **Borders** tab. Under *Lock size adjustments*, click to check **All**. Establish these borders:

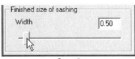

Step 2

ADJUST BORDER 1

   Style: **Mitered**

   Size: **0.50**

ADJUST BORDER 2

   Style: **Tile Squares**

   Blocks in border - Horizontal: **7**

A spacer will be added automatically to make the blocks fit evenly around the layout.

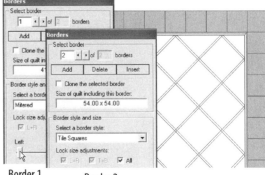

Border 1
Size: 0.50

Border 2
Blocks in border: 7

Lesson 6

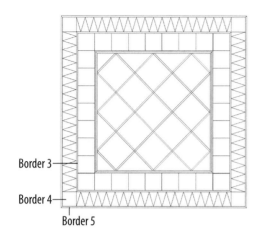

Border 3

Border 4

Border 5

Step 1

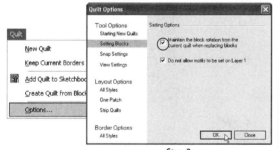

Step 2

Step 3
Set Block

ADD BORDER 3

Style: **Mitered**

Size: **0.50**

ADD BORDER 4

Style: **Points In**

Size: **5.00**

Blocks in border:

Horizontal: **18**

Vertical: **18**

ADD BORDER 5

Style: **Mitered**

Size: **0.50**

4 Click **Add to Sketchbook.**

Setting Designs in the Layout

1 Click the **Layer 1** tab.

> **Notes**
> If there are no lines in the layout, turn on the patch and block outlines, as described in Lesson 5, Removing Outlines from Quilts, step 2.

2 Before setting blocks in the layout, you will select the option to maintain block rotation. Click **QUILT > Options > Setting Blocks > click to check *Maintain the block rotation from the current quilt when replacing blocks >* OK**.

> **Notes**
> It is convenient to have this feature engaged when you are rotating designs on the layout because this makes it easy to replace designs in the same orientation.

3 Use the **Set Block** tool to set the blocks individually in the layout, as illustrated. **CTRL+click** to set the *Sunflowers* block in the corners of Border 2. **Add to Sketchbook.**

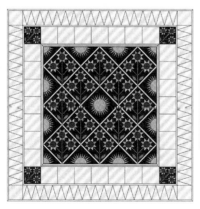

Lesson 6

4   Click the **Rotate Block** tool on the Quilt toolbar and rotate the ***Sunflowers*** blocks individually to the correct orientation, in the center of the quilt and in Border 2, as illustrated. **Add to Sketchbook**.

Rotate Block Tool

Step 4

5   Use the **Set Block** tool and **CTRL+click** to set the ***Pasture Fence*** block in Border 2. Use the **Rotate Block** tool and **ALT+click** to rotate each side of Border 2 to the correct orientation, as illustrated. **Add to Sketchbook**.

6   Use the **Eyedropper** to find the background color of the *Pasture Fence* block and **CTRL+click** to color the spacer in Border 2. Zoom in, if necessary. **Add to Sketchbook**.

Notes
- You learned in Lesson 3 that you can sort the Fabrics and Colors palette to place the most frequently used fabrics at the front of the palette.

- To find the size of the spacer in Border 2, click the Select tool, zoom in, and then click the spacer. Click FILE > Print > Block. Be sure that *Use size from quilt* is checked. You can read the settings under *Finished Block Size*, even though they are grayed out. Be sure to check the sizes of both the horizontal and vertical spacers in a rectangular layout since they can be different.

Eyedropper Tool

Steps 5 and 6

7   Click the **Paintbrush** tool and **CTRL+click** a different color to color the sashing strips. Zoom in, if necessary. Repeat this action to color the remaining sashing strips in the layout.

Notes
When selecting small or narrow designs on the layout, be sure that the tip of the tool that you are using is touching the design or space. Zoom in, if necessary.

Paintbrush Tool

Step 7

Step 8

8   Click a different color and **CTRL+click** to color the sashing squares. Zoom in, if necessary. Repeat this action to color the remaining sashing squares in the layout.

9   **CTRL+ click** with the **Paintbrush** to color Borders 1, 3, and 5. **Add to Sketchbook**.

Paintbrush Tool

Step 9

Step 10

Step 12

Layer 3

Step 13

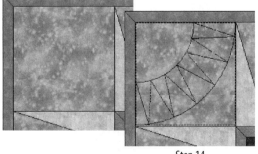

Set Block
Tool

Step 14

10 Use **CTRL+click** to color one series of triangles in Border 4. Click another color sample and **CTRL+click** to color the remaining series of triangles in Border 4. **CTRL+click** to color the corner blocks. **Add to Sketchbook**.

11 In Lesson 4, you learned about the *Nudge and Grid Settings* in **QUILT > Options > Snap Settings**. The Nudge Setting is the distance that the Adjust tool will move a design when you use the arrows on the Graph Pad or the arrow keys on the keyboard. Set this value to **1/8** inch for this particular layout.

Step 11

12 The Grid Settings control the size and position to which a design will snap on the layout when you set it or adjust it manually. Specifically, the *Snap block position to grid* setting controls the increment to which a design will snap into position when you set it on the layout with the Set Block tool or when you click and drag a design to move it. The default setting of **1/8** inch is recommended for this particular layout.

The *Snap block size to grid* setting controls the increment to which a design will resize when you use the nodes on the design to adjust the size. For this particular layout, click to **uncheck this option > OK**.

13 Click the **Layer 3** tab. Click the **Zoom In** tool and click and drag to form a selection box around the upper-left corner of Border 4. When you release the mouse button, this portion of the quilt will be magnified.

14 Click the **Set Block** tool, click the **Stencils** tab, and click the *Modified Radiant Beauty* stencil. Hold down the **SHIFT** key and **click and drag** to set a stencil in this corner.

Lesson 6

15 Click the **Adjust** tool and click the ***Modified Radiant Beauty*** stencil. Set the block size to **5.000 x 5.000** on the Graph Pad. The Block Size section is the third section from the left on the Graph Pad. Adjust the stencil so that it is correctly positioned over the corner square.

16 With the ***Modified Radiant Beauty*** still selected with the **Adjust** tool, **CTRL+C** to copy and then **CTRL+V** to paste another copy on the worktable.

Adjust Tool

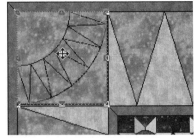

Step 15

Notes
To view the entire quilt, click the Fit to Worktable tool on the Project toolbar.

17 **Click and drag** the new copy of the ***Modified Radiant Beauty*** stencil to the upper-right corner block in Border 4. Visually position it over the upper-right corner block. You can use the stencil in the upper-left corner of Border 4 as a reference for this second stencil and **Align Top**. Click off of the stencils to deselect them.

18 Click the **Rotate Block** tool on the Quilt toolbar. Click the second stencil to rotate it to the correct orientation for the upper-right corner.

19 Repeat this procedure to set stencils in the lower-left and right corners of this layout. Visually place the stencils and then fine tune their positions using the appropriate **Align** tools, if necessary. Rotate the corner stencils, as illustrated. **Add to Sketchbook**.

Your *Nebraska Sunrise* quilt is finished!

Align Top

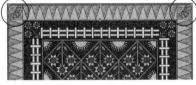

Step 17

Rotate Block Tool

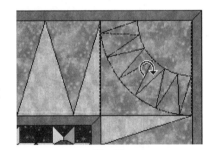

Step 18

Step 19

Lesson 6

Quilt: 66.00 by 66.00 (ins)
Status Bar

Step 1

Step 1
Layout Options

Step 1
Border Options

Step 2

Designing a Quilt Backing

You know by now that EQ6 is the perfect tool for helping you to design fabulous quilts. What you may not have realized yet is that the program can also help you to create unique backings for your quilts!

In this lesson, you will plan a simple backing of three wide fabric strips for your *Nebraska Sunrise* quilt. You will use Custom Set for this task because this layout style allows you much more freedom and flexibility than any of the traditional layout styles.

> **Notes**
> **With a little practice, you will be able to use Custom Set to design unique quilt backings that include leftover fabric yardage and blocks from your project!**

In a Custom Set layout, you can combine any arrangement of block styles and sizes to fill the central design area. To design the Custom Set backing for your *Nebraska Sunrise* quilt, you will use the same method and tools that you used to set and adjust stencils on Layer 3 in this lesson and in Lesson 4.

Notice that the finished size of your quilt is *66" x 66"*. This information is displayed on the Status bar on the lower-right side of the Quilt worktable. The standard rule in quilting is to *add at least 8" to the length and width* of your quilt for the backing.

1   Click **QUILT > New Quilt > Custom Set**. The Quilt worktable will open to an empty layout. On the **Layout** tab, set the *Size of center rectangle* to *75" x 75"*. Click the **Borders** tab and use the **Delete** button on the palette to remove all borders.

2   If there is no quilt outline on the worktable, right-click to open the **Quilt Worktable Context Menu**. Click **Outline Border** so that it is checked. You will now see a dotted line around the layout.

3 Click the **Layer 1** tab. You will need a plain block in the Blocks palette to set the three strips that you will need to form your quilt backing. Click the **Set Block** tool, click the **Blocks** tab in the palette, and then right-click on the Blocks palette to open the Blocks, Motifs & Stencils Palette Context Menu. Click **Add Plain Block** and a plain block will be added to the Blocks palette.

4 Click the **plain block** in the Blocks palette. Hold down the **SHIFT** key and **click and drag** to set the plain block on the layout. Click the **Adjust** tool, click the plain block on the layout, and set the size to **25.000 x 75.000** on the Graph Pad. Don't worry about exact placement at this point. Click the **Paintbrush** tool and color this plain block on the layout. **Add to Sketchbook**.

Selected Block Coordinates

Now you will learn how to set your designs precisely on this Custom Set layout using the coordinate positions of your blocks. For this, you will use the first section on the left on the Graph Pad, the *Selected Block* coordinates.

These two numbers are the X and Y coordinates that mark the specific location of the upper-left corner of the selected block in relation to the upper-left corner of the quilt's center design area.

The upper-left corner of the center design area on the quilt layout is the Zero Point. This is 0.000 at the left edge (X) and 0.000 at the top edge (Y) of the center design area. All designs placed in a Custom Set layout are measured in relation to this point.

The white dot that you see on the small block diagram to the left of the *Selected Block* coordinates is the reference point on the selected block for these X and Y values.

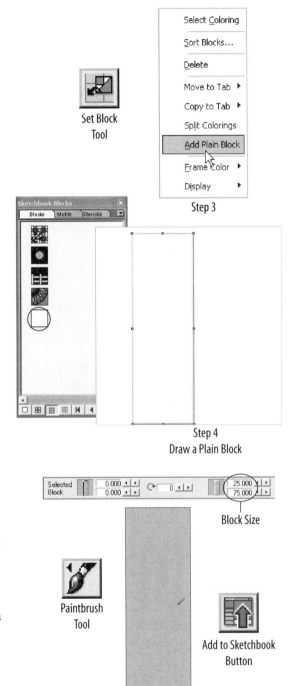

Set Block Tool

Select Coloring
Sort Blocks...
Delete
Move to Tab ▶
Copy to Tab ▶
Split Colorings
Add Plain Block
Frame Color ▶
Display ▶

Step 3

Step 4
Draw a Plain Block

Selected Block | 0.000 | 0.000 | 0 | 25.000 / 75.000

Block Size

Paintbrush Tool

Add to Sketchbook Button

Step 4
Color Plain Block

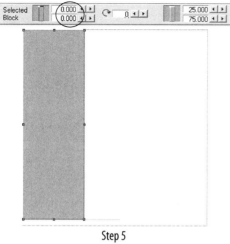

Step 5

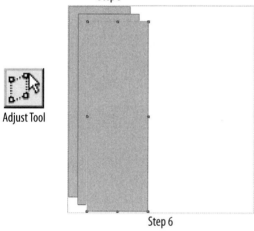

Adjust Tool

Step 6

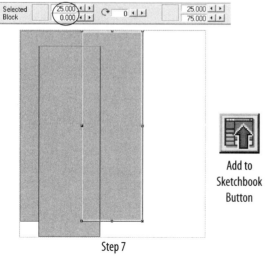

Step 7

5 Select the **plain block** with the **Adjust** tool. Use the arrows on the *Selected Block* coordinates to set the values to **0.000** and **0.000**. The upper-left corner of the plain block will now be perfectly aligned at the Zero Point.

Notes

• Block coordinates in the Custom Set layout reflect the location of the upper-left corner of the selected block, relative to the Zero Point (0,0). Measuring from this Zero Point, you can easily calculate the correct X and Y coordinates for each new block that you add to the layout. Simply total the sizes of the blocks that are between the Zero Point and the upper-left corner of the new block.

• All blocks along the left edge of the center design area have 0.000 as the X coordinate. X indicates a point on the *horizontal* axis.

• All blocks along the top edge of the center area have 0.000 as the Y coordinate. Y indicates a point on the *vertical* axis.

6 Now you will copy and paste to set two more 25" x 75" plain blocks on the Quilt worktable to form your quilt backing. Click the **Adjust** tool and click the **plain block**. **CTRL+C** to copy and **CTRL+V** to paste a second plain block on the worktable. **CTRL+V** again to paste a third plain block on the worktable.

7 Click the **second plain block** to select it. Since the first plain block is 25" wide, the upper-left corner of the second plain block should be 25" from the Zero Point. Set the *X coordinate* of the second plain block to **25.000**. Set the *Y coordinate* to **0.000** because the top edge of this block is on the vertical axis. The second plain block will be positioned perfectly on the layout. **Add to Sketchbook**.

Add to Sketchbook Button

Lesson 6

8 Since the first and second plain blocks together are 50" wide, the upper-left corner of the third plain block should be 50" from the Zero Point. Set the *X coordinate* of the third plain block to **50.000**. Set the *Y coordinate* to **0.000** because the top edge of this block is on the vertical axis. The third plain block will be positioned perfectly on the layout. **Add to Sketchbook**.

9 Recolor the **center plain block** with a different color. **Add to Sketchbook**.

Your quilt backing is now finished! In designing this simple Custom Set layout, you have discovered the *Selected Block* coordinates, a very important Graph Pad tool that will help you to place your designs easily and precisely on Layer 1 (Custom Set only), Layer 2 (appliqué) and Layer 3 (quilting stencils and embroidery). You will use this tool extensively in Lessons 7 and 8.

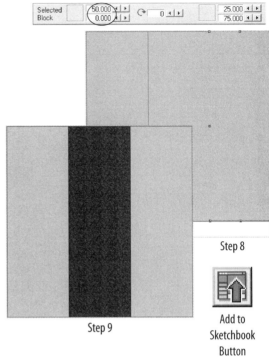

Step 8

Add to Sketchbook Button

Step 9

Designing a Quilt Label

Now that you have designed the backing, you will need a lovely customized label to attach to your *Nebraska Sunrise* quilt! You can use any of the layouts in EQ6 as a base for a label. In this lesson, you will create a simple quilt label using a Horizontal layout.

1 Click **QUILT > click to uncheck** *Keep Current Borders*, if necessary.

Step 1

> **Notes**
> You can make *Keep Current Borders* when starting a new quilt your default option in QUILTS > Options > Starting New Quilts. This feature allows you to keep the border designs from the worktable quilt when you create a new quilt layout.

2 Click **QUILT > New Quilt > Horizontal**.

3 Click the **Layout** tab and change the *Number of blocks Horizontal and Vertical* to **1**. Keep the *Finished size of blocks* set to **9.00**. Set *Finished size of sashing* to **0.00**.

Step 2

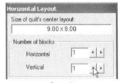

Step 3

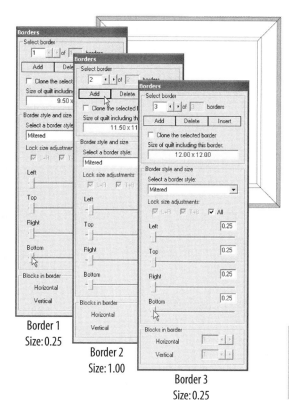

Border 1
Size: 0.25

Border 2
Size: 1.00

Border 3
Size: 0.25

Step 6

Add to
Sketchbook
Button

Work on Block
Button

Step 1

4 Click the **Borders** tab. Under *Lock size adjustments*, click **All** so that it is checked. Set these borders:

ADJUST BORDER 1 (default)

> Style: **Mitered**

> Size: **0.25**

ADD BORDER 2

> Style: **Mitered**

> Size: **1.00**

ADD BORDER 3

> Style: **Mitered**

> Size: **0.25**

5 Click **Add to Sketchbook**.

Notes
You can print this label in any size, so the values that you set here are not important, as long as the proportions are pleasing to you.

6 Click **Layer 1** and color the quilt. **Add to Sketchbook**.

The basic design of your quilt label is complete. The next step is to add appliqué motifs.

Designing with WreathMaker

EQ6's WreathMaker is a wonderful tool that allows you to generate perfect wreath designs easily from a single patch or a group of patches. You will use this feature now to create a sunflower motif for your *Nebraska Sunrise* quilt label. You will start with one simple shape and create a complex design that will add depth and dimension to your quilt label.

1 Click the **Work on Block** button on the Project toolbar. Click **BLOCK > New Block > PatchDraw Motif**. If the Precision Bar is not open at the top of the worktable, click **VIEW > click to check** *Precision Bar*.

Lesson 6

Pick Tool

Step 2

2   Click the **Pick** tool and the Precision Bar will be in the *Drawing Setup* mode. Set these values on the Precision Bar:

- Block Width and Height: **8**

- Snaps Horizontal and Vertical: **16**

- Graph Paper: **ON**, Horizontal and Vertical: **8**

Oval Tool   Step 3

3   **Click and hold down** the **Oval** tool, the sixth tool on the PatchDraw toolbar. The flyout toolbar will open. Click the third oval shape from the right so that it is selected.

4   Start in the center of the graph paper grid and draw the **first oval** to the *top of the vertical grid line that ends two units from the right corner*, as illustrated. When you release the mouse button, a closed patch will be on the worktable. **Add to Sketchbook**.

5   Start in the center of the graph paper grid and draw a **second oval** to the *top of the center vertical grid line*, as illustrated. **Add to Sketchbook**.

6   Start in the center of the graph paper grid and draw a **third oval** to the *top of the vertical grid line that ends two units from the left corner*, as illustrated. **Add to Sketchbook**.

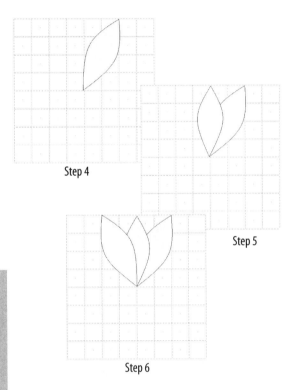

Step 4

Step 5

Step 6

Notes
- Remember to use EDIT > Undo or CTRL+Z to undo an action or series of actions.

- Always add your basic unit to the Sketchbook before applying WreathMaker. This will make it easy to experiment with your wreath because you can return to the original motif to try different settings.

- In PatchDraw, patches are layered in the order in which they are drawn.

Lesson 6

Step 7

7   Click the **Pick** tool and **CTRL+A** to select the three ovals. Click **BLOCK > WreathMaker**. The WreathMaker box will open. You can also right-click on the worktable to select WreathMaker on the PatchDraw Worktable Context Menu.

Notes
The WreathMaker box contains three settings:
- *Number of clusters* - This is the number of times the selected image is repeated as a cluster in the wreath. A cluster can be one or more patches. Acceptable values are 3 to 20.

- *Cluster spacing* - This percentage represents the position of the lower center point of each cluster selection box in relation to the center of the design area.

- *Resize cluster* - This is the percentage that the cluster size will change, based on its original size.

- See the EQ6 Help file and the *EQ6 User Manual* for more information about WreathMaker settings.

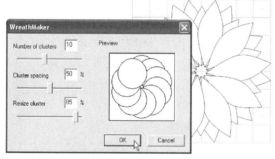

Step 8

8   Type in these settings in the WreathMaker box or use the palette sliders:

- Number of clusters: **10**

- Cluster spacing: **50**

- Resize cluster: **85**

Click **OK**. The new wreath will be on the worktable.

Notes
Remember to use EDIT > Undo or CTRL+Z to undo an action or series of actions.

Step 9

9   **Click and hold down** the **Oval** tool button to open the flyout toolbar. Click the first **oval** shape on the left of the flyout toolbar. **Click and drag** to form a large oval over the petals, as illustrated.

10   Click the **Centering** button, the fifth button from the right on the Precision Bar to center the oval. **Add to Sketchbook**.

Centering Button

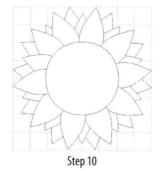

Step 10

11 Color your *Sunflower* motif. **Add to Sketchbook**.

Add to Sketchbook
Button

Step 11

Notes
Always record the WreathMaker settings on the wreath's notecard.

12 Open the **Quilts** section of the Sketchbook and double-click to place the quilt label on the worktable. Click **Layer 2**.

13 Click the **Set Block** tool, click the **Motifs** tab, and click the *Sunflower* motif.

14 Hold down the **SHIFT** key as you **click and drag** to set this design on the worktable. Click the **Adjust** tool, click the *Sunflower* motif and set the size to **5.500 x 5.500** on the Graph Pad. **Click and drag** the motif to the upper-left corner of the quilt layout, overlapping the borders, as illustrated. Use the left arrow keys on the *Selected Block* coordinates to set the values to **-3.125, -3.125**. **Add to Sketchbook**. The screen will resize to include the motif that extends over the borders. The dotted border outline will expand to include this motif.

Step 11

15 Select the motif with the **Adjust** tool, **CTRL+C** to copy and **CTRL+V** to paste another motif on the worktable. Move this second *Sunflower* motif to the lower-right corner of the quilt layout, overlapping the borders, as illustrated. Set the *Selected Block* coordinates to **6.750, 6.750**. **Add to Sketchbook**. The dotted border outline will expand to include this second motif.

Notes
The border outline is also called the virtual border because it defines the entire area of the quilt within a frame, whether it ends in a straight-edged border or in uneven edges.

Step 15

Step 1

Step 2

Customize Toolbar
Button

Step 3
Paintbrush

Set Appliqué Text
Tool

Step 4

Step 5

Adding Text with the Set Appliqué Text Tool

The next step in creating your quilt label is to add text!

1 Click the **Layer 2** tab.

2 To set the **Set Appliqué Text** tool on the Quilt toolbar, click **Customize Toolbar > Add/ Remove Buttons > Set Appliqué Text**. Click anywhere off of the list to close it. The Set Appliqué Text tool is now on the Quilt toolbar. The icon is a large letter "T" superimposed on a quilt layout.

3 Click the **Paintbrush** tool and click the color that you want to use for your text.

4 Click the **Set Appliqué Text** tool and the Appliqué Text box will open. EQ6 will list the TrueType fonts that you have available on your computer. Select the **font** that you want to use and use the slider button to set the **size**. You will have to experiment with the font size, depending upon the font that you use. Select any of the *Additional formatting* options: Bold, Italics, Underline, Align Left, Center, Align Right.

5 Use **SHIFT+drag** to form a text box on the worktable. As soon as you release the mouse the box will shrink, but it will expand as you type. **Type in the text** that you want on your quilt label. Use the **ENTER** key when you want to start another line of text.

Lesson 6

Notes

- To edit the text, click the Set Appliqué Text tool and then click in the text box.

- To resize the text box, select the Adjust tool and then click the box. Use the Block Size section on the Graph Pad or use the nodes on the text box to resize it.

- To move the text box, click the Adjust tool and then click the box. Click and drag or use the keyboard arrow keys to move it. You can also use the Selected Block coordinates to adjust its position in the layout.

- To delete the text box, click the Adjust tool, click the text box, and then press the DELETE key on your keyboard.

6   When you have finished typing in the text for your quilt label, click the **Adjust** tool and click the **text box**. Click the **Center** buttons on the Graph Pad to center the text within the layout. **Add to Sketchbook**.

Your quilt label is finished! You will print it later in this lesson.

Installing Rulers on the Quilt Worktable

You have the option to install rulers on the Quilt worktable. They can be helpful in many situations, especially when using the Custom Set layout or when designs extend over quilt borders, as they do in your quilt label. These rulers give you a point of reference that you can change.

1   Click **VIEW > click to check *Quilt Rulers***.

2   You can change the point of origin for these rulers so that they measure from various points in the upper-left corner. Click **QUILT > Options > View Settings > Ruler Origin**. You can set the rulers to measure your layout from the upper-left edge of the virtual border, the outer border, or the center design area. Experiment by selecting each option to see how the rulers change. If you are designing a large quilt, it may be neccessary to zoom in to the rulers to see them clearly.

Adjust Tool

Step 6

Step 6

Add to Sketchbook
Button

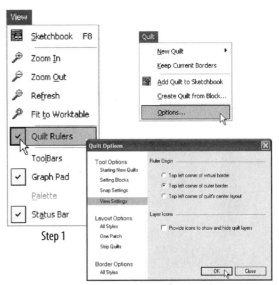

Step 1

Step 2

Select Tool

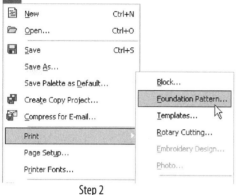

Step 2

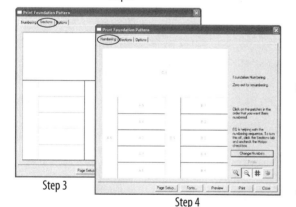

Step 3

Step 4

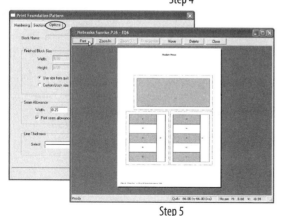

Step 5

Discovering More Complex Printing Options

You are ready to learn more about the printing options in EQ6.

Printing Complex Foundation Patterns

1   Open the **Quilts** section of the Sketchbook and double-click your *Nebraska Sunrise* quilt to place it on the worktable.

2   Click the **Select** tool and then click one of the *Pasture Fence* blocks in the top of Border 2. Click **File > Print > Foundation Pattern**. You can also click the **Print** button on the **Project toolbar > Foundation Pattern**. The Print Foundation Pattern box will open.

3   Click the **Sections** tab and you will notice that your *Pasture Fence* block is already divided into separate units by blue lines. You will print this block with EQ6's recommended sectioning and numbering then you will change it, dividing the block into different construction units.

4   Click the **Numbering** tab. Notice that EQ6 has already numbered the sequence of patches for you within defined sections that are marked by green lines.

5   Click the **Options** tab. Click **to check these options: Use size from quilt, Print seam allowance, Print numbering, Separate units, Mirror, Grayscale**, and **Print block name**. Click **Preview** and **Print**.

Lesson 6

Notes

- If you plan to move or delete any parts of a block on the Print Preview, be sure to check the option *Separate units* and uncheck *Print as many as fit.*

- With the Mirror option checked, the program will flip the units horizontally, in mirror image of their original orientation. This option is important if you are using the sew and flip method of paper foundation piecing, in which the fabrics are sewn on the back side of the foundation pattern. After these flipped units are sewn, the designs will be in the correct orientation.

- When the Grayscale option is checked, EQ6 will use shading to distinguish the different patches within the units to make the unit easier to construct. This coloring is automatic for library blocks.

- To get the same variation of shading in the foundation pattern of a block that you have drawn yourself, you must color the block with a special palette and this coloring must be the first coloring after the line drawing in the Sketchbook. You will get some degree of shading in the printout of this colored *Pasture Fence* block, even though it doesn't display the full range of shading that you would get if you used the special palette. See the EQ6 Help file for more information about the Grayscale feature.

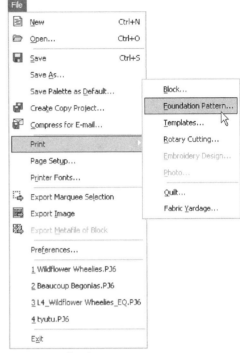

Step 6

6   Now you will resection and renumber the *Pasture Fence* foundation pattern differently than EQ6 suggests. With the block still selected in the layout, click **FILE > Print > Foundation Pattern**. Click **Start Over** on the **Sections** tab of the Print Foundation Pattern box. The blue lines that mark the suggested sectioning will disappear.

7   Be sure that *I want to section & number myself without EQ's help* is unchecked. With this option unchecked, EQ6 will allow you to choose only realistic sectioning and numbering. If this option is checked, then EQ6 will allow you to section and number the block in any way that you wish, even if it cannot actually be constructed in that sequence.

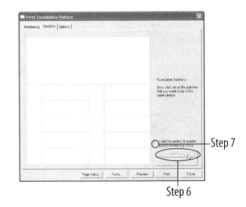

Step 7

Step 6

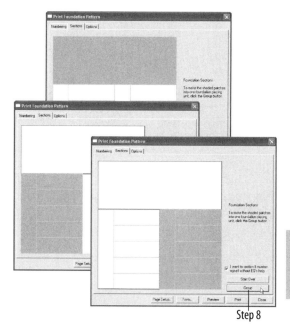

Step 8

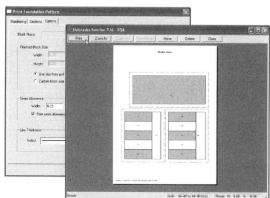

Step 10

Step 11
Save

Step 12

8 Click *the long strip above the fence* and then click **Group**. Click the *fence post on the left* and *all of the strips adjacent to it* and then click **Group**. Click the *center fence post* and *all of the strips to the right of that fence post* then click **Group**.

9 Click the **Numbering** tab. Since you defined the sectioning on the Sections tab, EQ6 assigned the numbers on the Numbering tab.

10 Click the **Options** tab. You can click the down arrow to change the **Line Thickness**, if you wish. Keep the remaining settings the same. **Preview** and **Print**.

> **Notes**
> **You learned how to move and delete foundation pattern units in Lesson 4, Printing Foundation Patterns, Templates, & Stencils.**

11 If you want to save your own sectioning and numbering with the project file, click the **Save** button on the Project toolbar after you Print Preview or Print. The icon is a disk. This sectioning and numbering will be saved with the block when you add it to My Library.

Now you will generate a foundation pattern for a block that contains an arc. In Lesson 2 you printed clipped blocks from your *Celtic Crossroads North* quilt. You learned that in an on-point layout, all triangular blocks on the outer edges of the center design area are setting triangles. When you set blocks in these spaces, EQ6 clips them automatically to fit. The *Dean's Sunflower Sun* blocks on the outer edges of your *Nebraska Sunrise* quilt are clipped.

> **Notes**
> **The side setting triangles are one half of the size of a full block. The corner setting triangles are one quarter of the size of a full block.**

12 With your *Nebraska Sunrise* quilt still on the worktable, click the **Select** tool and then click one of the *side setting triangles* of **Dean's Sunflower Sun** blocks in the layout.

13 Click **FILE > Print > Foundation Pattern**. The Print Foundation Pattern box will open.

EQ6 does not recognize a block that contains an arc as being able to be paper-pieced. As a result, this block will not be numbered or sectioned even though it is from the EQ6 Block Library. You can work around this limitation by grouping these patches yourself.

14 Under *Finished Block Size* on the **Options** tab, **Use size from quilt** should be selected.

15 On the **Sections** tab, click **Start Over** and then click *all the triangles within the arc*. Click **Group**.

16 Click the **Numbering** tab. The numbering tool is already engaged. The icon in this box is a number sign (#). Click *all of the triangles in sequence* and then click **Preview**.

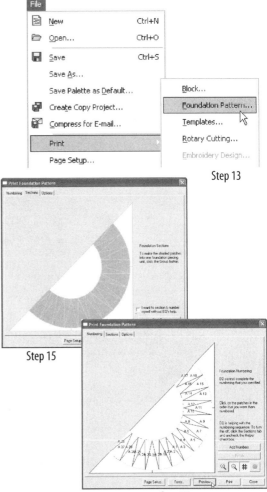

Step 13

Step 15

Step 16

Notes
If the foundation pattern is split over two pages, click Close. You will return to the Print Foundation Pattern box. Click Page Setup and change the orientation of the page to the appropriate setting: Portrait or Landscape > OK. You will return to the Print Foundation Pattern page. Click the Move button at the top of the Print Preview page, click the arc, and then move the arc so that it fits on the page. Print.

Notice that you were able to select and print only the part of the foundation pattern that you wanted. You have this option with any block that is able to be paper pieced.

You can generate a foundation pattern for the full *Sunflower Sun* block in the center of the layout by sectioning the arcs into two or more groups.

You can generate templates for the arc and background patches.

Printing Quilt Backing Information

1 Open the **Quilts** section of the Project Sketchbook and double-click to place your quilt backing on the worktable.

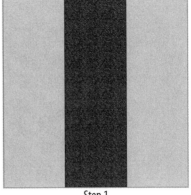

Step 1

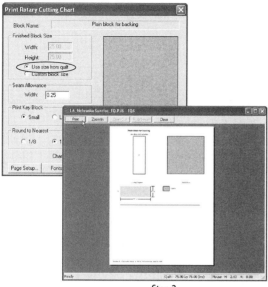
Step 2

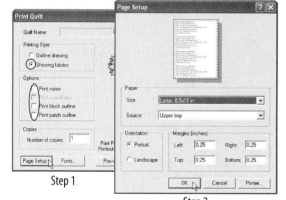
Step 1   Step 2

Step 2

2   To print the size of each backing strip, click the **Select** tool and click one of the strips. Click **FILE > Print > Rotary Cutting**. The Rotary Cutting Chart box will open. Under *Finished Block Size*, be sure that **Use size from quilt** is checked. **Preview**. Use the **Zoom In** tool to view the strip diagram. **Print**.

Notes
You can use this method to print the measurements for each panel of fabric in a quilt backing.

Printing a Quilt Label
You can print your quilt label from EQ6 directly onto one of the specially treated fabric sheets that are available on the market. The Electric Quilt Company markets EQ Printables inkjet fabric sheets, an excellent product that is specifically designed for printing quilt labels and photos with an inkjet printer.

1   Open the **Quilts** section of the Project Sketchbook and double-click to place your quilt label on the worktable. Click **FILE > Print > Quilt**. The Print Quilt box will open. Under *Printing Style*, click to check **Showing fabrics**. Click to **uncheck** *all selections under Options*.

2   You can print your label to any size. To restrict the printing to only part of a page, click **Page Setup** and adjust the margins accordingly. **Preview** and **Print** a test sheet before printing the final label on the treated fabric sheet.

Adding Designs to My Library
In Lesson 5, Adding Designs to My Library, you learned how to add your EQ6 Simplified designs to the Block, Fabric, and Layout Libraries. Refer to that section for detailed instructions as you add your Lesson 6 designs to My Library.

Exiting EQ6
Click **FILE > Exit**.

Lesson 6

Customizing with PatchDraw

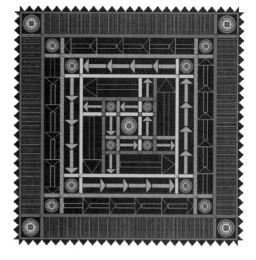

In this lesson, you will create *Gearing Up*, a dynamic quilt with a high-tech twist. This complex layout will be very easy to create because you will use a single pieced block as the base for the center design area. After you add a series of high impact borders and a chain of bold stencils, you'll have a quilt that really pops! This design will help you to develop your PatchDraw skills and give you more practice with EasyDraw™. You will also review many of the tasks that you have learned so far in this tutorial. You will:

- Draw a rectangular block in EasyDraw™

- Draw a rectangular motif in PatchDraw

- Draw a circular motif in PatchDraw

- Create a quilt layout from a block design

- Create a Prairie Points border

- Hide/show layers

Creating a New Project

Run EQ6 and create a new project with the file name *Gearing Up*.

Adding Designs from the Libraries

1 Open the **Block Library** and do a Notecard Search for the word *plaid*. Add the ***Plaid Lattice*** block to your Sketchbook. **Close** the Block Library.

2 Open the **Fabric Library** and choose new fabrics for your quilt. I recommend that you use bold colors for this design. For the design elements, you will need at least four colors that range in value from light to dark. You will need a high contrast color for the background.

3 Go to **by Category > 23 Geometric – Stripes** and add a striped fabric to use in Border 6. You can also use the Import feature in the Fabric Libraries box to add the striped fabrics that you used in Lessons 1 and 3. **Close** the Fabric Library.

4 Open the **Thread Library** and select a color for your quilting stencil that will contrast well with the background fabric in your quilt. **Add to Sketchbook**. **Close** the Thread Library.

Now you will create the designs that you will need for your *Gearing Up* quilt.

Drawing a Rectangular Block in EasyDraw™

You will start your drawing exercises by setting up the drawing board for the *EasyDraw Arrow* block. You will use this pieced block in the center design area and in Border 2.

1 Click the **Work on Block** button on the Project toolbar. Click **BLOCK > New Block > EasyDraw Block**. If the Precision Bar is not open at the top of the worktable, click **VIEW > click to check *Precision Bar*.**

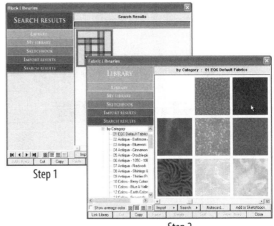

Step 1

Step 2

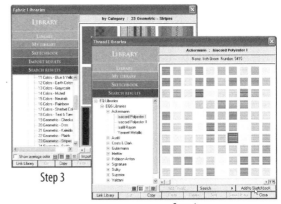

Step 3

Step 4

EasyDraw Arrow Block

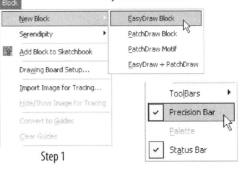

Step 1

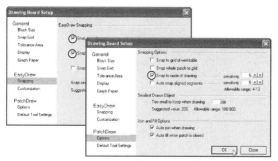

Drawing Board Setup

Before drawing, be sure that the Snapping options are set to the default settings: Click **BLOCK > Drawing Board Setup > Snapping >** *Snap to grid* and *Snap to nodes of drawing* should be checked. Click **Options > Snapping Options >** *Snap to node of drawing* should be checked. Click **OK**.

2   The *EasyDraw Arrow* block is based on a rectangular 4 x 8 grid structure, so you will draw this design as a rectangle. Set these values on the Precision Bar:

Step 2

- Block Width: **4.00**
- Block Height: **8.00**
- Snaps Horizontal: **8**
- Snaps Vertical: **16**
- Graph Paper: **ON**
- Horizontal: **8**
- Vertical: **16**

Notes
Use the TAB key to move through the settings on the Precision Bar.

3   The **Line** tool is engaged automatically. **Draw the block**, as illustrated. **Color the design** and **Add to Sketchbook**. This is your *EasyDraw Arrow* block. Name this design on the Notecard and close the Sketchbook.

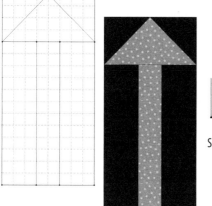

Step 3

Add to Sketchbook Button

Notes
- All designs in EQ6 save as squares in the Sketchbook and display as squares on the Notecard. If the EasyDraw™ worktable is set for the normal (square) configuration when you place a rectangular block there, you will have to change the Block Width and Block Height to the appropriate settings for this design.

- For example, when you open this *EasyDraw Arrow* design on the EasyDraw™ worktable, you will have to change the Block Width and Block Height to reflect the 1:2 ratio that you used to draw this block: 4" x 8". For this reason, you should always record the block ratio or size on the Notecard for a rectangular block.

EasyDraw Arrow Notecard

Lesson 7

Drawing a Rectangular Motif in PatchDraw

Now you will draw your *PatchDraw Arrow* motif. You will use this design as a stencil in the center design area and in Border 4.

Pick Tool

1 Click **BLOCK > New Block > PatchDraw Motif**. The worktable settings will define a rectangle if you have not changed them manually since you drew the *EasyDraw Arrow*. Click the **Pick** tool and the Precision Bar will change to the Drawing Setup mode. Set these values on the Precision Bar:

Step 1

- Block Width: **4.00**

- Block Height: **8.00**

- Snaps Horizontal: **8**

- Snaps Vertical: **16**

- Graph Paper: **ON**

- Horizontal: **8**

- Vertical: **16**

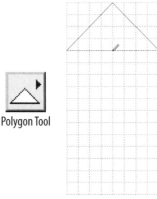

Polygon Tool

Step 2

2 Click the *first triangle on the left* in the **Polygon** tool on the PatchDraw toolbar. Click at the top of the center vertical graph paper line and, holding down the **CTRL** key, drag to form a triangle. Release the mouse button *four vertical units down from the top*. Release the **CTRL** key after releasing the mouse button.

Notes
Holding down the CTRL key ensures that the angle of the patch will be constrained to 15 degree increments. This will make it much easier to align the triangle perfectly on the worktable.

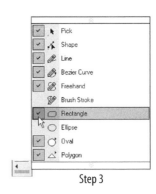

Step 3

3 You will need the **Rectangle** tool on the PatchDraw toolbar in order to draw the base of the arrow. On the PatchDraw toolbar, click **Customize Toolbar > Add/Remove Buttons > Rectangle**. You will need the **Ellipse** tool to draw the next block so check Ellipse to place it on the Quilt toolbar now. Click anywhere off of the list to close it.

Rectangle Tool

Ellipse Tool

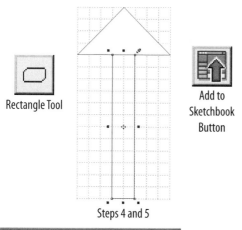

Rectangle Tool

Add to
Sketchbook
Button

Steps 4 and 5

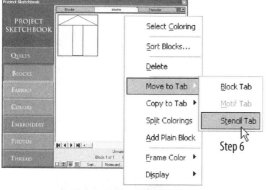

Step 6

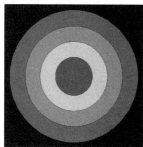

Bullseye Block

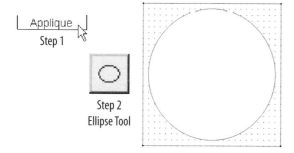

Step 1

Step 2
Ellipse Tool

4 Click the **Rectangle** tool on the PatchDraw toolbar. Click and drag to draw a rectangle on the worktable. Don't worry about exact size and placement at this point. You will adjust this rectangle in the next step.

5 Click the **Pick** tool and click the rectangle. Use the four-headed arrow in the center to move the rectangle into position. Use the nodes on the sides to expand or shrink the base of the rectangle to fit on the worktable, following the graph paper lines as illustrated. **Add to Sketchbook**.

6 Open the **Motifs** section of the Sketchbook and name the *PatchDraw Arrow* motif. Add the block size or 1:2 ratio to the Notecard. **Right-click** on the Sketchbook to open the Blocks, Motifs & Stencils Palette and Sketchbook Context Menu. Click **Move to Tab > Stencil Tab**. **Close** the Sketchbook.

Drawing a Circular Motif in PatchDraw

Now you will draw a series of concentric circles in PatchDraw to form your *Bullseye* block. You will use this appliqué block throughout the layout.

1 Click **BLOCK > New Block > EasyDraw + PatchDraw**. Click the **Appliqué** tab. Click the **Pick** tool. Set these values on the Precision Bar:

- Block Width and Height: **6.00**

- Snaps Horizontal and Vertical: **24**

- Graph Paper: **OFF**

2 Click the **Ellipse** tool on the PatchDraw toolbar. Position the crosshairs just within the upper-left corner of the block outline. **CTRL+click** and slowly drag the cursor diagonally to draw a circle on the worktable, stopping just within the lower-right corner of the block outline. Don't worry about exact placement at this point.

Lesson 7

Notes

- This step may take a little practice. If you go outside of the block outline on the lower-right, the circle will not form on the worktable when you release the mouse button. If you don't go far enough before releasing the mouse button, the circle will be too small. The edges of the circle should be close to the inside of the block outline.

- Use EDIT > Undo or CTRL+Z to undo your action, if necessary.

- Holding down the CTRL key constrains an ellipse to a perfect circle. Holding down the CTRL key when drawing a rectangle constrains the rectangle to a perfect square.

Step 3
Centering Button

Add to Sketchbook
Button

3   When you release the mouse button, the ellipse will be selected. Click the **Centering** button on the Precision Bar. This is the fourth button from the right. The icon is a square with four arrows. The circle will center on the worktable. **Add to Sketchbook**.

Step 4

Notes

Closed patch shapes can be filled or unfilled on the worktable. The default is filled. To turn off the Auto Fill feature, click BLOCK > Drawing Board Setup > Options > Join and Fill Options > click to uncheck *Auto fill when patch is closed* > OK. Now the circle will be transparent so you can see the grid points on the block background. This option is helpful when you want to see the overlapping lines, like those in an appliqué design or in a quilting stencil.

4   Click the **Pick** tool and click the circle. **Right-click** on the worktable to open the PatchDraw Worktable Context Menu. Click **Symmetry** and then click **Clone** to copy the circle.

5   With the second circle selected, **right-click** on the worktable to open the PatchDraw Worktable Context Menu. Click **Resize**. In the Resize box, type in **75** for the Horizontal percentage value. Press the **TAB** key on your keyboard twice to move to the Vertical percentage value and type in **75**, then click **OK**. The second circle will now be 75% of its original size. Click the **Centering** button on the Precision Bar.

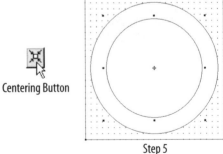

Centering Button

Step 5

Lesson 7

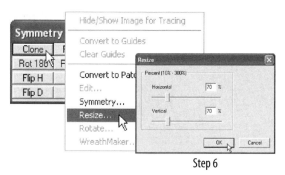
Step 6

Step 7

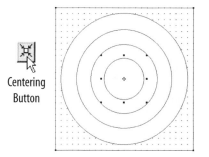

Centering Button

Add to Sketchbook Button

Work on Quilt Button

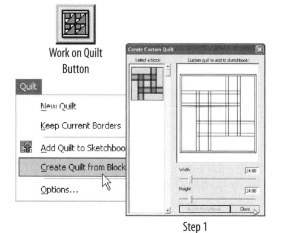
Step 1

6   With the second circle still selected, click **Clone** in the Symmetry menu to set a third circle on the worktable. **Right-click** to open the PatchDraw Worktable Context Menu and click **Resize**. In the Resize box, type in **70** for the Horizontal and Vertical percentage values, then click **OK**. With the third circle still selected, click the **Centering** button on the Precision Bar.

7   With the third circle still selected, click **Clone** in the Symmetry menu. **Right-click** to open the PatchDraw Worktable Context menu and click **Resize**. In the Resize box, type in **60** for the Horizontal and Vertical percentage values, then click **OK**. Click the **Centering** button on the Precision Bar. This is your *Bullseye* block. **Color the design** and **Add to Sketchbook**. Name the block in the Notecard and close the Sketchbook.

Creating a Quilt from a Block Design

EQ6 allows you to create a Custom Set layout from a single block design that contains only straight lines! The program will fill the spaces within the newly-defined layout with plain blocks that you can replace easily with other designs. You can do this without adjusting the size or the placement of each individual block like you would have to do in a typical Custom Set layout. In this lesson, you will create a Custom Set layout from the *Plaid Lattice* block, replacing the plain blocks in the newly-defined layout with new blocks.

1   Click the **Work on Quilt** button on the Project toolbar. Click **QUILT > Create Quilt from Block**. The *Plaid Lattice* block is selected. Set the size of this layout to **24 x 24**. **Add to Sketchbook** and **Close**.

2   Open the **Quilts** section of the Sketchbook, not the Blocks section, and double-click to put the *Plaid Lattice* layout on the Quilt worktable.

Lesson 7

3   Click the **Borders** tab. Under *Lock size adjustments*, click to check **All**. Establish these borders:

ADJUST BORDER 1

    Style: **Mitered**

    Size: **1.00**

ADD BORDER 2

    Style: **Blocks Aligned Inside**

    Size: **4.00**

    Blocks in border:

        Horizontal: **4**

        Vertical: **4**

ADD BORDER 3

    Style: **Mitered**

    Size: **1.00**

BORDER 4

- Do *not* click Add. Click to check **Clone the selected border**. Click **Border 2** to select it and then click **Add**. Border 4 will be added to the layout and it will be a clone of Border 2.

    Size: **4.00**

    Blocks in border:

        Horizontal: **5**

        Vertical: **5**

    You will use these blocks as placement guides for your stencils in this border. You will change this setting after your stencils are set on the layout.

- Click to *uncheck* **Clone the selected border**.

ADD BORDER 5

    Style: **Mitered**

    Size: **1.00**

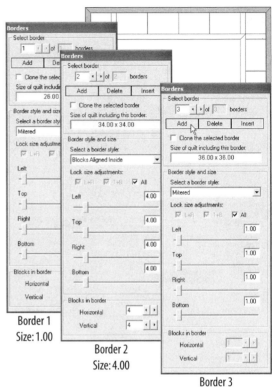

Border 1
Size: 1.00

Border 2
Size: 4.00

Border 3

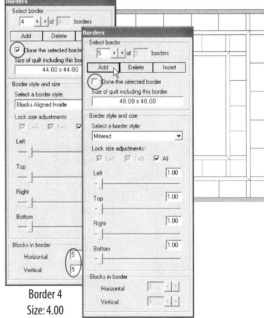

Border 4
Size: 4.00

Border 5

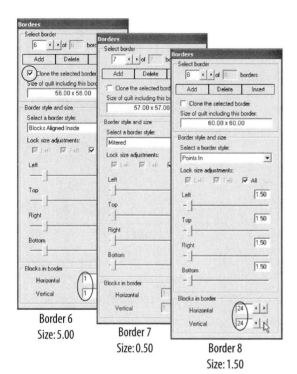

Border 6
Size: 5.00

Border 7
Size: 0.50

Border 8
Size: 1.50

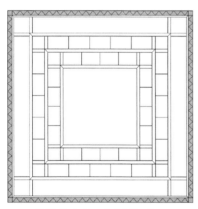

Quilt displaying all eight borders

Step 4
Add to
Sketchbook

BORDER 6

- Do *not* click Add. Click to check **Clone the selected border**. Click **Border 4** to select it and then click **Add**. Border 6 will be added to the layout and it will be a clone of Border 4.

    Size: **5.00**

    Blocks in border:

    Horizontal: **1**

    Vertical: **1**

- Click to *uncheck* **Clone the selected border**.

ADD BORDER 7

Style: **Mitered**

Size: **0.50**

ADD BORDER 8

Style: **Points In**

Size: **1.50**

Blocks in border:

Horizontal: **24**

Vertical: **24**

This border is intended to be Prairie Points.

4   Click **Add to Sketchbook**.

Setting Blocks in the Layout

When you create a quilt from a single block design, EQ6 defines the block as a Custom Set layout and fills the spaces in this new layout with plain blocks. ***It is important to remember to replace or erase, not delete, the blocks within a pre-set Custom Set layout.***

To *replace a block*, click the Set Block tool, click the new block in the Blocks palette, and then click the block that you want to replace in the layout. The new design will replace the previous design.

To *erase a block*, click the Erase Block tool and then click the block in the layout that you want to erase.

Be aware that if you remove a block from a Custom Set layout using the Adjust tool and the DELETE key, you will also remove the block definition. To refill this empty space with a block, you must click the Set Block tool, click the block, and then hold down the SHIFT key as you click and drag to place a new design. You must then adjust the size and the placement of the design within the space, using the Adjust tool and the Graph Pad.

REMEMBER: It is best to replace or erase, not delete, designs in a pre-set Custom Set layout! You will find this advice especially helpful when you use the quilt layouts in the Basics by Style category of the EQ6 Layout Library. These designs are all pre-set Custom Set layouts.

1   Click the **Layer 1** tab. Before setting blocks in the layout, you will turn on the convenient option to maintain block rotation. Click **QUILT > Options > Setting Blocks > click to check** *Maintain the block rotation from the current quilt when replacing blocks* **> OK.**

2   Click the **Set Block** tool, click the *EasyDraw Arrow*. Click to set this design in *eight spaces* in the center design area, as illustrated.

3   Click the **Rotate Block** tool on the Quilt toolbar and rotate the arrows to the appropriate orientation, as illustrated. **Add to Sketchbook.**

Step 1

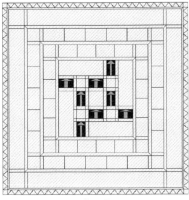

Step 2

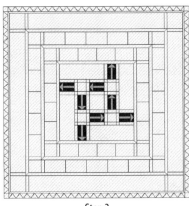

Step 3

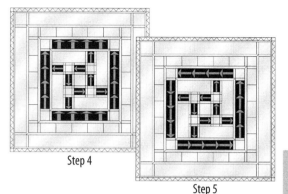

Step 4

Step 5

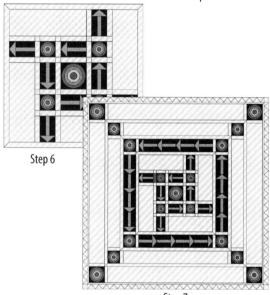

Step 6

Step 7

Add to Sketchbook
Button

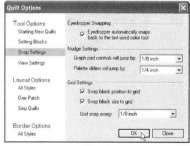

Step 1

4   Click the **Set Block** tool and click the *EasyDraw Arrow* block. **CTRL+click** on **Border 2** to set this block in each rectangular space.

5   Click the **Rotate Block** tool on the Quilt toolbar and **ALT+ click** each side of **Border 2** to rotate it to the correct orientation, as illustrated.

> **Notes**
> Use the Rotate Block tool and CTRL+click to rotate all sides of a border. Use the Rotate Block tool and ALT+click to rotate one side of a border.

6   With the **Set Block** tool, click the *Bullseye* block and set it in *five spaces* in the central design area, as illustrated.

7   **CTRL+click** to set this block in the *corners* of **Borders 2**, **4**, and **6**. **Add to Sketchbook**.

Setting Stencils on Layer 3

You learned about the Zero Point in a Custom Set layout in Lesson 6 when you designed the quilt backing for your *Nebraska Sunrise* quilt. You will use that reference point again here, as you place the stencils on your *Gearing Up* quilt layout.

It will be much easier for you to see the stencils if you set them on Layer 3 before you color the background patches and borders in Layer 1. After you have set the stencils on Layer 3, you will recolor all of the stencils simultaneously with the Spray Thread tool, and then you will color the rest of Layer 1.

1   Before setting stencil designs on this quilt, you will check the Nudge and Grid Settings to be sure that they are appropriate for this layout. Click **QUILT > Options > Snap Settings > Nudge Settings > *Graph Pad controls will jump by: 1/8 inch*.** Under **Grid Settings**, click to check **Snap block position to grid** and **Snap block size to grid. Grid snap every: 1/8 inch >** **OK**.

Lesson 7

Notes

- The *Nudge Setting* is the distance that the Adjust tool will move a design when you use the arrows on the Graph Pad or the arrow keys on the keyboard.

- The *Grid Settings* control the size and position to which a design will snap on the layout when you set it or adjust it manually. The *Snap block position to grid* setting controls the increment to which a design will snap into position on the worktable. The *Snap block size to grid* setting controls the increment to which a design will size when you set it on the layout with the Set Block tool or use the nodes on the design to adjust the size.

Step 2

2   Set the quilt rulers on the worktable. To set the quilt rulers, click **VIEW** > **click to check** *Quilt Rulers*.

3   The point of origin for the rulers should be the upper-left corner of the quilt's center layout. To set the point of origin for the rulers, click **QUILT** > **Options** > **View Settings** > **Ruler Origin** > **click to check** *Top left corner of the quilt's center layout*.

4   Under *Layer Icons*, click to check **Provide icons to show and hide quilt layers** > **OK**. You will return to the Quilt worktable and the quilt rulers will be installed. Notice that there are now small light bulb icons on each of the Layer tabs at the bottom of the worktable. These icons indicate that you can hide and show each layer on the worktable. You will experiment with this feature when you have finished setting stencils on Layer 3.

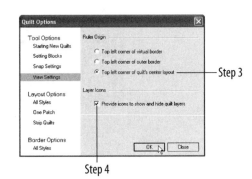

Step 3

Step 4

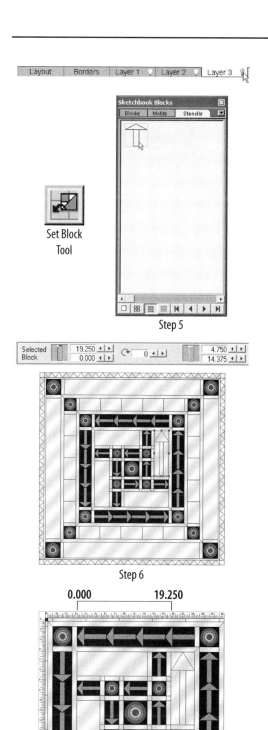

Set Block
Tool

Step 5

Step 6

0.000   19.250

Step 7

Notes

- **If you click one of these light bulb icons on the Layer tabs accidently, that layer will disappear. Simply click the light bulb again and it will reappear.**

- **Use the Zoom tools whenever you need them. Use EDIT > Undo or CTRL+Z to undo an action. Add to Sketchbook often when working on layers.**

- **Occasionally a design will disappear when you are working on layers. This may happen when you switch tools, change screens, or use the Zoom tools. To find a "lost" design on layers, highlight all of the designs on that layer. Click on the Adjust tool and, holding down the CTRL key, click on any design on the layer. All of the designs on that layer will highlight, including the "lost" design. Click off of the selected area to deselect.**

5   Click the **Layer 3** tab, click the **Set Block** tool, and click the **Stencils** tab in the Blocks palette. Click the *PatchDraw Arrow* design.

Notes

You will use a combination of methods to position the *PatchDraw Arrow* stencils on this layout: Align tools, Selected Block coordinates, and visual placement. You have already set the Nudge and Grid Settings to make your task even easier.

6   You will set the stencils in the center design area first. Hold down the **SHIFT** key and then **click and drag** to set the design over the *plain vertical block space on the right side of the center design area*, as illustrated. Click the stencil with the **Adjust** tool and set the size to **4.750 x 14.375** on the Graph Pad. Set the **Selected Block** coordinates to **19.250, 0.000**. Click **Add to Sketchbook**.

7   Click this **stencil** to select it and then **zoom in** to the upper-left corner of the center design area. Using the rulers as a measure, note that the upper-left corner of this stencil is 19.250 inches from the Zero Point (0,0) in the upper-left corner of the center design area. The position of this stencil aligns with 19.250 on the horizontal (X) ruler and with 0 (Y) on the vertical ruler. Click **Fit to Worktable** to return to normal viewing.

Lesson 7

8 Click the *PatchDraw Arrow* with the **Adjust** tool. **CTRL+C** to copy and **CTRL+V** to paste another stencil on the worktable. Use the left arrow on the **Graph Pad Rotation** tool to rotate this second stencil by **-90 degrees**. Notice that the original point of reference for this *PatchDraw Arrow*, the upper-left corner, is now in the lower-left corner. See the small white dot on the lower-left corner of the block diagram in the Graph Pad Block Position tool. This indicates that this is still the point of reference for this design, even though the design is now rotated.

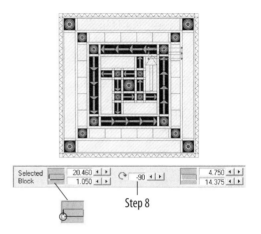

Step 8

9 Click the *second* **stencil** and move it over to the plain horizontal block space on the upper-left side of the center design area, as illustrated. The **Selected Block** coordinates are **0.000, 4.750**. These coordinates mark the current location of the *original* upper-left corner of the design (now showing as the lower-left corner after rotation), which is the point of reference for this stencil. **Add to Sketchbook**.

10 The first stencil is still on the Windows® clipboard, so **CTRL+V** to paste another copy of the first stencil on the worktable. Click this *third* **stencil** and move it over to the plain vertical block space on the lower-left side of the center design area, as illustrated. The **Selected Block** coordinates are **0.000, 9.750**.

11 Click the **Rotate Block** tool on the Quilt toolbar, not the Rotation tool on the Graph Pad. Click this *third* **stencil** twice to rotate it in the correct orientation. **Add to Sketchbook**.

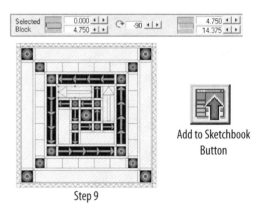

Step 9

Add to Sketchbook Button

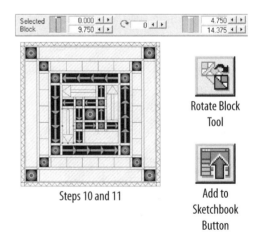

Steps 10 and 11

Rotate Block Tool

Add to Sketchbook Button

Quilt Toolbar
Rotate Block Tool

Graph Pad
Rotation Tool

Adjust Tool

Rotate Cursor

Align Right and
Align Bottom

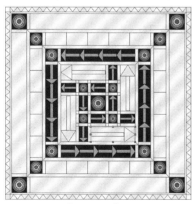

Steps 12 and 13

Add to Sketchbook
Button

Notes

There are three tools for rotating a design on layers:

- The Rotate Block tool on the Quilt toolbar rotates a design clockwise by 90 degrees with each click. The pivot point is the center of the design.

- The Rotation tool on the Graph Pad rotates the block by one degree increments, up to 180 degrees in either direction. The pivot point is the upper-left corner of the design.

- The Adjust tool rotates a design manually. The pivot point is the center of the design. Select a design with the Adjust tool. To rotate a design with the Adjust tool, hold down CTRL and click the directional arrows in the center of the design. A curved arrow will appear with the directional arrow cursor. Move the cursor over one of the corner nodes until only the rotation arrow remains. Drag the corner of the block clockwise or counter-clockwise to the desired orientation. Use the straight arrows to skew the design.

12 Click the **Adjust** tool and click the horizontal stencil in the upper-left center design area. **CTRL+C** to copy and **CTRL+V** to paste another copy of this stencil on the worktable. Click this *fourth* **stencil** and move it over to the plain space on the lower-right side of the center design area, as illustrated. Use the upper-right stencil as a reference for this stencil and **Align Right** using the Graph Pad. Use the lower-left stencil as a reference and **Align Bottom**.

13 Click the **Rotate Block** tool on the Quilt toolbar, not the Rotation tool on the Graph Pad. Click this *fourth* **stencil** twice to rotate it in the correct orientation. **Add to Sketchbook**.

Notes

Save often when setting designs on layers.

Now you are ready to set the *PatchDraw Arrow* stencils in Border 4. You selected the Blocks Aligned Inside style for this border and specified five blocks in each side. You will use these blocks as placement guides for the stencils. After you have set the stencils on Layer 3, you will change the number of blocks on Layer 1 so that the border is one strip of fabric, not five rectangles.

Lesson 7

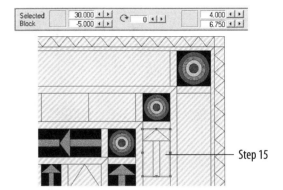

14 Click the **Adjust** tool and click the vertical *PatchDraw Arrow* stencil in the upper-right of the center design area. **CTRL+C** to copy and **CTRL+V** to paste another copy on the worktable.

15 With the design still selected, move this stencil to the first rectangle space in the right vertical side of Border 4. Set the size to **4.000 x 6.750** on the Graph Pad. Set the **Selected Block** coordinates to **30.000, -5.000**.

Step 15

16 With the stencil still selected, **CTRL+C** and **CTRL+V** *four times* to paste four copies of this design on the worktable. Use the first stencil as a reference to align the rest of these designs to left or to right. **Zoom in** and adjust each design vertically with the **Adjust** tool. You can click and drag each stencil or use the keyboard arrow keys to move them, one by one. **Add to Sketchbook**.

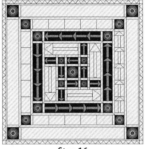

Step 16

Add to Sketchbook Button

17 Hold down the **SHIFT** key and click each stencil in this column. With the five stencils selected, **CTRL+C** to copy and **CTRL+V** to paste another column of stencils.

18 **Click and drag** this column to the left vertical side of Border 4. Fine tune the horizontal position of the first stencil and then use this stencil as a reference to align the rest of the stencils in the column. Fine tune the vertical position of each stencil visually so that each stencil fits within a rectangle. **Add to Sketchbook**.

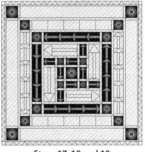

Steps 17, 18 and 19

Rotate Block Tool

Add to Sketchbook Button

19 Click the **Rotate Block** tool on the Quilt toolbar and rotate the *PatchDraw Arrow* stencils in the left side of Border 4, as illustrated.

20 Now you will set stencils in the top and bottom sections of Border 4. Set a *PatchDraw Arrow* on the worktable and position it over the first rectangle on the left in the top horizontal row of Border 4. Set the size to **6.750 x 4.000** on the Graph Pad. The **Selected Block** coordinates are **-5.000, -10.000**. **Add to Sketchbook**.

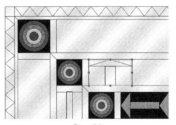

Step 20

Add to Sketchbook Button

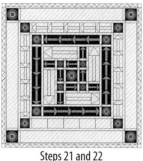

Steps 21 and 22

Rotate Block
Tool

Add to Sketchbook
Button

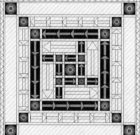

Steps 23 and 24

Rotate Block
Tool

Add to Sketchbook
Button

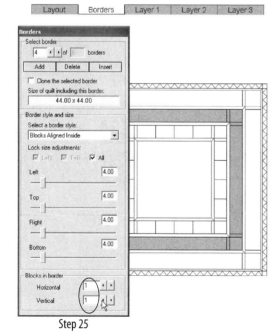

Step 25

21 Click the **Rotate Block** tool in the Quilt toolbar and rotate this stencil to the correct orientation, as illustrated.

22 With the **Adjust** tool, **CTRL+C** and **CTRL+V** *four times* to paste four copies of this stencil on the worktable. Use the first stencil as a reference to align the rest of the designs to top or to bottom. **Zoom in** and adjust each design horizontally with the **Adjust** tool. **Add to Sketchbook**.

23 Hold down the **SHIFT** key and click each stencil in this row. With the five stencils selected, **CTRL+C** to copy and **CTRL+V** to paste another row of stencils on the worktable. **Click and drag** this row to the bottom horizontal side of Border 4. Fine tune the vertical position of the first stencil and then use this stencil as a reference to align the rest of the stencils in the column. Fine tune the horizontal position of each stencil visually so that each stencil fits within a rectangle. **Add to Sketchbook**.

24 Click the **Rotate Block** tool in the Quilt toolbar and rotate the *PatchDraw Arrow* stencils on this side of Border 4. **Add to Sketchbook**.

25 You have placed your stencils on Layer 3 and no longer need the individual blocks that served as placement guides on Layer 1. Click the **Borders** tab and then click **Border 4** in the layout.

- Change:

    Blocks in border:

    Horizontal: **1**

    Vertical: **1**

Lesson 7

26 Now you will change the quilt rulers so that the point of origin is in the top-left corner of the outer border. This will generate an accurate display of your quilt measurement on the lower-right side of the screen. Click **QUILT > Options > Tool Options > View Settings > Ruler Origin > click to select** *Top-left corner of outer border* **> OK**.

Changing the Quilting Stencil Thread Color

Now you will change the color, weight, and style of all of the quilting stencils in the layout simultaneously, just as you did in your Lesson 4 *Wildflower Wheelies* quilt.

1 Click the **Layer 3** tab. If the **Set Thread** tool is not on the Quilt toolbar, click **Customize Toolbar > Add/Remove Buttons > Set Thread**.

2 On the Quilt worktable, **click** and **hold down the Set Thread** tool to open the flyout bar. Click the **Spray Thread** tool and the Thread palette will open. Under *Quilting Thread Properties*, click to check **Color**, **Style**, and **Weight**. Click the thread sample that you want to use in the layout. This color will display in the Color box. Click the **solid line** under *Style*. Click the **last line style** under *Weight*. This is the thickest, most visible stitching line. This option will make it much easier for you to see the stencils that you have set on the quilt layout. The cursor will change to a needle and thread on the worktable.

3 **CTRL+click** any stencil on the layout. All of the stencils will change to the color, style, and weight that you selected. **Add to Sketchbook**.

Notes
If you select the Swap Thread tool instead of the Spray Thread tool, then all of the stitches and outlines in the layout will recolor, including those on Layer 1. CTRL+Z to Undo.

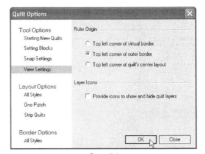

Step 26

Set Thread Tool

Spray Thread Tool

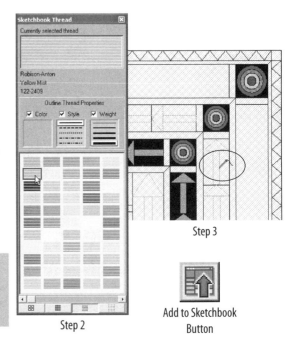

Step 3

Step 2

Add to Sketchbook Button

Paintbrush
Tool

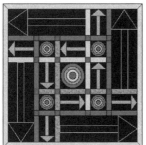

Quilt's Center Design Area

Add to
Sketchbook
Button

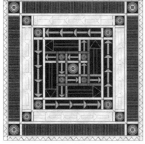

Step 3

Rotate Fabric
Tool

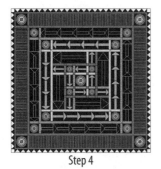

Step 4

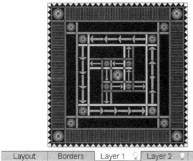

Step 6

Coloring the Background and Borders

1   Click **Layer 1**. Use the **Paintbrush** tool to color the lattice strips and squares in the quilt's center design area. **Add to Sketchbook**.

2   Color the **background patches** in the quilt's center design area. **Add to Sketchbook**.

3   Color **Border 6** with the striped fabric in your Fabrics and Colors palette. With the **Rotate Fabric** tool, use a simple rotation (90 degrees) on the striped fabric on two sides of this border. If the Rotate Fabric tool is not on the Quilt toolbar, click **Customize Toolbar > Add/Remove Buttons > Rotate Fabric**. **Add to Sketchbook**.

4   Click the **Paintbrush** tool and **CTRL+click** to color the remaining borders and the Prairie Points in the layout. **Add to Sketchbook**.

Your *Gearing Up* quilt is finished!

5   Before you print, you should go through your Sketchbook and name the designs that you want to keep. Delete any unwanted designs.

6   Before you set stencils on the layout, you turned on the option to show and hide quilt layers. Click the **small light bulb** on the **Layer 1** tab to turn off this layer. Click the small light bulb again to show this layer. Repeat this action with Layer 3 so that you can view Layer 1 without the stencils superimposed on the layout.

Paintbrush
Tool

Add to
Sketchbook
Button

Lesson 7

Printing Templates, Foundation Patterns, and Stencils

This quilt design offers you different printing possibilities, so you will explore them now.

Printing Circular Templates

1   With the quilt on the worktable, click the **Select** tool and then click any ***Bullseye*** block in the layout. Click **FILE > Print > Templates** or click the **Print** button on the **Project toolbar > Templates**.

Select Tool

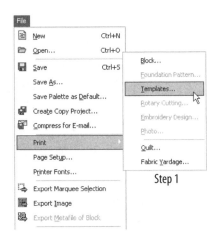

Step 1

2   In the Print Template box, **Use size from quilt** should be checked. Click to *uncheck* **Print seam allowance**. Under *Print Key Block*, click **None**. Click on the down arrow next to **Line Thickness** and choose one of the options. Click **Preview**. Click the **Delete** button in the Print Preview page, click the **background square** and press the **DELETE** key on your keyboard. **Print.**

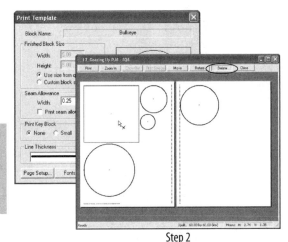

Step 2

Printing Foundation Patterns

You will experiment with different printing options for foundation patterns from this design.

3   Click one of the horizontal ***EasyDraw Arrow*** blocks in the top or bottom row of Border 2. Click **FILE > Print > Foundation Pattern** or click the **Print** button in the **Project toolbar > Foundation Pattern**.

Select Tool

Step 3

Lesson 7

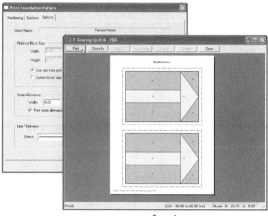

Step 4

4   In the Print Foundation Pattern box, notice that EQ6 has sectioned and numbered the block. Click the **Options** tab. Select **Use size from quilt** and click to check **Print seam allowance**. Use the down arrow to view and choose **Line Thickness**. Check *all selections* under the **Options** section on the Options tab. **Preview**. There will be two foundation patterns on the Print Preview page. **Print**.

Printing Stencils

5   Click the **Layer 3** tab. Click the **Select** tool and click one of the *PatchDraw Arrows* in the top or bottom row in Border 4. Click **FILE > Print > Block**. Under *Finished Block Size*, keep **Use size from quilt** checked. Under *Printing Style*, click **Outline drawing**. On the **Options** tab, **Print block name** and **Print as many as fit** should be checked. Choose **Line Thickness**. **Preview**. The stencil is drawn in solid lines. **Print**.

6   Click **FILE > Print > Block**. Under *Printing Style*, click **Quilting Stencil**. **Preview**. The stencil is drawn in dashed lines that resemble quilting stitches. **Print**.

Adding Designs to My Library

In Lesson 5, Adding Designs to My Library, you learned how to add your EQ6 Simplified designs to the Block, Fabric, and Layout Libraries. Refer to that section for detailed instructions as you add your Lesson 7 designs to My Library.

Exiting EQ6

Click **FILE > Exit**.

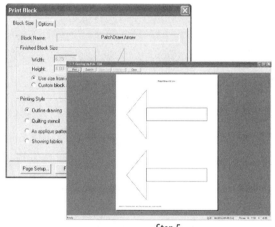

Step 5

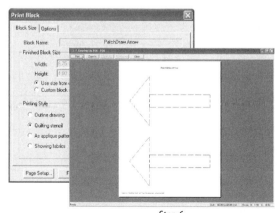

Step 6

Lesson 7

Continuing in Custom Set

In Lesson 8 you will continue to experiment with Custom Set, EQ6's most flexible layout style that gives you the freedom to combine blocks of different sizes in one design. The quilt for this lesson is *Shady Apple Farm* and it was inspired by our daughter Karen and our son-in-law David who live a lifestyle that respects the person and the planet.

This *Shady Apple Farm* quilt looks very complicated, but it will be easy to create with the EQ6 design skills that you have developed throughout this tutorial. You will set blocks of various sizes on Layer 1 (Custom Set) and superimpose a collection of appliqué designs on Layer 2. You will also modify several designs from the EQ6 Libraries and draw several simple designs in PatchDraw. You will review many of the tasks from previous lessons as you learn more advanced applications for EQ6's powerful design tools. You will:

- Draw with the PatchDraw tools:
    - Bezier Curve
    - Shape
    - Line
    - Brush Stroke
- Create a Custom Set layout
- Relayer in PatchDraw
- Experiment with advanced fabric rotation
- Add appliqué text to the quilt layout
- Enhance thread color
- Explore more printing options

Creating a New Project

Run EQ6 and create a new project named *Shady Apple Farm*.

Adding Designs from the Libraries

1   Click **LIBRARIES > Block Library > Search > by Notecard**. Search for these blocks and add them to your Sketchbook:

- *Harvest Sun*
- *Five Border Medallion*
- *Pig*
- *Tree of Life*
- *Round Basket*
- *Carrying Basket*
- *Farm House*

Step 1

2   Search for and add these motifs to your Sketchbook:

- *Three Clouds*
- *Apple*
- *Smoke*

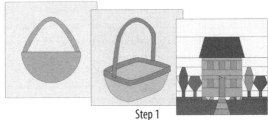

Step 2

3   With the Block Library still open, click the **Library** button on the left, then go to **6 Motifs > Silhouettes**. **CTRL+click** to select these designs and then add them to your Sketchbook:

- *Cat*
- *Cow*
- *Hen with Chicks*
- *Horse*
- *Man*
- *Woman*
- *Rooster*
- *Jumping Dog*

Step 3

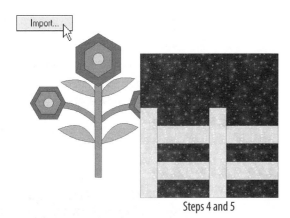

Steps 4 and 5

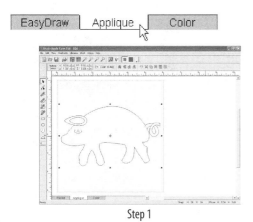

Step 6

Step 7

4 Click the **Import** button in the Block Library and navigate to your PJ6 directory. Open your **Lesson 5** *(Beaucoup Begonias)* project file and copy the *Flower from the 30s* motif from the Sketchbook. You will use this design as sunflowers on Layer 2.

5 Click **Import**, then open your **Lesson 6** *(Nebraska Sunrise)* project file and copy the *Pasture Fence* block from the Sketchbook. **Close** the Block Library.

6 Open the **Fabric Library** and browse **by Category** to select fabrics for *grass*, *leaves*, *sky*, *tree bark*, and *stone*. There are many appropriate samples in *12 Colors - Earth Colors* and in the *Nature* library styles. For Border 4, add a striped fabric from *23 Geometric - Stripes* or import samples from Lessons 1, 3, or 7. **Add to Sketchbook** and **close** the Fabric Library.

7 Open the **Thread Library** and select a medium yellow or orange thread, a medium blue thread, and a dark green thread to **Add to Sketchbook**. You will use these threads to enhance the appliqué stitching on several of your designs in the layout. **Close** the Thread Library.

Modifying Designs

Now you will modify some of the designs that you copied from the EQ6 Libraries and also draw several new designs.

Notes
Remember that in a PatchDraw block, the patches are on a background square. In a PatchDraw motif, the patches do not have a background square.

The Pig

1 You will convert the *Pig* block to a *Pig* motif. Open the **Blocks** section of your Sketchbook and double-click the *Pig* block to place it on the worktable. Click the **Appliqué** tab. Click **EDIT > Select All** or use **CTRL+A** to select all patches in the drawing. Click **EDIT > Copy** or use **CTRL+C** to copy.

Step 1

Lesson 8

2   Click **BLOCK > New Block > PatchDraw Motif**. Click **EDIT > Paste** or **CTRL+V** to paste the pig on the **Appliqué** tab of the PatchDraw Motif worktable. Click the **Centering** button on the Precision Bar. **Zoom in** on the Pig's head. With the **Pick** tool, click the eye, and delete it. Select the inner ear patch and delete it. **Add to Sketchbook**. Color this design with the fabric that you have chosen for your silhouettes and **Add to Sketchbook**.

The Tree of Life

3   You will convert the *Tree of Life* block to a motif. Open the **Blocks** section of the Sketchbook and double-click the *Tree of Life* to place it on the worktable. Click the **Appliqué** tab. **CTRL+A** to select all patches on this tab and **CTRL+C** to copy. Click **BLOCK > New Block > PatchDraw Motif**. **CTRL+V** to paste the *Tree of Life* on the Appliqué tab of the PatchDraw Motif worktable. Click the **Centering** button on the Precision Bar. **Add to Sketchbook**. Color this design and **Add to Sketchbook**.

The Baskets

4   You will convert the *Round Basket* and the *Carrying Basket* blocks to motifs. Open the **Blocks** section of your Sketchbook and double-click the *Round Basket* block to place it on the worktable. Click the **Appliqué** tab. **CTRL+A** to select all patches in the drawing. **CTRL+C** to copy. Click **BLOCK > New Block > PatchDraw Motif**. **CTRL+V** to paste the *Round Basket* on the Appliqué tab of the PatchDraw Motif worktable. Click the **Centering** button on the Precision Bar. **Add to Sketchbook**. Color this design with the silhouette color and **Add to Sketchbook**. The *Woman* will use this as an egg basket.

5   *Repeat step 4 to convert the **Carrying Basket*** from a block to a motif. **Add to Sketchbook.**

6   Now you will add apples to the *Carrying Basket* motif. Open the **Blocks** section of the Sketchbook, click the **Motifs** tab, and double-click the *Apple* design to place it on the worktable.

EasyDraw Block
PatchDraw Block
PatchDraw Motif
EasyDraw + PatchDraw

Centering Button

Step 2

Add to Sketchbook Button

Step 3

Step 4

Step 5

Add to Sketchbook Button

Apple Motifs

Lesson 8

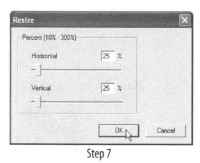

Step 7

Step 9

Add to
Sketchbook
Button

Pick Tool

Step 10

Step 11

Add to Sketchbook
Button

Colored Basket

7   **CTRL+A** to select all patches in the *Apple* design. Right-click to open the PatchDraw Block & Motif Worktable Context Menu and click **Resize**. In the Resize box, type in **25** for the Horizontal and Vertical percentage values, then click **OK**. The apple and leaves will be 25% of their original size. With the apple and leaves still selected, **CTRL+C** to copy the ***Apple*** design to the Windows® clipboard.

8   Open the **Motifs** section of the Sketchbook and double-click the ***Carrying Basket*** to place it on the worktable. EQ6 will ask if you want to save the resized apple. Click **No**.

9   The worktable will open with the *Carrying Basket* motif. **CTRL+V** to paste the resized apple on the worktable. With the *Apple* still selected, **click and drag** it to the back of the basket. **CTRL+V** to paste a second apple in the basket and position this apple next to the first apple. Paste three or four more apples in the basket, arranging each apple as you paste it. **Add to Sketchbook**.

10   Now you will relayer the design so that the basket patches are in the right order. Click the **Color** tab and then click the **Pick** tool. Click the bottom of the basket and it will highlight. Right-click on the worktable to open the Block Worktable Context Menu - Color tab. Click **Send to Front**.

11   Click the band of trim on the edge of the basket, right-click and **Send to Front**. **Add to Sketchbook**. Color the basket of apples and **Add to Sketchbook**.

Lesson 8

The Farm House

12   Now you will modify the *Farm House* block by adding a chimney. Open the **Blocks** section of the Sketchbook and double-click to place the *Farm House* on the worktable. Draw a chimney on the house, as illustrated. **Add to Sketchbook**. Color this block and **Add to Sketchbook**.

> **Notes**
> Remember that EQ6 recognizes a changed drawing as a new design.

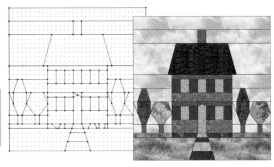

Step 12

Drawing with the PatchDraw Tools

Before you begin the next section, practice with the **Bezier Curve** tool and the **Shape** tool, drawing arcs and editing them until you are comfortable with the way that these tools work. The Bezier Curve is the fourth tool in the PatchDraw toolbar. The icon is a pencil drawing a curve containing a node.

  Bezier Curve Tool

  Shape Tool

> **Notes**
> • Before drawing, be sure that the Snapping options are set to the default settings: Click BLOCK > Drawing Board Setup > Snapping > *Snap to grid* and *Snap to nodes of drawing* should be checked. Click Options under PatchDraw. *Snap to node of drawing* should be checked > OK.
>
> • An object is automatically selected immediately after you draw it in PatchDraw.
>
> • You can toggle between a drawing tool and the Shape tool by pressing the SPACEBAR immediately after drawing.

Since you will be drawing arcs, you must know how to move, delete, and edit them in PatchDraw.

  Pick Tool

•   To **move an arc** that is not joined to another arc or line, click the **Pick** tool and then click the arc. It will be surrounded by nodes that form a selection box. Click the directional arrows in the center of the selection box and drag the arc to a new location. To delete the selected arc, press the **DELETE** key on your keyboard.

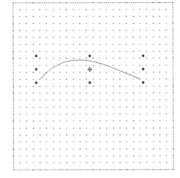

Move Arc

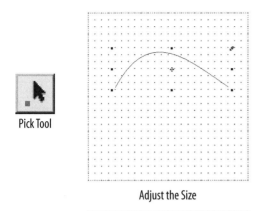

Pick Tool

Adjust the Size

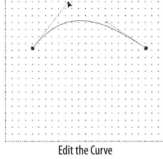

Shape Tool

Edit the Curve

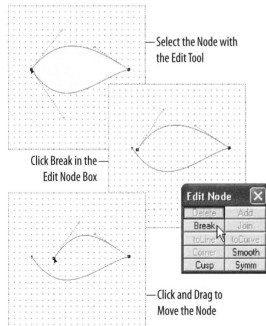

— Select the Node with the Edit Tool

Click Break in the — Edit Node Box

Edit Node ☒

Delete	Add
Break	Join
toLine	toCurve
Corner	Smooth
Cusp	Symm

— Click and Drag to Move the Node

- To **adjust the size of an arc** that is not joined to another arc or line, click the **Pick** tool, and then click the arc. The arc will be surrounded by nodes that form a selection box. Position your cursor on one of the nodes in the selection box. An arrow will appear that indicates the direction of adjustment for that node. Click the node and drag to shrink or enlarge the arc.

- To **edit the curve of an arc**, click the **Shape** tool, the second tool from the top in the PatchDraw toolbar. The icon is a black arrow pointing to a line containing nodes. Click the arc and two handles will appear on the nodes. These handles allow you to adjust the curvature of the arc. To move the end node of an arc, click the node and drag.

- To **move or delete an arc** that is joined to another arc or line, you must first separate the arc from the connected lines or arcs. Click the **Shape** tool and click one of the end nodes of the arc that you want to move or delete. Two handles will appear on the arc. Zoom in so that you are able to see the node clearly. Right-click on the node and the PatchDraw Worktable Context Menu will open.

Click **Edit** and the Edit Node box will open. Click **Break** in the Edit Node box and the selected joined nodes will separate. The arc is no longer connected to another object to form a closed curve. Repeat this process to break the node on the other end of the arc. Click the arc with the **Pick** tool and it will be selected. At this point, you can click and drag to move the arc or delete it by pressing the **DELETE** key on your keyboard.

Lesson 8

The Birds

1 Now you will draw a very simple bird for your *Shady Apple Farm* quilt. Click **BLOCK > New Block > PatchDraw Motif** and then click the **Pick** tool. On the Precision Bar, set the block size to **6 x 6**. Set the Snaps to **24 x 24**. Turn the Graph Paper on and set to **8 x 8**. Using graph paper gives you points of reference and makes it easier to draw balanced designs in PatchDraw.

2 This stylized bird is composed of four simple arcs drawn in sequence to form two closed patches. Click the **Bezier Curve** tool and, starting in the center of the graph paper, **draw one arc** to the left edge of the worktable. Release the mouse button at the end of this arc. Starting at this end point, **draw a second arc** that returns to the beginning point of the arc in the center of the graph paper. These two arcs form a closed shape that is a wing.

3 Starting at the center point again, **draw a third arc** to the right edge of the worktable. Starting at the end point of this arc, **draw a fourth arc** that returns to the center point of the graph paper. These four arcs form a closed shape that is a bird.

4 Click the **Shape** tool and click one of the arcs. Two handles will appear on the arc. Use the handles to edit the arc to your satisfaction. Be sure that the arcs do not overlap, as in a figure 8. **Add to Sketchbook**. Color the bird and **Add to Sketchbook**.

The Clothesline

5 The *Shady Apple Farm* family will need a clothesline for airing their quilts. Click **BLOCK > New Block > PatchDraw Motif** and then click the **Pick** tool. If you have not changed them, the Precision Bar settings are the same as they were for the *Bird* design above.

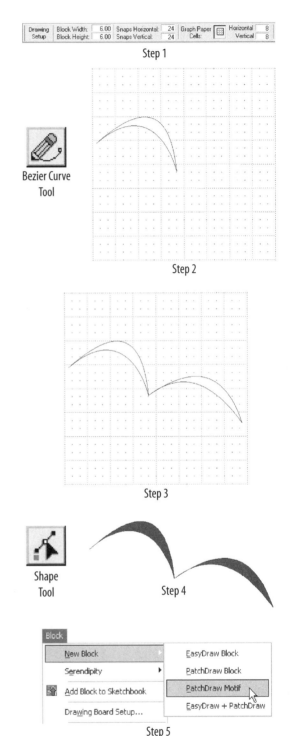

Step 1

Bezier Curve Tool

Step 2

Step 3

Shape Tool

Step 4

Step 5

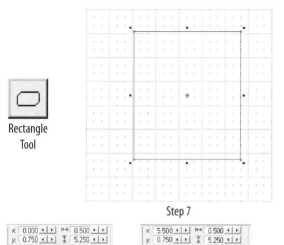

Rectangle Tool

Step 7

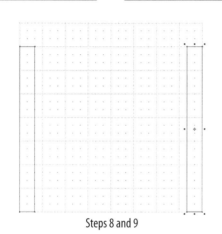

Steps 8 and 9

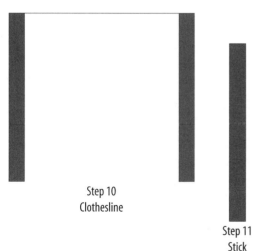

Step 10
Clothesline

Step 11
Stick

6 You will need the **Rectangle** tool on the PatchDraw toolbar in order to draw the clothesline poles. If the Rectangle tool is not on the PatchDraw toolbar, click **Customize Toolbar > Add/Remove Buttons > Rectangle**. Click anywhere off of the list to close it.

7 Click the **Rectangle** tool on the PatchDraw toolbar and then **click and drag** to draw a rectangle on the worktable. Don't worry about exact size or placement at this point.

8 Resize the clothesline pole by setting the size precisely on the Precision Bar. Click the **Pick** tool and then click the rectangle. On the Precision Bar, type in **0** for the X value and type in **0.750** for the Y value. Type in **0.5** for the width and **5.250** for the length.

9 Click the rectangle with the **Pick** tool, **CTRL+C** to copy and **CTRL+V** to paste another rectangle on the worktable. Click the second rectangle and move it to the opposite side of the block worktable. Type in **5.5** for the X value and **0.75** for the Y value.

10 Click the **Line** tool and draw the clothesline between the two poles. Color this design and **Add to Sketchbook**.

The Stick

The *Boy* will need a stick to herd the cows. You will copy one of the clothesline poles and use it for this new motif.

11 Click the **Appliqué** tab, click the **Pick** tool, and click one of the clothesline poles. **CTRL+C** to copy. Click **BLOCK > New Block > PatchDraw Motif** and then **CTRL+V** to paste the rectangle on the worktable. Click the **Centering** button on the Precision Bar. **Add to Sketchbook**. Color this design and **Add to Sketchbook**.

Lesson 8

The Rein / Ribbon

The *Man* will need a rein for the horse and the *Little Girl* will need a piece of ribbon to play with her cat. You will use the **Brush Stroke** tool to create one design for both the rein and the ribbon.

Brush Stroke
Tool

12 On the PatchDraw toolbar, click **Customize Toolbar > Add/Remove Buttons > Brush Stroke**. Click anywhere off of the list to close it.

13 Click **BLOCK > New Block > PatchDraw Motif**. Click the **Brush Stroke** tool, the sixth tool on the PatchDraw toolbar. The icon is a pencil drawing a wide, closed curve. On the Precision Bar, click the down arrow next to **Stroke Style** and click the last style. Click the down arrow next to **Stroke End** and click the last style. Set the *Minimum Width* to **1.000** and the *Boldness* to **3.000**. **Click and drag** to draw an object that resembles a soft "J," as illustrated. Color this design and **Add to Sketchbook**.

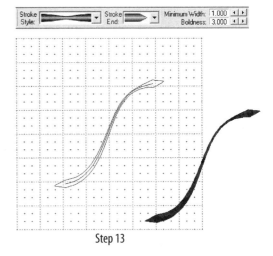

Step 13

The Tree of Life Background

14 You will need a landscape background block for the *Tree of Life* motif before you can set it into your quilt layout. Be sure that the **Block Rulers** are on the worktable. If the rulers are not on the worktable, click **VIEW > click to check *Block Rulers***.

Polygon Tool

15 Click **BLOCK > New Block > PatchDraw Block > Appliqué tab**. Click and hold down the **Polygon** tool. Click the first triangle on the left in the flyout toolbar. Hold down the **CTRL** key and, starting in the lower-left corner, drag the cursor up to draw a triangle on the worktable, as illustrated. Don't worry about exact size and placement at this point. When you release the mouse button, the triangle will be selected.

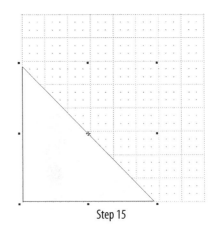

Step 15

Note
You learned in Lesson 7 that holding down the CTRL key ensures that the angle of the patch will be constrained to 15 degree increments. This will make it much easier to align the triangle perfectly on the worktable.

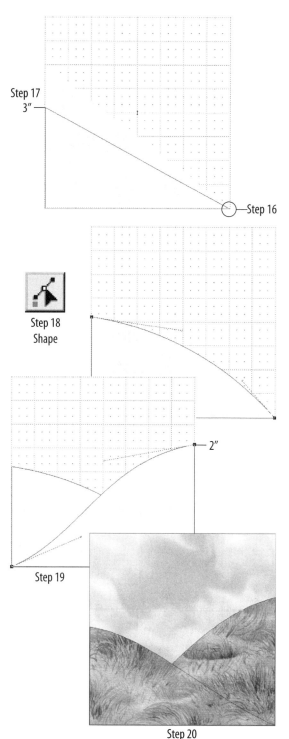

Step 17
3"

Step 16

Step 18
Shape

2"

Step 19

Step 20

16 Click the **four-headed arrows** in the center of the block and move the triangle into the lower-left corner. Click the **node** in the middle of the right side of the selection box and **drag** it to stretch the triangle to the lower-right corner of the block.

17 Click a **node** in the top of the selection box and **drag** to stretch the triangle so that the top of the selection box aligns with the **3"** mark on the left ruler.

18 Click the **Shape** tool. Click the diagonal side of the triangle to select it. Click **BLOCK > Edit > to Curve**. Use the two blue handles to adjust this curve, as illustrated.

19 Click the **Pick** tool and click the modified triangle to select it. Right-click and choose Symmetry. In the Symmetry box, click **Clone > Flip H** (horizontally). Move the second modified triangle to align with the right side of the block outline, as illustrated. Click one of the **nodes** at the top of the selected patch and **drag** so that the top of the selection box aligns at the **2"** mark on the left vertical ruler. Adjust the slope of the hill with the **Shape** tool so that it dips, as illustrated.

20 Now you will relayer the "hills" so that the hill on the left is in front of the hill on the right. Click the **Color** tab and click the **Pick** tool. Click the left hill and it will highlight in green. Right-click and **Send to Front**. **Add to Sketchbook**. Color this block and **Add to Sketchbook**.

21 Open the **Blocks** section of the Sketchbook and recolor the remaining designs on the Blocks and Motifs tabs and add them to your Sketchbook: *Harvest Sun*, *Five Border Medallion*, *Pasture Fence*, *Three Clouds*, and *Smoke*. The *Five Border Medallion* block will serve as the quilt that hangs on the *Clothesline*. You will recolor the silhouette motifs on the quilt layout.

You now have all of the designs that you need to create your *Shady Apple Farm* quilt!

Lesson 8

Creating a Custom Set Layout

In Lessons 6 and 7 you learned basic techniques for planning and filling a Custom Set layout. In this lesson, you will build on that experience and discover the full creative freedom of this flexible layout.

Step 1

1   Click the **Work on Quilt** button in the Project toolbar. Click **QUILT > New Quilt > Custom Set**.

2   Click the **Layout** tab and the Custom Set Layout box will open. Set these values for the center design area:

Size of center rectangle:

Width: **36.00**

Height: **36.00**

Step 2

3   Click the **Borders** tab and set these borders:

BORDER 1

Style: **Mitered**

Size: **0.50**

BORDER 2

Clone Border 1.

BORDER 3

Clone Border 2.

BORDER 4

Clone Border 3.

Adjust width to **4.50**.

BORDER 5

Clone Border 3.

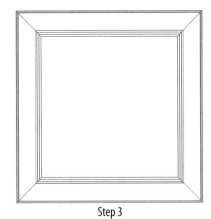

Step 3

4   Click **Add to Sketchbook**.

Step 4
Add to Sketchbook

Setting Designs on Layer 1 (Custom Set)

Throughout this tutorial, you have used a variety of tools to set appliqué and quilting stencils on layers. These tools include the Set Block tool, the Graph Pad, the Adjust tool, and the Zoom tools. In Lesson 6 you used these tools to create a quilt backing in Custom Set. In Lesson 7 you used these tools to set blocks on Layer 1 and quilting stencils on Layer 3 in a Custom Set layout that was based on a single block design. In this lesson, you will use the same tools and techniques to set blocks on Layer 1 (Custom Set) and motifs on Layer 2 of your *Shady Apple Farm* quilt.

Step 1

1   Click the **Layer 1** tab. If the Graph Pad is not open on the worktable, click **VIEW > click to check** *Graph Pad*. Remember that the Graph Pad will be activated only when a design is selected with the **Adjust** tool.

VIEW > Graph Pad

> **Notes**
> When planning a Custom Set quilt, you can streamline the placement process by keeping your block sizes at standard measurements. For example, by making each block in this quilt a whole size, all of the Selected Block coordinates will end with ".000". This will make design placement quick and easy because you can simply glance at the Selected Block coordinates to verify the positions.

Since all of the blocks in this Custom Set layout are whole sizes, you will change the Nudge and Grid Settings accordingly. These changes will make it very easy to set the blocks on Layer 1 because the designs will snap to the increments that you specify for size and placement.

2   Click **QUILT > Options > Snap Settings > Nudge Settings > Graph Pad controls will jump by** *1/4 inch*. This nudge setting ensures that the selected designs will move or resize in 1/4 inch increments when you use the arrow keys on the Graph Pad or on the keyboard. This is the largest value that you can choose for this setting.

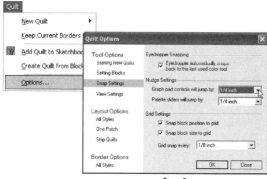

Step 2

Lesson 8

3 Under *Grid Settings*, click to check **Snap block position to grid** and **Snap block size to grid**. **Grid snap every: 1 inch > OK**. This grid setting ensures that the selected design will move or resize by 1" when you manually drag it or use the nodes to resize it, after its initial placement on the layout.

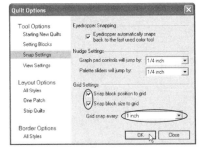

Step 3

I have included a Block Layout Chart and a Block Diagram (found on page 235 and 236, respectively) to help you in creating your *Shady Apple Farm* quilt. The Block Layout Diagram shows you the placement of each block in the layout. Each block in the Block Layout Diagram corresponds to a number in the Block Chart. The Block Chart lists:

- The block number assigned in the Block Layout Diagram

- The block name

- The Selected Block coordinates

- The block size

I have provided the Selected Block coordinates so that you can verify block placement when moving the blocks manually or when using the keyboard arrow keys to move them. You can also type in these coordinates to place the blocks quickly and accurately in the layout. You may not need to refer to them after you discover how easy it is to place blocks visually in this Custom Set layout. However, having all of this information at hand now will help you to understand and apply the Zero Point concept so that you can start designing your own Custom Set layouts.

Now it's time to start setting designs on Layer 1! Using the various tools, I will guide you through the sizing and placement of the first few blocks. After that, you should be able to place the rest of the blocks on Layer 1 yourself, using your experience with Custom Set and the layout information I have provided.

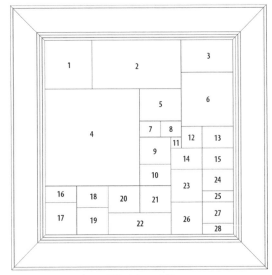

Layer 1 Block Layout Diagram
See page 235 for the Block Chart.

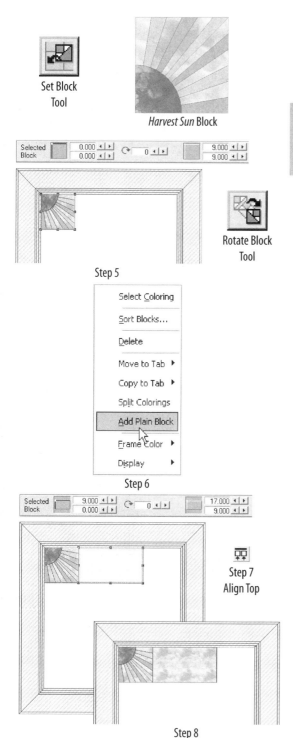

Set Block
Tool

Harvest Sun Block

Step 5

Rotate Block
Tool

Select Coloring

Sort Blocks...

Delete

Move to Tab ▶

Copy to Tab ▶

Split Colorings

Add Plain Block

Frame Color ▶

Display ▶

Step 6

Step 7
Align Top

Step 8

4 Click the **Set Block** tool, click the *Harvest Sun* block and, holding down the **SHIFT** key, **click and drag** to set it on the layout. Don't worry about exact size and placement now. You will adjust this design in the next step.

Notes
Remember that you must use the SHIFT key to set designs on layers: Layer 1 (Custom Set), Layer 2 (appliqué), and Layer 3 (quilting stencils and embroidery).

5 Click the **Adjust** tool, click the *Harvest Sun* block, and set the size to **9 x 9**. Move this block to the **Zero Point (0,0)** in the upper-left corner of the center design area. Click the **Rotate Block** tool on the Quilt toolbar and rotate the block, as illustrated. **Add to Sketchbook**.

6 You will need plain blocks for the grass and the sky patches in your *Shady Apple Farm* quilt. Click the **Set Block** tool and right-click on the **Blocks** palette. Click **Add Plain Block** and a plain block will be added to the end of the Blocks palette.

7 Set the **plain block** on the worktable. Set the size to **17 x 9**. Click off of the design to deselect it. Use the *Harvest Sun* as a reference and, holding down the **SHIFT** key, click **Block 2** (Sky) and **Align Top**. Click off of the blocks to deselect them.

8 With the **Adjust** tool engaged, use the arrow keys on the keyboard to move **Block 2** (Sky) into the correct horizontal position on the layout. The upper-left corner of this block should be **9"** from the Zero Point on the X axis. Block 2 (Sky) is on the Y axis, so the Selected Block coordinates are **9,0**. Color this block with the sky fabric that you have chosen and **Add to Sketchbook**.

Lesson 8

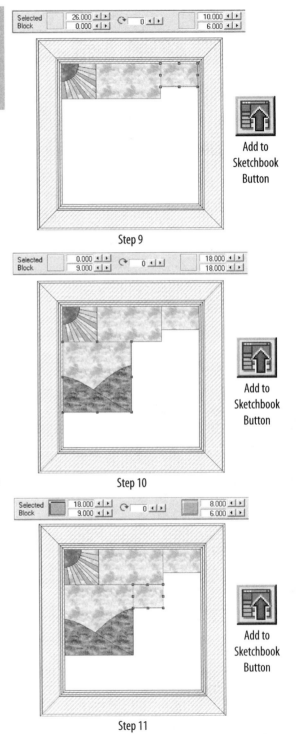

Notes
You learned in Lesson 6 that all blocks along the left edge of the center design area have 0 as the X coordinate. X indicates a point on the horizontal axis. All blocks along the top edge of the center design area have 0 as the Y coordinate. Y indicates a point on the vertical axis.

9   Select **Block 2** (Sky) with the **Adjust** tool and **CTRL+C** to copy and then **CTRL+V** to paste another copy on the worktable. Resize this block to **10 x 6** and use **Block 2** (Sky) to align **Block 3** (Sky) to the top of the layout. The horizontal distance from the upper-left corner of Block 3 (Sky) from the Zero Point is 26, which is equal to the width of Blocks 1 and 2. The vertical (Y) distance is 0 because Block 3 is on the Y axis. The Selected Block coordinates for Block 3 are **26**, **0**. **Add to Sketchbook**.

Notice how easy it is to set designs on Custom Set when you understand the Zero Point concept! It's also very helpful to have the proper Nudge and Grid Settings in place. With just a little practice, you will soon be able to position designs visually, without calculating the position of each block.

10   Set the *Tree of Life Background* block on the worktable. Set the size to **18 x 18**. Use the *Harvest Sun* block as a reference and **Align Left**. Adjust the position of this block vertically below the *Harvest Sun* block. The Selected Block coordinates are **0, 9**. The horizontal (X) distance of the upper-left corner from the Zero Point is **0** because this block is on the X axis. The vertical (Y) distance of the block's upper-left corner from the Zero Point is **9**, which is the height of the *Harvest Sun* block. **Add to Sketchbook**.

11   Copy **Block 2** (Sky) to set **Block 5**. Adjust the size to **8 x 6**. Adjust the placement and verify the Selected Block coordinates at **18, 9**. **Add to Sketchbook.**

Add to Sketchbook Button

Step 9

Add to Sketchbook Button

Step 10

Add to Sketchbook Button

Step 11

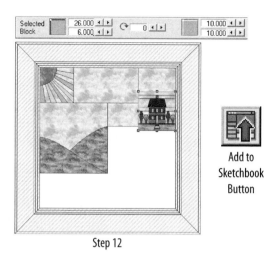

Step 12

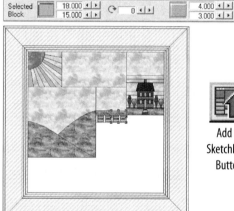

Steps 13 and 14

Step 16
Layer 1 is finished!

Add to
Sketchbook
Button

Add to
Sketchbook
Button

Add to
Sketchbook
Button

12 Set the *Farm House with Chimney* block on the layout for Block 6. Set the size to **10 x 10**. Adjust the placement and verify the Selected Block coordinates at **26, 6**. **Add to Sketchbook**.

13 Set the *Pasture Fence* on the layout for Block 7. Set the size to **4 x 3**. Adjust the placement and verify the Selected Block coordinates at **18, 15**. **Add to Sketchbook**.

14 Copy **Block 7** (*Pasture Fence*) on the layout to set **Block 8**. Adjust the placement and verify the Selected Block coordinates at **22, 15**. **Add to Sketchbook**.

15 Copy any **plain block** in the layout (Sky) to set **Block 9**. You will recolor this block with the grass fabric after you have resized and adjusted it. Adjust the size to **6 x 5**. Adjust the placement and verify the Selected Block coordinates at **18, 18**. Recolor this block with the grass fabric. **Add to Sketchbook**.

16 Continue to set blocks in the layout, referring to the Block Layout Diagram (page 222 and 236) and the Block Chart (page 235) for block size and placement. Use the full range of tools and features as you fill the layout, practicing the various techniques that you have learned.

Lesson 8

Setting Designs on Layer 2 (Appliqué)

Now you are ready to set the designs on Layer 2! The motifs that you have drawn may vary from my drawings so you might have to adjust the sizes and positions of your original drawings accordingly.

I encourage you to use the Appliqué Chart (found on page 237) only as a guide. Feel free to disregard the Appliqué Chart entirely and position your designs wherever you choose on the layout. With all of your experience in Custom Set, it should be easy for you to set and adjust these designs visually on the layout without limiting yourself to the sizes and positions that I have suggested.

After you are comfortable working on Layer 2, you can replace any of these motifs with different designs. You may want to have more kids, more dogs, no cats, all horses, no cows, a pear tree instead of an apple tree, a flag on the clothesline, a different style house, etc. The possibilities are endless!

1   The motifs on Layer 2 require different Nudge and Grid Settings so you will change that now. Click **QUILT > Options > Snap Settings > Nudge Settings > Graph Pad controls will jump by *1/8 inch*.** This nudge setting ensures that the selected designs will move or resize in 1/8 inch increments when you use the arrow keys on the Graph Pad or on the keyboard.

2   Under *Grid Settings*, click to check **Snap block position to grid** and **Snap block size to grid**. **Grid snap every: 1/8 inch > OK**. This grid setting ensures that the selected design will move or resize by 1/8 inch when you manually drag it or use the nodes to resize it, after its initial placement on the layout.

I will guide you through the sizing and placement of the first few motifs and then give you additional instructions for adjustments to specific motifs in this layout.

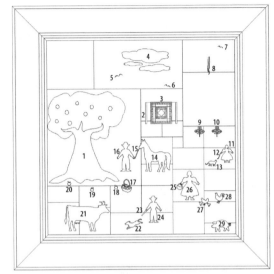

Layer 2 Appliqué Layout Diagram
See page 237 for the Appliqué Chart.

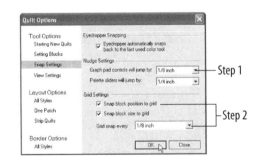

Motifs

Steps 3, 4 and 5

Add to
Sketchbook
Button

Flip Block
Tool

3 Click **Layer 2**. Click the **Set Block** tool and click the *Tree of Life* design on the **Motifs** tab in the Blocks palette. Hold down the **SHIFT** key as you **click and drag** to set this design on the worktable. Click the **Adjust** tool, click the *Tree of Life*, and set the size, as listed in the Appliqué Chart. Position the design visually on the layout or use the Selected Block coordinates on the Appliqué Chart on page 236. **Add to Sketchbook**.

4 Click the **Set Block** tool and click the *Clothesline* design on the **Motifs** tab in the Blocks palette. Hold down the **SHIFT** key as you **click and drag** to set this motif on the worktable. Click the **Adjust** tool, click the *Clothesline*, and set the size as listed in the Appliqué Chart. Position the design visually on the layout or use the Selected Block coordinates on the chart. **Add to Sketchbook**.

5 Now you will use the *Five Border Medallion* design as a quilt and hang it on the clothesline. Set this design on the worktable. Adjust the size and position as suggested on the Appliqué Chart. **Add to Sketchbook**.

6 Set, size, and position the remaining motifs on **Layer 2** of your *Shady Apple Farm* quilt. Use the size and Selected Block coordinates as suggestions.

Notes
When you click on a block to adjust its size, drag from any corner and watch the size change on the Graph Pad. When you're close to the desired size, click the Graph Pad arrows to adjust the size up or down as needed.

7 Flip these motifs using the **Flip Block** tool on the Quilt toolbar:

- Motif 5: Bird 1
- Motif 13: Cat
- Motif 14: Horse
- Motif 17: Apple Basket
- Motif 18: Apple 1
- Motif 20: Apple 3

Lesson 8

8 **Add to Sketchbook**.

9 Use the Graph Pad Rotation tool to **rotate** these motifs:

- Motif 23 - Stick: **45 degrees**

- Motif 25 - Round Basket: **17 degrees**

10 **Add to Sketchbook**.

11 Use the **Spraycan** tool and **CTRL+click** to recolor all of the silhouettes simultaneously. **Add to Sketchbook**.

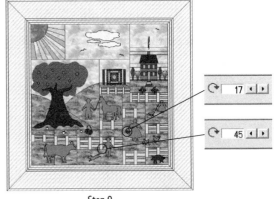

Step 9

Experimenting with Advanced Fabric Rotation

1 Click **Layer 1** and color the quilt borders. Color **Border 4** with the striped fabric in your Sketchbook.

2 If the Rotate Fabric tool is not on the Quilt toolbar, click **Customize Toolbar > Add/ Remove Buttons > Rotate Fabric**. Click **Rotate Fabric > Advanced > type in *45***. **CTRL+click** twice to rotate all sides. **Add to Sketchbook**.

Rotate Fabric Tool

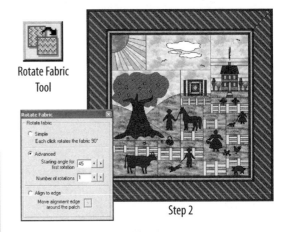

Step 2

Notes
Feel free to experiment with this advanced application of the Rotate Fabric feature by changing the degree of rotation or by rotating the striped fabric differently on each side of the layout.

3 If the Fussy Cut tool is not on the Quilt toolbar, click **Customize Toolbar > Add/Remove Buttons > Fussy Cut**. Use the **Fussy Cut** tool to arrange the fabric so that the stripes match around all sides of the quilt layout, as illustrated. **Add to Sketchbook**.

Fussy Cut Tool

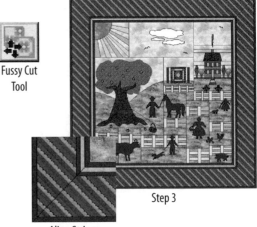

Step 3

Align Stripes

Label

Step 1

Adding Appliqué Text to the Quilt Layout

In keeping with the style of *Shady Apple Farm*, you will now create a decorative label for the front of your quilt. You will construct this label by layering two rectangles on the bottom of Border 4 and then adding text on top of them.

1 Click **Layer 2**. Zoom in and set a **plain block** on the bottom of Border 4. Set the size to **17 x 3** and color it as a background rectangle. Manually center this rectangle on the bottom of Border 4. Click the horizontal **Centering** button on the Graph Pad or set Selected Block coordinates to **9.5** and **38.125**.

2 With the rectangle selected, **CTRL+C** to copy and **CTRL+V** to paste another rectangle on the worktable. Set the size of this rectangle to **16 x 2.5** and color this second rectangle with a contrasting color. Manually center this rectangle on top of the first rectangle. Click the horizontal **Centering** button on the Graph Pad or set the Selected Block coordinates to **10** and **38.375**. **Add to Sketchbook**.

Add to Sketchbook Button

Step 2

Set Appliqué Text Tool

Step 6

3 Use Customize Toolbar to add the **Set Appliqué Text** tool to the Quilt toolbar, if necessary.

4 Click the **Paintbrush** tool and click the color that you want to use for your text.

5 Click the **Set Appliqué Text** tool and the Appliqué Text box will open. EQ6 will list the TrueType fonts that you have available on your computer. Select a font and set the size and any additional formatting options. You may have to experiment with the font size, depending upon the particular font that you use.

6 Use **SHIFT+drag** to form a text box on the worktable. Type in *Shady Apple Farm*. The text box will expand as you type.

Lesson 8

Notes

- To edit the text, click the Set Appliqué Text tool and then click in the text box.

- To resize the text box, select the Adjust tool and then click the box. Use the Block Size tool on the Graph Pad or use the nodes on the text box to resize it.

- To move the text box, click the Adjust tool and then click the box. Click and drag or use the keyboard arrow keys to move it. You can also use the Selected Block coordinates to adjust its position in the layout.

- To delete the text box, click the Adjust tool, click the text box, and then press the DELETE key on your keyboard.

Step 7

7 Click the **Adjust** tool, click the text, and move it on top of the layered rectangles in Border 4. Set the size of the text box to **15.25 x 2.75**. Click the horizontal **Centering** button on the Graph Pad or set the Selected Block coordinates to **10.375** and **38.250**. **Add to Sketchbook**.

Enhancing the Thread Color

In Lessons 4 and 7, you recolored stencils on Layer 3. Now you will use the Set Thread tools to recolor and enhance appliqué stitching on the layout. To experiment with this technique, you will enhance the thread color in three large patches and in one line in this layout: the *Harvest Sun*, the *Three Clouds*, the *Tree of Life*, and the *Clothesline*.

1 With your *Shady Apple Farm* quilt on the worktable, click **Layer 1**. Click the **Spray Thread** tool and click to check **Color**, **Style**, and **Weight** under Outline Thread Properties in the Thread palette. Click the medium yellow or medium orange thread sample that you added from the EQ6 Thread Library. Click the solid line in the Style list and click the thickest line in the Weight list. Zoom in to the ***Harvest Sun*** block and click within each patch to recolor the patch outlines in this block. **Add to Sketchbook**.

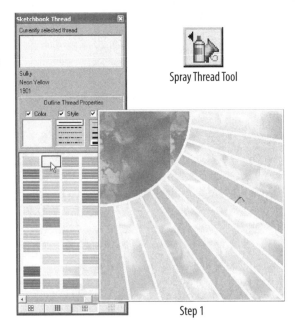

Spray Thread Tool

Step 1

Brush Thread Tool

Step 3

Brush Thread
Tool

Step 4

Step 5

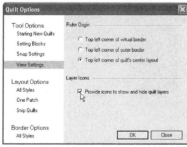

Step 7

2 Click the **Layer 2** tab and click the blue thread sample. Keep the thickest solid line selected for thread style and weight. Click and hold the **Spray Thread** tool to open the flyout toolbar. Click the **Brush Thread** tool and click the blue thread sample. Click within one of the cloud patches.

> **Notes**
> Notice that the Brush Thread tool recolors a single patch in a design.

3 Click the **Spray Thread** tool and then click another cloud. All of the identically colored patches in the *Three Clouds* design will recolor. **Add to Sketchbook**.

4 Click the **Brush Thread** tool. Keep the thickest solid line selected for thread style and weight. Click the green sample and zoom in to the *Tree of Life*. Click within the leaf canopy to recolor the outline of this large patch. **Add to Sketchbook**.

5 With the **Brush Thread** tool still engaged, select a color for the clothesline. Zoom in and click the clothesline to thicken it. **Add to Sketchbook**.

You can use this technique to recolor all patch and block outlines throughout the quilt layout, as I have done in my quilt. This will enhance or blend the outlines in the quilt layout.

Your *Shady Apple Farm* quilt is finished!

6 Before printing, go through your Sketchbook and name the designs that you want to keep, deleting any unwanted designs in the process.

7 In Lesson 7, you turned on the option to show and hide quilt layers. If that feature is still on, there are small light bulbs on each of the Layer tabs at the bottom of the Quilt worktable. If this feature is turned off, click **QUILT > Options > View Settings > Layer Icons > click to check** *Provide icons to show and hide quilt layers* **> OK**.

Lesson 8

8 Click the small light bulb on the **Layer 1** tab to hide this layer so that you can view Layer 2 only. Click the small light bulb again to show this layer. Repeat this action with Layer 2 so that you can view Layer 1 only.

Step 8

Exploring More Printing Options

In Lesson 6, you learned how to print directly onto specially treated fabric sheets. You can use this method to print the *Five Border Medallion* quilt as a single patch that you can appliqué to your *Shady Apple Farm* quilt.

1 With the ***Five Border Medallion*** quilt selected on Layer 2 of the Quilt worktable, click **FILE > Print > Block**. The Print Block box will open. Click to check **Use size from quilt**. Be sure that the colored version is displayed in the Print Block box. Click to check **Showing fabrics**.

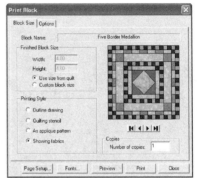

Step 1

2 On the **Options** tab, click to **uncheck all selections** under *Pattern Style Options*. Choose the options that you want under *Showing Fabric Style Options*.

Step 2

3 Remember that you can restrict the printing to only part of a page by adjusting the margins in Page Setup. **Preview** before printing on the treated fabric sheet.

4 You can use an inkjet printer to print the silhouette templates and the letter templates onto a paper-backed bonding agent. You can then press this bonding agent onto the appropriate fabrics, cut out the templates, and then press them onto the background fabric. You can stitch around the edges of the templates with a straight or satin stitch, if you wish. There are a variety of paper-backed bonding agents available on the market. Be sure that the product that you choose is appropriate for your particular printer.

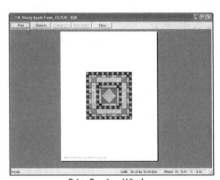

Print Preview Window

FILE > Exit

Finished *Shady Apple Farm* Quilt

Notes

- When using detailed appliqué motifs, it is easiest to use an application technique that avoids seam allowances that must be turned under. Uncheck *Print Seam Allowances* in the Print Template box to eliminate seam allowances.

- Be sure to select your printer's mirror image option before printing any asymmetrical templates, including letters.

- Remember that EQ Printables are available through The Electric Quilt Company. This product is specifically designed for printing quilt labels and photos with an inkjet printer.

Adding Designs to My Library

Add your Lesson 8 designs to My Library as you've done in the previous lessons.

Exiting EQ6

Click **FILE > Exit**.

CONGRATULATIONS! You are now an experienced EQ6 user who has collected an impressive list of accomplishments. You have:

- Created project files for a series of sophisticated quilt designs in increasing levels of complexity.

- Used pre-set layouts, adjusted and cloned borders, added sashing to quilts, installed Auto Borders, and created Prairie Points.

- Experimented with EQ6's broad range of border styles.

- Explored the EQ6 Libraries in depth and added many layouts, blocks, fabrics, and threads to your Sketchbook to use in your designs.

- Learned how to search the libraries by name and by category to find appropriate designs for your quilts.

- Created your own libraries in EQ6 and learned how to store and retrieve your designs from them easily.

- Fully documented your designs on notecards.

- Discovered the drawing distinctions in EQ6, analyzed designs in preparation for drawing, and drawn blocks, quilting stencils, and motifs.

- Modified many library blocks and drawn many designs in EasyDraw™ and PatchDraw using a variety of tools.

- Resized and combined designs and experimented with WreathMaker.

- Colored your designs with various EQ6 coloring tools and then fussy cut and rotated fabrics in your blocks and quilts.

- Converted blocks to motifs, motifs to blocks, and also converted a block design to a quilt layout.

- Rotated and flipped individual designs on layouts, used the Symmetry tool to systematically rotate blocks, and maintained the rotation of designs on layouts.

- Used the Serendipity tool to merge, tilt, and frame the designs in your quilts.

- Worked extensively with several Custom Set layouts and superimposed appliqué motifs and quilting stencils on your quilt.

- Created quilt labels and planned a quilt backing.

- Set appliqué text on layouts and changed and enhanced quilting thread color, style, and weight.

- Experimented fully with EQ6's printing options as you printed blocks, templates, motifs, quilting stencils, foundation patterns, quilts, and clipped designs.

- Learned that you can print from EQ6 onto specially treated fabric sheets and on bonding agents that you can then press onto your fabrics.

- Exported a design and prepared a project for emailing.

- Generated fabric yardage requirements and rotary cutting instructions.

- Discovered the wide range of resources that are available to you for learning to use EQ6 to its full potential: the *EQ6 User Manual*, the EQ6 Help file, the EQ6 videos within the program, the Dynamic Help tool, the Electric Quilt website, the free Info-EQ mailing list, and QuiltUniversity.com.

With your new EQ6 skills and experience, you can unleash your creativity and design with total confidence and freedom!

GOOD LUCK!

Lesson 8: *Shady Apple Farm*
Layer 1 Block Chart

Number	Name	X	Y	Size (inches)
1	Harvest Sun	0	0	9 x 9
2	Sky	9	0	17 x 9
3	Sky	26	0	10 x 6
4	Tree of Life Background	0	9	18 x 18
5	Sky	18	9	8 x 6
6	Farm House with Chimney	26	6	10 x 10
7	Pasture Fence	18	15	4 x 3
8	Pasture Fence	22	15	4 x 3
9	Grass	18	18	6 x 5
10	Pasture Fence	18	23	6 x 4
11	Grass	24	18	2 x 2
12	Pasture Fence	26	16	4 x 4
13	Pasture Fence	30	16	6 x 4
14	Pasture Fence	24	20	6 x 4
15	Grass	30	20	6 x 4
16	Pasture Fence	0	27	6 x 3
17	Grass	0	30	6 x 6
18	Pasture Fence	6	27	6 x 4
19	Grass	6	31	6 x 5
20	Pasture Fence	12	27	6 x 5
21	Pasture Fence	18	27	6 x 5
22	Grass	12	32	12 x 4
23	Grass	24	24	6 x 6
24	Pasture Fence	30	24	6 x 4
25	Grass	30	28	6 x 2
26	Pasture Fence	24	30	6 x 6
27	Pasture Fence	30	30	6 x 4
28	Grass	30	34	6 x 2

Refer to the "Setting Designs on Layer 1 (Custom Set)" section on page 222.

Lesson 8

Lesson 8: *Shady Apple Farm*
Layer 1 Block Diagram

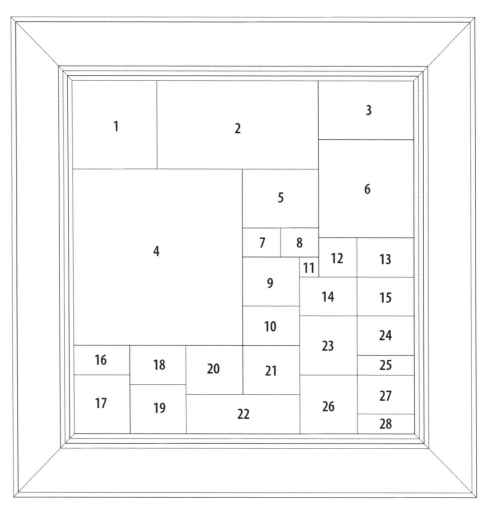

Refer to the "Setting Designs on Layer 1 (Custom Set)" section on page 222.

Lesson 8: *Shady Apple Farm*
Layer 2 Appliqué Chart

Number	Name	X	Y	Size (inches)
1	Tree of Life	-.250	9.250	15.50 x 17.50
2	Clothesline	18.875	11.000	6.00 x 4.50
3	Five Border Medallion	19.875	11.500	4.00 x 4.00
4	Three Clouds	14.000	1.500	10.00 x 4.50
5	Bird 1 (Flip)	13.000	5.875	1.50 x 1.50
6	Bird 2	22.500	8.000	1.25 x 1.25
7	Bird 3	32.750	0.875	1.00 x 1.00
8	Smoke	30.000	3.000	2.00 x 3.50
9	Sunflower (use Flower from the 30s)	28.250	16.000	2.00 x 2.00
10	Sunflower (use Flower from the 30s)	31.500	16.000	2.00 x 2.00
11	Little Girl (use Woman)	32.750	19.500	3.25 x 3.25
12	Ribbon	32.125	20.625	1.75 x 1.75
13	Cat (Flip)	30.250	21.750	2.25 x 2.25
14	Horse (Flip)	17.500	18.250	6.25 x 6.25
15	Rein	15.750	19.500	3.00 x 3.00
16	Man	12.750	18.875	4.50 x 5.50
17	Apple Basket (Flip)	13.750	25.625	2.75 x 2.75
18	Apple 1	12.750	26.875	0.75 x 0.75
19	Apple 2	8.125	27.250	0.75 x 0.75
20	Apple 3	3.750	26.125	0.75 x 0.75
21	Cow	3.000	28.125	9.00 x 9.00
22	Dog	14.500	32.000	4.00 x 4.25
23	Stick (Rotate 45 degrees)	18.500	30.750	1.75 x 1.75
24	Boy (use Man)	18.250	28.875	4.00 x 5.00
25	Round Basket (Rotate 17 degrees)	24.750	26.125	1.75 x 1.75
26	Woman	24.750	24.250	5.00 x 5.50
27	Hen & Chicks	29.000	29.000	2.25 x 2.25
28	Rooster	32.000	28.375	2.00 x 2.00
29	Pig	31.250	32.500	4.00 x 4.00

Refer to the "Setting Designs on Layer 2 (Appliqué)" section on page 226.

Lesson 8

Lesson 8: *Shady Apple Farm*
Layer 1 Appliqué Diagram

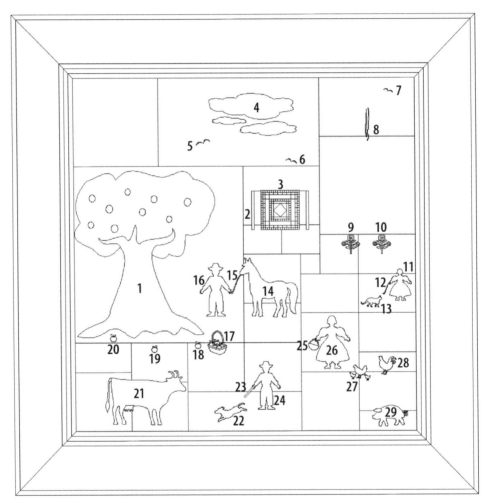

Refer to the "Setting Designs on Layer 2 (Appliqué)" section on page 226.

EQ SIMPLIFIED

An Easy Learning Guide by Fran Iverson Gonzalez

Index

Index

Index

The Toolbars

Project Tools

 New

 Open

 Save

 Create Copy Project*

 Compress for E-mail*

 Print

 Export Selection*

 Export Image*

Export Metafile of Block*

 Undo*

 Cut*

 Copy*

 Paste*

 Add to Sketchbook

 View Sketchbook

 Zoom In

 Zoom Out

 Refresh

 Fit to Worktable

 Watch a Video

 Display Dynamic Help

 Work on Block

 Work on Quilt

 Customize Toolbars

> * These tools are not on the toolbar by default. To add them to the toolbar, click the Customize Toolbars button > click Add/Remove Buttons > click to put a check next to the tools you want to add. Click away from the list to close it. (To restore the default tools at any time, click Customize Toolbars > Restore Default Tools.)

The Toolbars

Quilt Tools

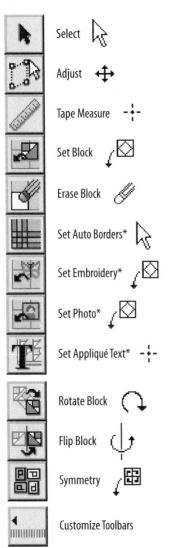

Select

Adjust

Tape Measure

Set Block

Erase Block

Set Auto Borders*

Set Embroidery*

Set Photo*

Set Appliqué Text*

Rotate Block

Flip Block

Symmetry

Customize Toolbars

> * These tools are not on the toolbar by default. To add them to the toolbar, click the Customize Toolbars button > click Add/Remove Buttons > click to put a check next to the tools you want to add. Click away from the list to close it. (To restore the default tools at any time, click Customize Toolbars > Restore Default Tools.)

Color Tools (Quilt worktable)

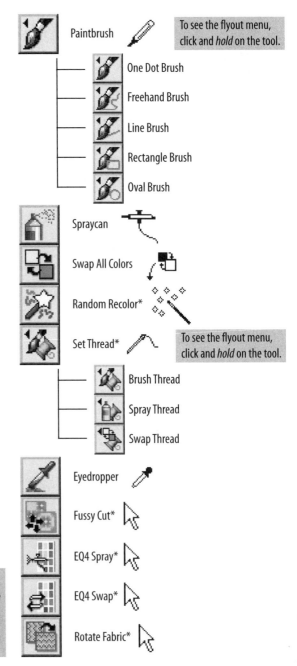

Paintbrush

> To see the flyout menu, click and *hold* on the tool.

One Dot Brush

Freehand Brush

Line Brush

Rectangle Brush

Oval Brush

Spraycan

Swap All Colors

Random Recolor*

Set Thread*

> To see the flyout menu, click and *hold* on the tool.

Brush Thread

Spray Thread

Swap Thread

Eyedropper

Fussy Cut*

EQ4 Spray*

EQ4 Swap*

Rotate Fabric*

The Toolbars

EasyDraw™ Tools

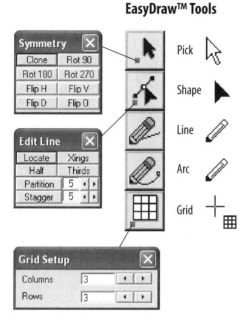

Pick

Shape

Line

Arc

Grid

Tracing Tools

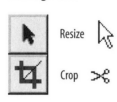

Resize

Crop

Color Tools (Block worktable)

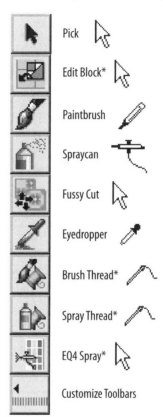

Pick

Edit Block*

Paintbrush

Spraycan

Fussy Cut

Eyedropper

Brush Thread*

Spray Thread*

EQ4 Spray*

Customize Toolbars

> * These tools are not on the toolbar by default. To add them to the toolbar, click the Customize Toolbars button > click Add/Remove Buttons > click to put a check next to the tools you want to add. Click away from the list to close it. (To restore the default tools at any time, click Customize Toolbars > Restore Default Tools.)

The Toolbars

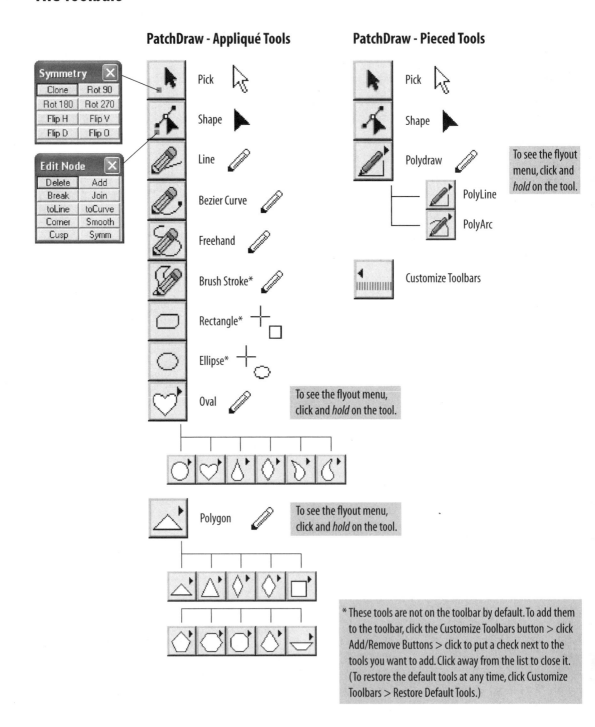

PatchDraw - Appliqué Tools

Pick

Shape

Line

Bezier Curve

Freehand

Brush Stroke*

Rectangle*

Ellipse*

Oval

To see the flyout menu, click and *hold* on the tool.

Polygon

To see the flyout menu, click and *hold* on the tool.

Symmetry

Clone	Rot 90
Rot 180	Rot 270
Flip H	Flip V
Flip D	Flip O

Edit Node

Delete	Add
Break	Join
toLine	toCurve
Corner	Smooth
Cusp	Symm

PatchDraw - Pieced Tools

Pick

Shape

Polydraw

PolyLine

PolyArc

To see the flyout menu, click and *hold* on the tool.

Customize Toolbars

* These tools are not on the toolbar by default. To add them to the toolbar, click the Customize Toolbars button > click Add/Remove Buttons > click to put a check next to the tools you want to add. Click away from the list to close it. (To restore the default tools at any time, click Customize Toolbars > Restore Default Tools.)